The A/UX™ Handbook

Also by Jan L. Harrington

Microsoft Works: A Window to Computing

Making Database Management Work

Database Management with Double Helix II for the Macintosh and VAX

Relational Database Management for Microcomputers: Design and Implementation

Macintosh Assembly Language: An Introduction

The A/UX™ Handbook

Jan L. Harrington
Marist College
Division of Computer Science and Mathematics

Brady
New York

BRADY

Simon & Schuster, Inc.
15 Columbus Circle
New York, New York 10023

DISTRIBUTED BY PRENTICE HALL TRADE

Manufactured in the United States of America

1 2 3 4 5 6 7 8 9 10

Library of Congress Cataloging-in-Publication Data

Harrington, Jan L.
The A/UX Handbook / Jan Harrington.
p. cm.
ISBN 0-13-054826-X
1. A/UX (Computer operating system) I. Title.
QA76.76 063H35 1989 89-38383
005.4'469—dc20 CIP

Contents

Preface

Prefaces are handy things. They give me the only chance I have to talk to you directly (first person in the body of a book being somewhat tacky), to explain about this book and what it can do for you. This book discusses A/UX™, Apple's implementation of the UNIX™ operating system for Macintosh computers. A/UX runs on a Macintosh II with a PMMU (paged-memory management unit), a Macintosh IIx, a Macintosh IIcx, or a Macintosh SE/30.* Although A/UX will run in 2 Mb of main memory, the computer needs more for acceptable performance when more than one person is using the machine or when it is part of a local area network.

A/UX users fall into three general groups: productivity users (people who use A/UX to perform their jobs), system administrators (people whose jobs include managing an A/UX installation), and developers (people who are writing software to run under A/UX). Although these groups are by no means mutually exclusive, this book has been written for the first two. If you have some knowledge of the Macintosh but little or no knowledge of UNIX, then this book is for you.

Why is this book not targeted at developers? Certainly one of the things that makes A/UX unique is its support for the Macintosh ToolBox. However, using that ToolBox is a complex task (the ROM routines require the five volumes of *Inside Macintosh* for complete documentation). Any attempt to cover A/UX software development would be cursory at best; it is simply beyond the scope of this book. If you will developing A/UX software, you may wish to consult many of the fine books that are available about Macintosh software development to learn about using the Macintosh ToolBox.

---

* If you a using an SE/30, you should look at Chapter 7 immediately after completing the A/UX installation procedure. Because Apple does not explicitly support the SE/30, A/UX has no terminal emulator for that machine's small screen. You should therefore use the `term` utility described in Chapter 7. `Term` windows are small enough to fit within the SE/30 screen. You will also need more than 2 Mb of main memory, because the `term` utility places additional overhead on the system. Performance on a 2 Mb SE/30 running `term` is unacceptable.

For each A/UX command and major feature, *The A/UX Handbook* displays a reference to where additional information can be found in the documentation, using a grey box such as this one. References include the documentation volume, and where available, a page number (much of the documentation is organized in alphabetical order by command, without page numbers).

The A/UX Handbook is divided into three sections. Part I (Understanding and Using UNIX) provides an introduction to A/UX for the productivity user. In Part I you will find discussion of topics such as:

- Background information about the UNIX operating system.
- Instructions on how to log in to A/UX, change a password, and log out .
- Creating, editing, formatting, and manipulating text files. (UNIX, and, therefore, A/UX provides a wealth of tools for working with text files.)
- Telecommunications, including electronic mail and file transfer.

To benefit from Part I, you need no background other than some familiarity with standard Macintosh techniques and some basic computing principles. In particular, you should understand the characteristics of RAM and ROM, know what a CPU does, and be familiar with both hard and floppy disks.

Part II (Focusing on A/UX) is also aimed at the productivity user. It turns to some of the things that separate A/UX from other UNIX implementations. (Most of what appears in Part I applies to UNIX systems in general.) The material in Part II is more advanced than that in Part I. In particular, it covers:

- Transferring files between the Macintosh Operating System and A/UX..
- Running Macintosh Operating System Programs under A/UX
- Running A/UX commands in multiple windows (the `term` utility).
- Programming A/UX's default shell (the Bourne shell).
- Using A/UX's implementation of the Korn shell.
- Using A/UX's implementation of the C shell

Part III (Administering A/UX) is designed for the individual who has been given the responsibility of maintaining an A/UX system. Within Part III you will find discussions of:

- System startup and shutdown issues, including ways to configure the system to automatically perform tasks at specific times.
- Maintaining user accounts.
- Managing peripherals such, as disks and printers.
- System security.
- Administering telecommunications.
- System accounting procedures.

Part III does not discuss installing A/UX. The installation process is documented thoroughly in the *A/UX Installation Guide*. There really is no way that a book like this one could do a better job of taking you through the installation process than Apple's document. Therefore, if you've been given an A/UX system that is still in the box (literally or figuratively), follow the step-by-step instructions in the installation guide before you attempt to perform any of the functions discussed in Part III.

The C programming language is UNIX's native language. Although this book makes no attempt to teach C programming, you may be interested in compiling C programs that you receive, for example, over a UNIX network such as USENET. For that reason, Appendix A discusses compiling C programs. If you are comfortable with BASIC, Pascal, FORTRAN, or COBOL, you may wish to examine the source code to understand how it works. Appendix A, therefore, ends with a summary of C syntax and the source code of a short utility program (`ytree`). `Ytree` is short enough to type in and compile if you so desire.

How This Book Was Produced

Because, in this day of desktop publishing, some people really care how books were put together, I thought you might like to know how this book was produced. It was written using Interleaf Publisher, running on a 5 Mb Macintosh II with Virtual memory software and a Radius Two-Page display. The A/UX screen shots were taken using the StarNine Utilities. Modification of graphics was handled by MacPaint, MacDraw II, and Interleaf Publisher. The type pages for this book came from a Merganthaler L300 Laser Imagesetter.

For about 90 percent of the development process, A/UX ran on the Macintosh II. At the very last, I switched the A/UX drive to an SE/30. I wish I'd done it sooner, because using one machine for both writing and A/UX meant an awful lot of rebooting.

Acknowledgments

There are a number of people who helped me put this book together. All of them have my undying thanks:

Marjorie Gursky, my editor at Brady
Tom Dillon, production editor
Elizabeth McGee, StarNine, who provided the StarNine Utilities as well as acted as a knowledgeable reviewer
Bruce Webster, who also reviewed the manuscript
Tom Stoehn, Michael Morrell, and the cast of thousands who wrote and upgraded the `month` program. I only wish the source code had been short enough to include in the book
Gene Lee, the author of the `ytree` program.
All the A/UX wizards on USENET who frequent the comp.unix.aux newsgroup. They answered lots of questions, both intelligent and stupid, without ever asking for anything in return.

JLH

Part I

Understanding and Using UNIX

Chapter 1

UNIX and A/UX

UNIX was born in the late '60s at AT&T Bell Laboratories. Since the first working version appeared in early 1970, the operating system has been implemented on an extraordinarily wide variety of computers. Nonetheless, the basic concepts behind the operating system have remained essentially the same.

Until recently, UNIX has been used primarily in colleges and universities for teaching purposes and in industry for intensive program development. In the past two years, it has begun to make inroads into business as well.

The operating system was written by programmers for their own use. In its native form, it is therefore both powerful and complex. UNIX's attractiveness stems from both power and portability. It runs on more different types of hardware than any other operating system. Software that uses no graphics can generally be recompiled[1] for each individual computer and run with few modifications.

In addition, UNIX provides extensive support for telecommunications. Because implementations are very similar, UNIX has become the ideal operating system for use in environments where hardware from many different vendors is in use. For example, A/UX systems often share networks with Sun and Apollo workstations as well as Digital Equipment Corp. (DEC) VAX minicomputers.

This chapter provides an overview of UNIX, starting with a look at its history and how it has evolved since it was created. It then presents some introductory operating system concepts and the basics of UNIX. A/UX specifics are discussed as appropriate.

Some UNIX History

During 1969, researchers at AT&T Bell Laboratories in Murray Hill, NJ were involved in a project to develop an operating system that would

---

1. Compile:Translate a program written in a programming language such as C, COBOL, Pascal, or FORTRAN into a binary form that can be executed by the computer. Because the binary codes that a computer understands differ from one CPU to another, programs must be recompiled if they are to run on different machines.

support on-line program development and also provide text processing capabilities. The project, known as Multics, was canceled primarily because it seemed that there was no way that the desired end product could be delivered in a reasonable amount of time. Some of the researchers (K. Thompson, D. M. Ritchie, M. D. Mellroy, and J. F. Ossana) wanted to continue to work to develop some sort of operating system, but were unable to present management with a project plan that would justify the requested expenditure on computer hardware.

Rather than giving up completely, the researchers began to design their operating system on paper. During 1969, the way in which UNIX handles files was developed, written on blackboards and scraps of paper. At the same time, Thompson wrote a version of a "Space Travel" game for a DEC PDP-7 minicomputer already owned by Bell Labs.

Although the game was amusing (it simulated the movements of planets), it also gave the research team experience in working with the PDP-7. It seemed a natural step to implement the file handling method developed on paper for the machine. Soon afterwards, the research team also added utility programs to do things such as copy and edit files. All of the programs that went into the prototype operating system were written in assembly language.

UNIX was actually named in 1970, when B. Kernighan came up with the name as a jab at the failed Multics project. Although UNIX has evolved and grown since the 1970 PDP-7 version, its basic concepts (file handling and program control) are essentially the same.

Because of their success on the PDP-7, the UNIX research team was able to convince AT&T to purchase additional, more powerful hardware for the product. During 1971, UNIX was transferred to the DEC PDP-11 and then to the PDP 11/45. During this same period, Bell Labs' researchers were working on a high-level programming language that was eventually called C. In 1973, all but a small portion of UNIX was written in C, making it possible to easily transfer UNIX from one computer to another.

Originally, UNIX was not intended to be a commercial product. (Government regulations prevented AT&T from selling computer products.) Early implementations were, therefore, given away to many academic institutions. The most well-known academic version is Berkeley UNIX (BSD UNIX, a product of the University of California at Berkeley). The version currently marketed by AT&T is known as UNIX System V. A/UX is based on System V, but contains a number of the Berkeley extensions. (The implications of merging both versions under A/UX is discussed later in this chapter.)

Operating System Basics

An operating system is a program, just like any other program you use on a computer. It belongs to a class of programs known as *systems programs*. System programs perform management tasks for the computer. In contrast, the programs that do work for a computer's end users (e.g., word processors, spreadsheets, graphics programs) are known as *application programs*.

Among the things that an operating system does are:

1. Launch (begin the execution of) application programs.
2. Manage disk and tape storage, including keeping a directory of files on storage media, reading files, and writing files.
3. Allocate and manage main memory.
4. Communicate with other peripherals, such as printers, plotters, and modems.

Typical microcomputer operating systems (e.g., MS-DOS and the Macintosh Operating System[2]) are designed to support one user running a single application program at one time. However, the operating systems found on mainframes, minicomputers, and some microcomputers can handle multiple users and programs.

An operating system that can manage more than one application program at the same time is known as a *multitasking* operating system. Multitasking operating systems may be single user (e.g., OS/2) or they may be *multiuser* (e.g., UNIX, mainframe, and minicomputer operating systems).

---

2. The Macintosh Operating System does provide a primitive form of multitasking using MultiFinder. However, since MultiFinder does not schedule which task should run when, some people do not consider it to be true multitasking.

Multitasking

A multitasking operating system can have more than one program in the execution phase at the same time. This does not, however, mean that the computer is simultaneously running more than one program.

The majority of today's computers have only one central processing unit (CPU). A CPU can only do one thing at a time, including running only one program. Multitasking, therefore, requires that programs take turns with the CPU. For that reason programs running in a multitasking environment are often said to be running *concurrently*.

Each concurrent program is called a *task*, or *process*.[3] At any given time, one process will have control of the CPU and will therefore be executing. The other processes will be frozen somewhere in the midst of execution.

To manage multitasking, an operating system must:

1. Allocate a separate (but not necessarily contiguous) portion of main memory to each process.
2. Decide which process will have access to the CPU at any given time.
3. Handle the swapping of processes in and out of the CPU, including saving information about processes that must wait.

Every concurrent process must have its own, inviolable area of main memory. This is because a given RAM location can only hold one value at a time. If another value is written to a RAM location, it will erase the previous value. Therefore, if one process encroaches on the location of a second process, it will destroy a portion of the second process. A multitasking operating system, therefore, allocates blocks of main memory to every process that begins execution and protects that process from being overwritten by any other process.

A/UX uses memory management routines found in a Paged Memory Management Unit (PMMU). If A/UX is run on a Macintosh II, the PMMU

3. Multitasking is occasionally called *multiprocessing*. However, that term also refers to a computer that has more than one CPU.

must be added separately, since the Motorola 68020 microprocessor does not provide memory management. If A/UX is run on any of the 68030 Macintoshes (the IIx, IIcx, or SE/30), then an external PMMU is not required; memory management is built into the 68030 chip.

A multitasking operating system assigns priorities to the processes that are competing for control of the CPU. Generally, systems processes (i.e., programs run by the operating system rather than by users) have highest priority. In addition, processes that require smaller amounts of main memory are assigned higher priority than processes that require large amounts. Finally, the longer a process waits for control of the CPU, the higher its priority becomes. The operating system applies these rules in such a way that the greatest amount of work is produced in the shortest amount of time (i.e., it attempts to maximize *throughput*[4]).

The operating system will give control of the CPU to the highest priority process that is ready to run. If a process is waiting for some external event (e.g., reading from or writing to a disk drive), then it is not ready to run and will not be given access to the CPU, even if it has the highest priority. The priorities assigned to processes are maintained in a list called the *priority queue.*

Once a process gains control of the CPU, it will execute until one of three things happens. If the process must wait for a peripheral (e.g., disk drive, tape drive, or printer), it must relinquish the CPU and will be placed on a waiting list (the *sleep queue.*) If the activity for which another process is waiting (e.g., a disk read) is completed, the second process will *interrupt* the running process to regain CPU control. Finally, if no I/O is required and no other process sends an interrupt, the running process will give up the CPU when a predetermined time interval has passed. Operating systems that allocate blocks of CPU time to processes are known as *time–sharing* operating systems.

Virtual Memory

Programs run in main memory, not from external storage such as disk or tape. However, using a technique known as *virtual memory*, an operating

4. Throughput refers to the amount of data processed per unit time.

system can have more processes in the execution phase than will fit completely in RAM.

In computing, the word "virtual" is defined as simulated, or imaginary. A virtual memory operating system divides RAM into blocks called *pages*. Most UNIX systems use 512 byte pages.

When a new process is generated, the operating system loads as many pages into RAM as it can fit. The remaining portion of the program remains on an external storage medium (usually a disk drive). When pages on disk are needed in RAM, the operating system flags some of the pages in RAM and writes those that have been modified to disk. It then copies the needed pages from disk into main memory (*paging*). The disk drive, therefore, acts as a simulated extension of RAM. It is the virtual memory.

There are two major advantages to virtual memory. First, it allows programmers to write programs that are larger than the amount of main memory available on a computer. Second, it permits the operating system to place more processes in the execution phase than could be handled if no virtual memory were available.

Virtual memory operating systems, however, are subject to a problem called *thrashing*. Thrashing occurs when the operating system does nothing but swap pages in and out. In other words, it swaps a page to disk to make room for a needed page and then discovers that the page it just swapped out is also needed in main memory.

Foreground and Background Processes

A process may run in the *foreground* or the *background*. A foreground process retains control of the user terminal, preventing the user from entering additional commands until the process has terminated. A background process releases the user terminal and runs without user intervention until completion.

A number of A/UX system processes always run in the background. These include one or more *getty*s, processes that poll terminals attached to the A/UX machine to determine if someone is attempting to log in. A process known as the *Tool Box daemon* also runs in the background to act as an interface between A/UX and the Macintosh ToolBox.

A process is placed in the background from ending the command line with an ampersand (&). For example, if the ToolBox daemon has stopped running for some reason, it can be restarted and sent to the background by typing:

```
/etc/toolboxdaemon &
```

Multiuser Support

In addition to providing multitasking, operating systems such as UNIX and those found on minicomputers and mainframes also support more than one user at a time. These *multiuser* operating systems use multitasking to handle the actions requested by more than one concurrent user.[5]

Because multiuser systems must be available to many people using many different terminals, they require security measures to ensure that only those people authorized to use the system are actually able to do so. The first line of defense is a combination of a user name (sometimes also known as a "login ID") and password. To gain access to the system, a user must first supply a valid user name and password pair. In many cases, the security of the entire system rests on how difficult it is to guess passwords. A/UX security, which is typical of the security features found on UNIX systems, is discussed in Chapter 13.

Spooling

Spooling is a term that refers to using a disk as a temporary holding area for work that is waiting for something. For example, when a user requests that a file be printed, the file will not be sent directly to the printer. In most cases, the printer attached to a multiuser system is shared by all the system's users. Therefore, the file that is to be printed will be written to a special area on disk set aside as a waiting area for files to be printed. The

---

5. Keep in mind that an operating system may be multitasking but not multiuser, as in the Macintosh operating system's MultiFinder. However, if an operating system is multiuser, it will be multitasking.

waiting list of print requests is known as the *print queue* (from the British expression for a waiting line).

On small systems, print queues are emptied in *first in, first out* order; a print request simply waits until all requests that precede it in the queue have been printed. However, many large mainframes have complicated rule systems that determine when a file will be printed based on the size of the file (small files print sooner) and how long the file has been in the queue (the longer a file waits, the higher its position in the queue).

UNIX also uses spooling to help manage electronic mail. Outgoing messages are collected in a special area on disk until such time as they can be transmitted.

Spooling is not restricted to output. Mainframes that processes work as a batch (i.e., not interactively from a terminal) may use input spooling. Requests to run programs are stored on disk in an input queue. The computer uses a set of rules to determine which program will run at any given time (e.g., programs that require less CPU time run before longer programs; as a program waits, it moves forward in the queue).

The major advantage to spooling is that it frees the user's terminal (or the batch input device), making it unnecessary for the user to wait for the work to actually gain access to the hardware it needs. The user is free to continue his or her work; the spooled activity will take place in the background as the needed device becomes available.

The UNIX Operating System

UNIX has three major components: the kernel (routines that must always stay in main memory), a shell (a command interpreter), and utility programs.

The Kernel

The UNIX kernel is written primarily in C[6]; a very small portion (less than 1,000 lines) is written in assembly language. Although the functions it performs are essential, the kernel represents only about ten percent of the entire operating system. It is responsible for:

1. Creating new processes when requested by either the operating system or the user.
2. Swapping processes in and out of the CPU.
3. Swapping pages to and from external storage (i.e., managing virtual memory).
4. Scheduling process access to the CPU.
5. I/O transfers to external devices (e.g., disk drives, tape drives, networks, and printers).
6. Organizing and keeping track of files.

Shells

The commands that a user issues to UNIX are intercepted by a command interpreter known as a *shell*. There are three shells available:

1. The Bourne shell
2. The Korn shell
3. The C shell

At any given time, a user works with only one type of shell. The Bourne shell is the default under A/UX, although both the Korn shell and the C shell are available. (The first portion of this book focuses on the Bourne shell; the differences between the Bourne shell and the other two shells appear in Chapter 9 [the C shell] and Chapter 10 [the Korn shell].)

---

6. C might well be considered UNIX's native language. Not only is the operating system itself primarily written in C, but most UNIX application programs are also written in C.

Each shell supports a programming language that can be used to write programs known as *shell scripts*. Shell scripts are *interpreted*: each line of the program is translated to binary as the program is run, without ever creating a binary version of the entire program.

A shell is actually a UNIX program. A default shell is run automatically when you log in to the system. Because UNIX is multitasking, more than one shell can be running at any given time. One way to run another shell is to use the shell as a command (`sh` for the Bourne shell, `ksh` for the Korn shell, and `csh` for the C shell). In addition, whenever a command is executed, the default shell spawns a *daughter shell*, another shell under which the command actually runs. (Commands can be run without creating daughter shells by preceding the name of the command with a period.)

Most UNIX systems provide *shell layers*. With shell layering, a user can run up to seven separate shells. A separate program or command is run under each shell; the user switches between shells as needed. Through A/UX's shell–layering command (`shl`), you can interact with a maximum of seven shells. (The `shl` command is discussed later in this chapter.) However, A/UX's `term` utility provides up to 16 Macintosh-style windows. Each window will run its own command or program and also supports some Macintosh-like editing. (For details on the `term` utility, see Chapter 7.)

Utility Programs

The majority of commands that a user issues to UNIX are not part of the kernel. Rather, they are stand-alone utility programs. Some have been written in C and exist on disk in their compiled (binary) form. Others are shell scripts, written in a shell's programming language.

Because most of UNIX's commands are not part of the kernel, but contained in separate files, UNIX can easily be customized. Undesired commands can be removed from the system. Additional commands can be added whenever needed by simply writing programs that perform the required function. Shell programming, using the Bourne shell, is discussed in Chapter 8; C and Korn shell programming is discussed in Chapters 9 and 10, respectively.

Automatic Program Execution

One of the powerful features of UNIX is its ability to execute commands and programs without direct user intervention. This facility, known as `cron`, allows the system administrator and other authorized users to record the dates and times on which specific commands and functions should be executed in `crontab` files.

`Cron` is managed by a process named `cron` that is always running. Each minute, `cron` checks the `crontab` files to see if there is something that should be done. For example, most UNIX systems check to see if there is any electronic mail to be sent twice every hour. Typical `crontab` entries also include daily commands to clean out log files that tend to grow large and programs to print reports about system accounting data. (Using `cron` is discussed in detail in Chapter 11).

Directing Input and Output

UNIX views all hardware devices–terminals, disk drives, printers, and modem—as files. Input and output are therefore streams of characters that are coming from or sent to some file. By default, input comes from the user's terminal keyboard (*standard input*); output is directed to the user's terminal screen (*standard output*). However, both input sources and output destinations can be changed, or *redirected.*

If, for example, the contents of a file should be listed to another file rather than to the screen, the command could be written:

```
cat inventory >new.file
```

The > redirects the output of the `cat` command to the file whose name follows it; no output appears on the terminal screen. If the file `new.file` already exists, its contents will be replaced by the output of the command. However, if >> is used instead of >, the output will be *appended* to the file.

Input redirection is indicated by <. For example, if a modem is represented by the file name `/dev/tty1`, then the following command will display the characters being received from the modem on the terminal screen:

Place
First Class
Postage
Here
Post Office
Will Not
Deliver
Without Postage

Brady Books
One Gulf+Western Plaza
New York, NY 10023

```
cat </dev/tty1
```

Input and output redirection can be combined in the same command. The modem input displayed on the standard output in the above example can be directed to a disk file:

```
cat </usr/dev/tty1 >modem.capture
```

Pipes and Tees

Among the features included in the first versions of UNIX were *pipes* and *tees*. A pipe sends the output of one command as input to a second. For example, assume that you wish to search a text file containing a listing of a supply room's inventory for all the pencils and then count the number of types of pencils found. The `grep` command will locate every line in the file that contains *pencil*; the `wc`[7] command will count the number of times *pencil* is found:

```
grep pencil inventory | wc -l
```

The pipe is indicated by the vertical bar (|). The typical output of the `grep` command is every line in the file that contains the string for which the command is searching. However, in this case, the output from `grep` is sent directly to `wc`, rather than appearing on standard output. The result of the command is, therefore, a single number, the result of `wc` counting the number of lines submitted to it through the pipe.

A tee is used to capture the output of a command in the middle of a pipe. For example, the command:

```
grep pencil inventory | tee pencil.list | wc -l
```

will take the output of the grep command, write it to a file named pencil.list and then pass it on to the wc, where the number of lines are counted.

---

7. The `grep` and `wc` commands are discussed in Chapter 3.

Introducing A/UX

This section presents an overview of A/UX and some basic techniques for actually working with A/UX. As well as discussing the format of A/UX commands, logging in and out, changing your password, and managing shell layers, it introduces some A/UX commands that provide information about the system.

What You Get with A/UX

As mentioned earlier in this chapter, A/UX is based on UNIX System V, but includes a number of the Berkeley (BSD) extensions. The result is a UNIX implementation that is exceedingly rich.

Among the features of A/UX you will find:

1. A variety of telecommunications options
   a. `B-NET` (the BSD implementation of TCP/IP)
   b. `NFS` (a BSD feature not generally included with System V)
   c. `uucp` (standard with all UNIX systems)
   d. `kermit` (a public domain file transfer protocol supported by both UNIX and nonUNIX systems)
   e. AppleTalk (Apple's proprietary network; requires an expansion board for use under A/UX)
2 Extensive text management tools
   a. editors (e.g., `ed`, `ex`, `vi`, `sed`)
   b. formatters (e.g., `nroff`. `troff`, `psroff`)
3. Program development tools
   a. C compiler (`cc`)
   b. FORTRAN compilers (`f77`[8] and `efl`)
   c. specialized languages
      i. pattern matching (`awk`)
      ii. arbitrary-precision arithmetic (`bc`)

---

8. At the time this books was written (shortly after A/UX 1.1 was shipped), `f77` still had problems and was considered unusable by many developers.

4. Access to the Macintosh ToolBox ROM: The Macintosh ToolBox ROM contains routines that support Macintosh features, such as graphics (i.e., QuickDraw), windows, menus, and dialog boxes. A/UX programmers can include calls to these routines in their programs to produce the standard Macintosh user interface.

Entering A/UX Commands

Most of the commands that you issue to A/UX are actually utility programs. A command is invoked by typing its name and pressing RETURN or ENTER. Many commands also take one or more optional *arguments* or *flag options* that affect the action of the command. Arguments are generally the name of something (e.g., a file, user, or system). Flag options are preceded by a hyphen. They control how a command will operate and/or the type of output that will be provided.

The `ps` command, for example, displays a listing of current processes. When used without options, `ps` shows only those processes created by the user issuing the command. However, if the command is issued as:

```
ps -e
```

the command displays all current processes. The `e` is a flag option to the `ps` command. Like all flag options, it is preceded by a hyphen (-).

In addition to flag options, some commands also require arguments. For example, one of the functions of the `cat` command is to list the contents of a text file on the screen. The command must, therefore, be followed by a file name, as in

```
cat inventory
```

The range of options and arguments available with A/UX commands is extensive. This book does not attempt to present every option or argument to every command, but instead focuses on those used most often.

Sometimes you may wish to cancel a command while it is still executing. To do so, type CTRL-C.

Finding A/UX Documentation

The documentation for A/UX is available in two different formats: on paper and on disk. The contents of both are identical.

The reference portion of the documentation is divided into a number of *sections*:

User Commands (1): Describes commands that are useful to, and can be issued by, users working with a standard shell.

Maintenance Commands (1M): Describes commands that are used for system maintenance and administration and can only be run by a privileged user.

System Calls (2): Describes calls to A/UX system functions that can be made from C programs.

Subroutines (3): Describes subroutines that are available for use in C programs.

File Formats (4): Describes the format of system files.

Miscellaneous Facilities (5): Describes system commands and features that don't fit into any other section.

Special files (7): Describes files that support disk drives and other hardware devices.

System Maintenance (8): Describes additional maintenance and administrative commands, including utilities that start A/UX and run Macintosh Operating System programs.

A given name may appear in more than one section. For example, *passwd* refers to the command that a user can use to change his or her password, as well as to the file that contains user account and password data.

To find which portion of the on-line documentation contains a given command or topic, use the `apropos` command to perform a keyword

search of the commands and their descriptions. For example, if the command is typed as

```
apropos passwd
```

the screen will display

```
passwd(1)         - change login password
passwd(4)         - password file
yppasswd(1)       - change login password in yellow pages
yppasswd(3N)      - update user password in yellow pages
yppasswd(1M)      - server for modifying yellow pages password file
```

Note that `apropos` searches for any entry that contains the text that follows it (either whole or partial words).

The `apropos` command is documented in *A/UX Command Reference (A–L)*. See the section *User Commands(1)*; the commands are in alphabetical order.

To see manual pages, use the `man` command followed by the name of the command or file whose documentation you would like to see. For example,

```
man passwd
```

will display the manual pages for passwd (1) (the command) and passwd(4) (the file). To restrict the manual page to just one section, precede the file name with the section number, as in

```
man 1 passwd
```

The `man` command is documented in *A/UX Command Reference (M–Z and Games)*. See the section *User Commands(1)*; the commands are in alphabetical order.

A/UX Users

Because A/UX is a multiuser operating system, users must supply a valid user name and password pair to gain access to the system. (A given user name is also often called an *account*.) However, once users are logged on, who is using the system is not a secret.

Types of Users

UNIX systems have two broad types of users: the *superuser* and everyone else. The superuser has access to every part of the system and cannot be prevented from gaining access to any file. A/UX has one superuser account with a user name of *root*. However, regular users can become the superuser temporarily and obtain superuser privileges by supplying the root's password (see Chapter 11 for details).

Superuser privileges are used primarily for system administration. Because the root is so powerful, its password is guarded very carefully. Usually, only the system administrator and one or two other people in an organization will be able to become the superuser. The type of user described in this chapter, the remainder of Part 1, and Part 2 is a regular user, not a superuser.

Groups

Each A/UX user name belongs to one or more *groups*. A group represents a collection of user names that should have the right to access the same files. For example, if the same A/UX system is used by both accounting and sales, the accounting users would be assigned to an accounting group, giving them access to accounting files but restricting them from using sales files. Sales users would be part of a sales group, with access to the sales files but not the accounting files.

Although an A/UX user name can belong to more than one group, one group will be specified as the user's default group. More information about groups appears later in this chapter.

Logging In

When ready to accept a user, A/UX displays the prompt:

```
login:
```

In response, type your user name, as in:

```
login: jon
```
[9]

A/UX will then ask for a password:

```
password:
```

Type your password and press RETURN or ENTER. The password will not appear on the screen as it is typed, preventing anyone who might be looking over your shoulder from discovering the password.

If the password and user name do not match, A/UX will respond with:

```
Login incorrect
login:
```

The system will not tell you whether the user name, password, or both were wrong. This makes it a bit more difficult for anyone trying to guess passwords and user names to gain unauthorized entry to the system.

When the user name and password match, A/UX logs you into the system. Assuming that the account will be using the Bourne shell, a successful login presents the user with the Bourne shell's default prompt (a dollar sign). The prompt means that the shell is ready to accept input.

---

9. Unlike operating systems such as MS-DOS, UNIX knows the difference between uppercase and lowercase letters. When logging in, be sure to match the capitalization in your user name and password exactly.

Changing Your Password

Because a password is the key to A/UX security, it should be changed frequently. Preferably, a password should not be written down at it. If you feel you must put it on paper, carry the paper in your wallet rather than leaving it lying around in a desk.

Assuming that you are logged in under a user name of `jon`, to change your password, type:

```
passwd
```

A/UX responds with:

```
Changing the password for jon
```

and then prompts for the old password:

```
Old password:
```

Enter your current password. A/UX will then ask for the new password:

```
New password:
```

Enter the new password. You will then be asked to enter the new password once more to ensure that the new password is exactly what you intended. This is very important, because A/UX encrypts passwords. No one other than A/UX, not even the superuser, can decrypt a password. If a password is forgotten, the only alternative is to request a new password from the system administrator.

A/UX enforces some rules about how passwords can be constructed.[10] These rules are designed to make passwords hard to guess (e.g., to prevent you from using your spouse's name for a password):

---

10. The superuser is exempt from the password restrictions. The superuser may set a password for any account, using any combination of characters.

1. A password must have at least six characters. Although there is no upper limit to the length, A/UX will use only the first eight.
2. A password must have at least two letters (uppercase or lowercase).
3. A password must have at least one number or special character (e.g., a period or underscore).
4. A password must not be the same as the user name, either frontwards, backwards, or circularly.
5. A new password must have at least three characters that are different from the old password. When making the comparison between the old and new password, A/UX will ignore differences between uppercase and lowercase.

The `passwd` command is documented in *A/UX Command Reference (M–Z and Games)*. See the *User Commands (1)* section; commands are in alphabetical order.

Logging Out

To log out, type a `CTRL-D` at the dollar sign prompt. A/UX will log you out and respond with another `login:` prompt.

Why a `CTRL-D` works as a logout command isn't particularly obvious. To A/UX, `CTRL-D` actually means "end–of-input" or "terminate this process." It is used in several instances to signal that a process should be completed. For example, it is used to signal the end of input to a message that is to be sent by electronic mail. At the shell's prompt (the dollar sign), the only process running for the logged-in user is the shell itself.[11] The `CTRL-D`, therefore, indicates that the shell should stop running, effectively logging the user out.

As an alternative to `CTRL-D`, you may log out by simply typing:

```
exit
```

---

11. The major exception to this statement are processes that have been instructed to run in the background.

Working with Shell Layers

As discussed earlier in this chapter, A/UX's shell–layering capabilities provide up to seven shells in which you can run commands and programs. To work with layers, type:

```
shl
```

A/UX will respond with `shl`'s prompt, >>>. Until such time as you return to the default shell's prompt (`$`), you will be working within `shl`.

To create a new layer, type:

```
create <layer name>
```

Layer names can contain any printing character except a blank. Although there is no limit to the length of the name, A/UX will recognize only the first eight characters. For example,

```
create layer1
```

defines a layer named `layer1` and runs a shell for that layer.

Immediately after creating a layer, A/UX will clear the screen and display the name of the layer in the upper left corner; the layer's name is its prompt. You can then interact with the layer just as you would with the default shell.

To return from a layer to `shl`, type a `CTRL-Z`. The >>> prompt will return. At that point you may:

1. create another layer (up to a total of seven)
2. make another layer active (make it the *current* layer) by typing:

   ```
   resume <layer name>
   ```

   as in:

   ```
   resume layer6
   ```

3. delete a layer by typing:

   ```
   delete <layer name>
   ```

   as in:

   ```
   delete layer2
   ```

4. return to working with the layer with which you last worked by typing:

   ```
   toggle
   ```

5. exit `shl` and return to the default shell by typing `quit`

The `shl` command is documented in *A/UX Command Reference (M–Z and Games)*. See the section *User Commands (1)*: the commands are in alphabetical order.

Looking at System Information

By default, a UNIX system is very open. Users can gain a great deal of information about what the system is doing at any time. This includes seeing what processes are running and checking the date and time.

Seeing the Logged-in Users

Like most UNIX systems, A/UX is generally open about allowing users to view parts of the system and what the system is doing. That includes seeing exactly who is logged in at any given time.

A list of all current users is produced by typing:

```
who
```

The `who` command will list each user name, followed by the line that he or she is using to connect to the system, and the time that he or she logged in. The listing below shows three users, one of whom is working at the system console (the Mac II itself):

```
sysop    console        Apr 11  15:25
parker   tty1           Apr 11  20:20
chang    tty0           Apr 11  21:00
```

The who command is documented in *A/UX Command Reference (M–Z and Games)*. See the *User Commands (1)* section; commands are in alphabetical order.

Managing Processes

To see the processes that he or she has created, a user types:

```
ps
```

The output appears as:

```
PID TTY      TIME COMMAND
 20 tty1     0:01 sh
 44 tty1     0:00 ps
```

The leftmost column contains the process ID. Processes are numbered consecutively, beginning with 0, at the time A/UX is booted. The second column from the left identifies the port through which the user's terminal is connected to the Macintosh II on which A/UX is running. The amount of CPU time the process has consumed appears in the third column, followed by the name of the command that was issued to initiate the process. The `ps` process represents the `ps` command itself; `sh` is the Bourne shell.

To see *all* running processes, type:

```
ps -e
```

As mentioned in the previous section, the `-e` is a flag option that instructs A/UX to display *every* running process. If the user issuing the command is using tty1 and the system administrator is using the console (the Macintosh II's monitor and keyboard), the output might be:

```
PID   TTY       TIME  COMMAND
  0   ?         0:00  swapper
  1   ?         0:00  init
  2   ?         0:00  vhand
 15   console   0:01  sh
 36   ?         0:00  toolboxd
 37   ?         0:00  errdemon
 38   ?         0:00  cron
 39   ?         0:00  lpsched
 46   console   0:00  sh
 47   console   2:41  vi
 50   tty1      0:02  sh
 70   tty1      0:00  ps
109   ?         0:00  getty
110   ?         0:00  getty
```

Processes 0, 1, and 2 are started automatically when A/UX is booted. The `swapper`, for example, is the process that swaps processes in and out of the CPU; `init` is the process initializer. Processes 36, 37, 38, and 39 are started automatically when A/UX is brought from single user to multiuser mode. In addition, there are two `getty`s running, each of which is polling a line where a terminal is connected to A/UX. The system administrator is running `vi`, one of A/UX's text editors; the user who issued the command is running `ps`. Note that both the system administrator and the remote user also have a copy of the shell (`sh`) running.

Processes 36 through 39 belong to a special group of processes known as *daemons* (pronounced "demons"). A daemon is a process that runs alongside everything else the system is doing. For example, the printer daemon (`lpsched`) manages the waiting list (or *queue*) of files to be printed on a shared printer. `Cron`, the program that manages automatic program execution, is the clock daemon. The ToolBox daemon, `toolboxd`, acts as an interface between A/UX and the ToolBox routines in the Macintosh ROM.

The `ps` command is documented in *A/UX Command Reference (M–Z and Games)*. See the section *User Commands (1)*; the commands are in alphabetical order.

A user can stop any process that he or she has started with the `kill` command:

```
kill <process ID number>
```

For a regular user, `kill` is most useful for aborting processes that are running in the background. For example, assume that you have obtained a public domain C program from a UNIX network. You compile the program in the background by typing:

```
cc sample.prog &
```

While the compilation is in progress, you decide that you don't want to let it finish. The `ps` command indicates that its process ID is 1045. It can then be killed with:

```
kill 1045
```

The `kill` command is documented in *A/UX Command Reference (A–L)*. See the section *User Commands (1)*; the commands are in alphabetical order.

Dates and Times

The command `date` will print the current date and time, as in:

```
Wed May 10 10:34:53 EDT 1989
```

This same command can also be used to set the date and time, but only by the system administrator (see Chapter 9 for details).

The `date` command is documented in *A/UX Command Reference (A–L)*. See the section *User Commands (1)*; the commands are in alphabetical order.

---

12. In most cases, a user can only kill processes that he or she has created. The exception is the superuser, which is discussed in Chapter 2 and throughout Part III. The superuser can kill any process.

If you need to see more than the current date, use the `cal` command. Used without arguments, `cal` will print a calendar of the current month, as in:

```
                   1
 2  3  4  5  6  7  8
 8  9 10 11 12 13 14
15 16 17 18 19 20 21
22 23 24 25 26 27 28
29 30 31
```

`Cal` takes arguments that instruct it to print calendars for any given month or year. For example,

```
cal 2001
```

will print the calendar for the entire year 2001;

```
cal 10 1950
```

will print the calendar for October 1950. A/UX will accept any year between 1 and 9999.

The `cal` command is documented in *A/UX Command Reference (A–L)*. See the section *User Commands (1)*; the commands are in alphabetical order.

Chapter 2

Organizing a UNIX System

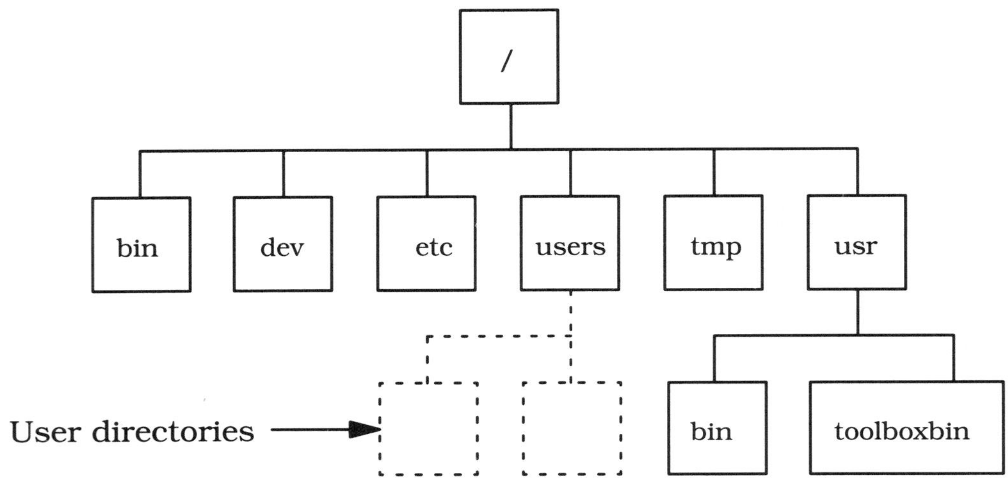

Figure 2.1 A/UX's default file structure.

This chapter looks at how A/UX systems are organized. In particular, it focuses on file systems. Before reading this chapter, you should read Chapter 1 to understand basic UNIX concepts and how to log in to A/UX.

File Systems

A/UX, like all UNIX systems, organizes its files into one or more *file systems*. From the user's point of view, a file system consists of *directories* arranged in a hierarchical, or tree, structure. Each directory can contain both files and other directories (*subdirectories*).[1] The directory, its files, and its subdirectories all have names.

---

1. To be technically correct, a directory is no different from any other kind of file. Its contents include a list of the files and subdirectories that are assigned to the directory, the access rights assigned to the files and subdirectories, and the dates the files and subdirectories were last modified.

A/UX is shipped with one file system. Figure 2.1 shows some of its directories. Each box represents a directory and contains the directory's name; subdirectories are attached to their parent directory by a line.

At the top of the hierarchy is the root directory with the name "/." The root directory contains a number of subdirectories, some of which are used for A/UX system files:

1. bin: Contains binary system utilities (commands).
2. dev: Contains special files that correspond to hardware devices like disk drives, tape drives, and terminals.
3. etc: Contains system files, such as the list of user names and encrypted passwords.
4. users: The parent directory of the directories assigned to system users (this is the directory not used for A/UX system files).
5. tmp: Contains temporary system files.
6. usr: The parent of additional system directories, including:
   a. bin: Contains additional binary system utilities. Utilities developed by users are often placed in this directory so they can be used by everyone on the system and
   b. toolboxbin: Contains utility programs written to give A/UX a bit more of a Macintosh flavor (e.g., providing multiple windows for running more than one program at a time)

The complete name of a file or directory is made up of all the directories through which the system must traverse down the file system's hierarchy, starting at the root, to reach the file or directory. This complete name is known as a *path name.*[2] For example, the bin directory that is a subdirectory of usr has the path name /usr/bin.

A/UX maintains a list of path names, the *default path*, for each user account. These path names represent the directories that A/UX will search to find commands that are typed at the shell's prompt. The default path is retained in a system variable named PATH. PATH can be changed

---

2. If you have used MS-DOS, then all of this may sound somewhat familiar. Keep in mind, however, that MS–DOS is a bit like UNIX, and not vice versa.

to include the path names of directories needed by a specific user (see Chapter 8 for details).

A directory is associated with each user name (the user's *home directory*). By convention, all user directories are subdirectories of /users. When the user logs in, he or she is placed in that directory.

A/UX keeps track of the directory in which you are working at any given time. This directory is known as the *current*, or *working*, directory.

Checking File System Disk Usage

To see the amount of disk space remaining for a file system, use the `df` command. If used without arguments, `df` will display the number of 512K– byte blocks available for the the file system. For example, if A/UX's default file system (/) is the only file system known to A/UX, then `df`'s output might be:

```
/    /dev/dsk/c1d0s0      42315
```

This output indicates that the root file system has just over 20 Mb of free space (remember that each megabyte is made up of two 512K byte blocks). The sequence `/dev/dsk/c1d0s0` is the path name of the file that A/UX uses to represent the disk on which the root file system can be found. (The number following `c` is the SCSI address of the drive.)

The `df` command is documented in *A/UX Command Reference (A–L)*. See the section *User Commands (1)*; the commands are in alphabetical order.

Working with Directories

When you log in to A/UX, you will be placed in the directory assigned to your user name (the *home* directory). In most cases, you will keep personal files in that directory.

Listing the Contents of a Directory

The `ls` command displays the contents of a directory. Used without any flag options, it displays the names of all files and subdirectories in the current directory except those whose names begin with a period, as in

```
author_copy
aux.dimmer
ds.script
inventory
logs
saved_mail
usage
```

Names appear in alphabetical order in a single column. If there are more names than there are lines on the screen, the listing will scroll. However, the default A/UX screen is different from a Macintosh document window; once lines scroll off the top, they cannot be recovered.[3]

The output of `ls` can be formatted to make it easier to read. A flag option of `C`[4] will display file names in columns. Therefore,

```
ls -C
```

will produce

```
author_copy          inventory       saved_mail
aux.dimmer           logs            usage
df.script
```

---

3. A/UX 1.1 provides a way to capture lines off the top of the screen through its `term` utility. See Chapter 3 for details.

4. Keep in mind that A/UX is case sensitive. Uppercase flag options and arguments must be entered in uppercase; lowercase flag options and arguments must be entered in lowercase. Otherwise, A/UX will not recognize them.

Note that the columns read down. To obtain a directory listing where names are alphabetized across the screen, use the x argument:

```
ls -x
```

which produces:

```
author_copy        aux.dimmer ds.script
inventory          logs       saved_mail
usage
```

The directory listings presented to this point do nothing but list the names of files and subdirectories. There is no way to differentiate between files and subdirectories, see file sizes, or obtain information about file names that begin with periods. To see all file and subdirectory names, use the a argument; to see additional file information, use the l argument. In most cases, they are used together:

```
ls -al
```

will produce a listing like:

```
drwxr-xr-x   2 jon    users     144 Apr 11 16:13 .
drwxr-xr-x   5 root   root       80 Apr 11 10:06 ..
-rw-r--r--   1 jon    users      28 Apr 11 16:23 .clipboard
-rw-r--r--   1 jon    users      22 Apr 11 16:20 .profile
-rw-r--r--   1 jon    users     256 Mar 15 03:25 author_copy
-rw-r--r--   1 jon    users   11461 Jun 22 16:10 aux.dimmer
-rw-r--r--   1 jon    users     500 Apr 11 16:07 ds.script
-rw-r--r--   1 jon    users     296 Apr 11 16:22 inventory
-rwxr-xr-x   1 jon    users      39 Apr 06 15:32 logs
-rw-r--r--   1 jon    users    2408 Aug 30 14:30 saved_mail
-rwx------   1 jon    users     540 Jan 15 15:25 usage
```

The a argument controls the display of four additional file/directory names:

```
.
..
.clipboard
.profile
```

The single period refers to the directory being listed; the double period refers to its parent directory The files names .clipboard and .profile are part of the directory along with all the other files. However, they do not appear in listings without the `a` argument because their names begin with periods.

The additional information that appears about each file and directory is the result of the `l` argument. The columns in the listing are:

1. File type and permissions: The first character in column 1 represents the type of file. A `d` indicates a directory; a `-` indicates a regular file (either text or binary). The remaining nine characters represent file access permissions. These will be discussed in more detail shortly.
2. The number of links to the file: A files that already exists on disk can be added to a directory without making a copy of the file by *linking* the file to the directory. The second column represents the number of links that exist. (Linking is discussed later in this chapter).
3. The owner of the file.
4. The group to which the file belongs.
5. The size of the file in bytes.
6. The date the file was last modified.
7. The time the file was last modified.
8. The name of the file or directory.

Unless you tell it otherwise, `ls` will always list the contents of the current directory. To see the contents of a different directory, add the path name of the directory to the `ls` command. For example,

```
ls -al /usr/spool/uucp/amcad
```

will list the contents of the directory with the path name /usr/spool/uucp/amcad.

The `ls` command is documented in *A/UX Command Reference (A–L)*. See the *User Commands (1)* section; the commands are in alphabetical order.

Managing a Long Listing

Many A/UX directories contain more files than the number of lines on the screen. The output of an `ls -l` command will, therefore, scroll off the screen. Ideally, there should be some way to freeze a screen full of data and leave it there until the user is ready to proceed. The solution is a rather handy program called `more`. If the output of a command is piped into `more`, A/UX will pause after printing a screen full of data, display `--More--` at the bottom of the screen, and wait for a press of the RETURN key or space bar before continuing.

For example, the command

```
ls -al | more
```

will take the listing of all files in the current directory and display one screen of data. If the RETURN key is pressed, `more` will display one additional line; if the space bar is pressed, `more` will display another screen full of data. (`More` can also be used without a pipe to view the contents of a file. See Chapter 4 for details.)

The `more` command is documented in *A/UX Command Reference (M–Z and Games)*. See the *User Commands (1)* section; the commands are in alphabetical order.

Finding Files

The A/UX file system is quite extensive. It's not uncommon to be mystified about the exact location of some file. To make it easier to locate files, A/UX supports the `find` command. In its barest form, `find` has the format:

```
find <path to search> arguments
```

Although find takes a wide variety of arguments, the most common argument is -name, which instructs find to match a particular file or directory name. For example,

```
find / -name hfx
```

will search the A/UX file system beginning with the root directory (/), traversing all subdirectories of /, looking for a file with the name hfx.

Unfortunately, finding a file is *all* find does. It does not print the path names of the files that it finds. One way to see the result of find is to add the -exec flag option to the command.

```
find / -name hfx -exec echo "{}" ";"
```

Echo is a command from the Bourne shell's programming language; it displays whatever follows on the standard output. In this particular case, the curly braces in double quotes represent the path name of a file returned by find. The semicolon within double quotes signals find that the end of the command has been reached and is required as a terminator for all -exec commands.

As an alternative, find can be used with its -print flag option. This option displays the name of every file that find checked while looking for the file you have requested. The result is, therefore, piped into grep, a command that matches patterns and only returns input items that match the pattern. (Grep is discussed in detail in Chapter 3.) Using -print, the command is issued as:

```
find / -name hfx -print | grep hfx
```

The find command is documented in *A/UX Command Reference (A–L)*. See the section *User Commands (1)*; the commands are in alphabetical order.

The whereis command can also be used to locate files. It has the general format:

```
whereis <file name>
```

The output is the path name of the file and the path name of the file's on-line manual entry.

The `whereis` command is documented in *A/UX Command Reference (M–Z and Games)*. See the section *User Commands (1)*; the commands are in alphabetical order.

Checking File and Directory Disk Usage

To quickly see the number of 512–byte blocks used by files and/or directories, use the `du` command. If used without arguments, `du` reports the number of blocks used in the current directory. For example,

```
du
```

will print just a single number:

```
53
```

The current directory, therefore, occupies 53 * 512 bytes or 27,636 bytes.

By default, `du` does not display information about the files within a directory. However, if the `-a` option is added, it will display the disk usage of each file within the directory. Therefore, the command:

```
du -a
```

will produce a listing of the sizes (in blocks) of all files in the current directory.

If `du` is followed by one or more file or directory names, it will print the disk usage of those items. In addition, it will print the disk usage of any subdirectories of directories in the command line. This ability to traverse subdirectories can lead to unexpected results. For example, `du /` will display the names and sizes of every directory in the root file system. By the same token, `du -a /` will display the names and sizes of every file in the root file system.

The du command is documented in *A/UX Command Reference (A–L)*. See the section *User Commands (1)*; the commands are in alphabetical order.

File and Directory Permissions

Although the UNIX operating system has a reputation for not being secure, it nonetheless has a system for controlling access to files and directories. Each file and directory has three categories of access rights–for its owner (by default, the user that created the file or directory), for its group (by default, the group to which the owner belongs), and for the rest of the world (all users not the owner or members of the owner's group). Within each category, a user may be permitted to perform any combination of reading, writing, or executing the file or directory.

The permissions assigned to a file or directory are visible in the leftmost column when the `l` argument is used with the `ls` command:

```
-rw-r--r--   1 jon      users    2408 Aug 30 14:30 saved_mail
-rwx------   1 jon      users     540 Jan 15 15:25 usage
```

Assuming that the characters in the leftmost column are numbered from the left, character 1 indicates whether the item is a directory (a *d*) or a regular file (a –). The remaining nine characters are the access rights. Characters 2 through 4 refer to the owner, 5 through 7 to the group, and 8 through 10 to the rest of the world.

Within each group of three characters, the leftmost will contain an *r* if the user is able to read the file or directory. The center character will contain a *w* if the user can write to the file or directory. The rightmost character will contain an *x* if a file is executable (i.e., is a program that can be run); it will contain an *x* for a directory if the user has permission to make that directory its working directory or to use the directory in a path name. A dash (–) indicates the absence of an access right.

In the example above, the `saved_mail` file has the default permissions assigned to any newly created file. The owner is given the right to read and write the file; the owner's group and the rest of the world can read the file (including the right to copy it into their own directories), but cannot modify it.

The file named `usage` is a shell script that was written by a system administrator to collect data for a report on all the people who have logged into the system. Because it cleans out a system file, destroying the information about who has logged in, it must be very carefully protected. For that reason, only the owner has the right to read, write, or execute the file. Although the script itself is not proprietary, if any other user were to copy the file into his or her account, there would be nothing to prevent that user from running the script and destroying valuable information before the system administrator had run the report.

Changing File and Directory Permissions

File and directory permissions are changed with the `chmod` command. A user can change the permissions only for those files and directories for which it is the owner. The one exception is the superuser, which can change permissions on any files and directories in the system.

The `chmod` command can be used by either supplying numbers for the new access rights or by using letters to represent the permissions. When numbers are used to assign access rights, each type of permission is given a value:

4	read the file or directory
2	write the file or directory
1	execute the file or search (execute) the directory

The rights given to a user category are determined by adding the values for the individual permissions. For example, if the owner of a file is to have the right to read and write the file, then the owner's rights have the value of 6. However, if the file is also executable, then the owner's rights will be 7.

The numbers are supplied as arguments to `chmod` in the following manner:

```
chmod <owner rights><group rights><world rights> file_name
```

Therefore, if the owner of a file named `inventory` is to have read and write permissions, the owner's group read permission, and the rest of the world no permission, the command is written:

```
chmod 640 inventory
```

When letters are used to assigned permissions, each type of access right has a unique character:

r read
w write
x search or execute

If the permission is to added, then it is preceded with a plus (+); if it is to be removed, then it is preceded with a minus (–). The user category to which a permission applies is also indicated by a letter:

u user (the owner)
g group
o other (the rest of the world)

If used without a user category, then the permission is applied to all three user categories. For example,

```
chmod +x usage
```

would have the unfortunate effect of making `usage` executable by not only its owner, but by all members of the owner's group, and everyone else on the system.

Instead, the command can be issued as:

```
chmod o+x usage
```

The presence of the `o` restricts the execute access to just the owner of the file.

The `chmod` command is documented in *A/UX Command Reference (A–L)*. See the *User Commands (1)* section; the commands are in alphabetical order.

Changing File Owners and Groups

The owners and groups to which files and directories belong may be changed by either the file or directory owner or the superuser. Changing owners requires the `chown` command, changing groups, the `chgrp` command. Both have a similar syntax:

```
chown <new owner name> file_name

chgrp <new group name> file_name
```

For example, the current owner of `usage` may wish to further restrict use of that file by changing its owner to the system's administration account, sysadm. To do so, the `chown` command is written:

```
chown sysadm usage
```

The `chown` and `chgrp` commands are documented in *A/UX Command Reference (A–L)*. See the `chown` command in the *User Commands (1)* section; the commands are in alphabetical order. (`chgrp` is documented on the same page as `chown`.)

Moving Between Groups

As discussed in Chapter 1, each user on an A/UX system belongs to one or more groups. The group in which you are working in part determines the access that you have to files. When you log in to A/UX, you will be a member of your default group.

To change groups and gain the access rights associated with a different group, use the `newgrp` command. The command has the general format:

```
newgrp <group name>
```

For example, if an account's default group is `users` and the user wishes to gain access to files available only to members of the group `proposal`, he or she would type:

```
newgrp proposal
```

If the group has a password, the user will be prompted for it. The group change will be permitted only if the correct password is supplied.

Issuing the command without a group name returns the user to his or her default group.

The `newgrp` command is documented in *A/UX Command Reference (M–Z and Games)*. See the section *User Commands (1)*; the commands are in alphabetical order.

Moving Between Directories

To change the working directory, use the `cd` command:

```
cd <path name of new working directory>
```

as in,

```
cd /usr/toolboxbin
```

The command above will make the user's working directory the directory in which A/UX's ToolBox utilities are stored.

To return quickly to your home directory, enter

```
cd $HOME
```

or more simply:

```
cd
```

`HOME` is a shell variable that contains the path name of each user's home directory. Placing a dollar sign in front of the variable instructs A/UX to use the contents of the variable as an argument to the command.

The cd command is documented as part of the sh command in *A/UX Command Reference (M–Z and Games)*. See page 10 of the sh command in the *User Commands (1)* section; the commands are in alphabetical order.

In the midst of a long session working with A/UX, it is possible to forget exactly which directory is the current directory. Although the ls command will tell you, it is easier to use pwd (print working directory). The pwd takes no arguments. It simply displays the complete path name of the current directory.

The pwd command is documented in *A/UX Command Reference (M–L and Games)*. See the *User Commands (1)* section; the commands are in alphabetical order.

Creating and Removing Directories

New directories are created with the mdkir command:

```
mkdir <new directory name>
```

The command line

```
mkdir my.mail
```

will create a subdirectory of the current directory with the name my.mail.

The new directory can be created as a subdirectory of a directory other than the current directory by including a complete path name, as in:

```
mkdir /usr/bin/DumpFiles
```

The directory DumpFiles will be created as a subdirectory of the /bin directory, which in turn is a subdirectory of /usr.

The mkdir command is documented in *A/UX Command Reference (M–L and Games)*. See the *User Commands (1)* section; the commands are in alphabetical order.

To remove a directory, use `rmdir`:

```
rmdir <path name of directory to be removed>
```

As a safeguard, A/UX will not remove directories that contain files.

Maintaining Files

A/UX files can be copied, renamed, moved from one directory to another, and deleted.

Naming Files and Directories

A/UX offers a great deal of flexibility in choosing file and directory names. With a very few exceptions, names can contain any character that can be typed from the keyboard; uppercase and lowercase characters are different. Names are limited to 14 characters.[5] (Although A/UX will not report an error if a file or directory name is longer than 14 characters, it will truncate the extra characters.)

The characters that cannot be used in file and directory names are:

1. blanks: Although file names may contain multiple words (e.g., separated by periods or underscores), they may not contain embedded blanks. This is in direct contrast to the Macintosh Operating System, which does permit blanks within file names.
2. \: The backslash is used to remove the effect of characters that have special meaning to A/UX, including all of those listed below, so that they can be used in text files.
3. /: The slash is used to separate directories in a path name.
4. @: The *at* is used to erase a command line.
5. #: The pound sign is used to erase the character directly to the left.

---

5. Other UNIX implementations permit longer file names (e.g., up to 256 characters). The 14– character limit is specific to A/UX.

6. |: The line is used to indicate a pipe.
7. < and >: The greater than and less than signs are used to indicate input and output redirection.
8. $: The dollar sign is the Bourne shell prompt and is also used to indicate that A/UX should use the contents of a variable rather than interpreting the variable name as text.
9. quotes: Quote marks (‘, ’, and ") are used to identify text strings or to instruct the shell to process the expression within the quotes.

File Name Wildcards: Metacharacters

A large portion of the commands that you will read about in this book require one or more file names as arguments. A/UX recognizes several *metacharacters*, characters that can be used to substitute for portions of a file name.

The most well–known metacharacter is the asterisk (*). The asterisk stands for zero or more characters in a file name. For example, the file name `*` will match every file in a directory that is made of a single word. The file name `.*` will match every file name that begins with a period and `*.*` will match every file name that contains a period somewhere within it. The asterisk can also be used more restrictively. For example, `program*` will match every file that begins with the characters `program`, as in `program`, `program1`, `program2`, and `program3`.

The asterisk is not a particularly discriminating metacharacter (i.e., it matches any character). A/UX can instead be given a list of characters that are acceptable for matching with file names by surrounding the list with brackets ([and]). For example, to specify either `program3` or `program7`, the file name is written `program[37]`. However, to indicate `program1` through `program10`, the file name can be written `program[1-10]`.

The `?` metacharacter is even more discriminating. It will match only one character. For example, `prog?` will match `prog1`, `prog2`, and `proga` but not `prog1a`, `program`, or `program1`.

Copying and Linking Files

Files are copied with the cp command:

```
cp <path name of existing file> <path name of copy>
```

For example,

```
cp aux.dimmer /usr/bin/dimmer
```

will copy the file aux.dimmer from the current directory to the /usr/bin directory and give it the name dimmer. If the command was issued as

```
cp aux.dimmer /usr/bin
```

it will be copied into /usr/bin with the same name (aux.dimmer).

> The cp command is documented in *A/UX Command Reference (A–L)*. See the section *User Commands (1)*; the commands are in alphabetical order.

The cp command makes a physical copy of a file. There are two drawbacks to that action. First, it uses unnecessary disk space. Second, it uses something known as an *i–node*. An i–node represents a place for a file within a file system; each system has a fixed number of i–nodes available. When the i–nodes are used, no more files can be added to the file system, regardless of whether or not there is free disk space.

The alternative to copying is linking. Linking creates an entry in a directory for the linked file without making a physical copy of the file or using an i–node. To link a file, use the ln command:

```
ln <path name of existing file> <path name for link>
```

as in

```
ln aux.dimmer /usr/bin/dimmer
```

The file aux.dimmer will be linked to the /usr/bin directory with the name dimmer. If the file name is omitted from the path name of the link, then the file will be linked with the same name as the original.

There is one limitation to the use of linking. Links can only be made within the same file system. If the same file must exist in two different file systems, then there is no alternative but to copy it.

The ln command is documented in *A/UX Command Reference (A–L)*. See the *User Commands (1)* section; the commands are in alphabetical order.

When used as discussed earlier in this chapter, the ls command does not provide information about which files in a directory are actually links to files stored elsewhere. If you need to identify links and see the path names of the files to which links refer, use ls's -L flag option, as in:

```
ls -alL
```

Wherever ls encounters a link, it will display the path name, permissions, links, and so forth for the file which the link refers.

Moving and Renaming Files

A/UX uses the same command, mv, for both renaming files and moving files from one directory to another. This is because UNIX views renaming a file as moving it from one name to another within the same directory. The general format of the mv command is:

```
mv <existing path name> <new path name>
```

To rename the file aux.dimmer, the command is written:

```
mv aux.dimmer dimmer
```

Because the path name for both files is the same (the current directory), the file is effectively renamed.

To actually move a file from one directory to another, the path names of the two files must be different, as in:

```
mv aux.dimmer /users/jon/dimmer
```

The above command will move the file `aux.dimmer` from the current directory and place it in the `/users/jon` directory under the name `dimmer`. If the file name is omitted from the destination path name, the file will be moved with the same file name.

There is one important limitation to `mv`: Files can only be moved within a single file system. If you need to transfer a file to another file system, copy it to the destination directory with `cp` and then delete the original. (See the next section for details on deleting files.)

The `mv` command is documented in *A/UX Commands Reference (M–Z and Games)*. See the section *User Commands (1)*; the commands are in alphabetical order.

Deleting Files

To delete a file, use the `rm` command:

```
rm <path name of file>
```

as in:

```
rm aux.dimmer
```

If the file name mentioned in the command is the last link to a file, then the file is physically removed from disk and its i–node freed. However, if additional links exist, `rm` merely deletes the link.

The `rm` command is documented in *A/UX Commands Reference (M–Z and Games)*. See the section *User Commands (1)*; the commands are in alphabetical order.

Chapter 3

Manipulating Text Files

A/UX provides a rich array of utilities that manipulate text files. These include commands to look at file contents, cut and paste files, and count characters, words, and lines. In addition, there are special utilities for checking spelling and style and for managing a bibliography.

Viewing File Contents

As discussed earlier in this book, the `cat` command can be used to "concatenate" a copy of a file to the standard output (the terminal screen), providing a quick way to view an entire file. However, `cat` displays a file without stopping; if the file contains more lines than will fit on a single screen, the lines will simply scroll off the top. To solve the problem, A/UX contains commands that either freeze after displaying one screen full of data or view only a portion of a file.

Paging

Two commands–`more` and `pg`–freeze the screen after a screen full of data has been displayed. To use them, type

```
more <file name>
```

or

```
pg <file name>
```

`More` will display `--More--` on the bottom line of the screen and wait for a press of either the RETURN key or space bar. Each press of RETURN displays one more line; each press of the space bar displays another screen.

The `more` command is documented in *A/UX Command Reference (M–Z and Games)*. See the section *User Commands (1)*; the commands are in alphabetical order.

`Pg`, on the other hand, displays a colon (:) on the bottom line of the screen. Pressing the RETURN key displays another screen full of data. In

addition, `pg` can be instructed to scroll forward and backward by whole or half screens. To do so, enter the amount that is to be scrolled at the colon and press RETURN:

`+n`	Scroll *n* screens forward.
`+-n`	Scroll *n* screens backward.
`+d`	Scroll one-half screen forward.
`+CTRL-d`	Scroll one-half screen backward.
`.`	Redisplay the current screen.
`$`	Display the last screen.

The `pg` command is documented in *A/UX Command Reference (M–Z and Games)*. See the section *User Commands (1)*; the commands are in alphabetical order.

Tops and Bottoms

The `head` command displays a specified number of lines from the beginning of a file. For example,

```
head aux.dimmer
```

will display the first ten lines of the file `aux.dimmer`. The default of ten lines can be overridden by including the number of lines to display in the command:

```
head -20 aux.dimmer
```

In this case, the first 20 lines of the file will be displayed.

The `head` command is documented in *A/UX Command Reference (A–L)*. See the section *User Commands (1)*; the commands are in alphabetical order.

To see the bottom of a file, use the `tail` command. When used without any options, `tail` will display the last ten lines of a file, as in:

```
tail aux.dimmer
```

The number of lines displayed can be changed by including a number as an option to the command. If the number is preceded by a minus sign (-), `tail` will count lines from the bottom on the file. However, if the number is preceded by a plus sign (+), `tail` will count lines from the beginning of the file. For example, assume that you are working with a 100 line file. In that case,

```
tail -20 100.lines
```

will display the bottom 20 lines of the file. On the other hand,

```
tail +20 100.lines
```

will display the bottom 80 lines of the file. `Tail` will count down 20 lines from the beginning of the file and then display the remainder.

The `tail` command is documented in *A/UX Command Reference (M–Z and Games)*. See the section *User Commands (1)*; the commands are in alphabetical order.

Comparing Files

Within A/UX's array of text manipulation tools are commands that compare files and report the differences between them. The simplest of these is `cmp, which` locates and reports the first difference it finds. As an example, consider the text file `story1` that can be seen in Figure 3.1 and the slightly altered version, `story2`, that appears in Figure 3.2. If `cmp` is written as:

```
cmp story1 story2
```

A/UX will respond with

```
story1 story 2 differ: char 186, line 4
```

```
     On the 24th of February, 1815, the Marseilles port lookouts
signaled that the three-master Pharoah was coming up the
harbor. She belonged to Morrel and Son, and was homeward bound
from Smyrna, Triest and Naples. The pilot boat ran out to meet
her, and the the idlers congregated on the waterside to see her
come into her mooring-place, with the more interest as she had
been built, launched and fitted out from this ancient port.
     She came in so slowly that it was easy to guess that she
had met some mishap, not to herself, as she was in trim
condition, but to some one aboard. By the pilot was seen,
standing to transmit his orders, a bright-eyed and active young
man.
```

Figure 3.1 The file `story1`.

```
     On the 24th of February, 1815, the Marseilles port lookouts
signaled that the three-master Pharoah was coming up the
harbor. She belonged to Morrel and Son, and was homeward bound
from Paris, Amsterdam and Naples. The pilot boat ran out to
meet her, and the the idlers congregated on the waterside to
see her come into her mooring-place, with the more interest as
she had been built, launched and fitted out from this ancient
port.
     She came in so slowly that it was easy to guess that she
had met some mishap, not to herself, as she was in trim
condition, but to some one aboard. By the pilot was seen,
standing to transmit his orders, a dark-eyed and quiet young
man.
```

Figure 3.2 The file `story2`.

Note that `cmp` stops processing when it detects the first difference between the two files. In this particular example, it does not report that there is also a difference between the files on line 11.

The `cmp` command is documented in *A/UX Command Reference (A–L)*. See the section *User Commands (1)*; the commands are in alphabetical order.

To receive a more complete analysis of the difference between two files, use the `diff` command. The command line

```
diff story1 story2
```

will produce the output in Figure 3.3. Each < precedes a line from the first

```
4c4
< from Smyrna, Triest and Naples. The pilot boat ran out to meet
---
> from Paris, Amsterdam and Naples. The pilot boat ran out to meet
11c11
< standing to transmit his orders, a bright-eyed and active young
---
> standing to transmit his orders, a dark-eyed and quiet young
```

Figure 3.3 The output of the `diff` command.

file that is not the same as a line in the second; the text from the second file follows a >. Above each pair of lines are the `ed` commands that might be used to change the first file to match the second. Unlike `cmp`, `diff` finds every line that is different.

If `diff` is used on long files that have many different lines, the output may scroll off the screen. To prevent that, use the `-l` flag option. `Diff` then automatically pipes its output to `pg`, freezing each screen full of data. A command with that option might appear as:

```
diff -l story1 story2
```

You may also wish to write `diff`s output to a text file. If issued as:

```
diff -l story1 story2 >diff.file
```

output will be written to `diff.file` but not on the screen. However, if used with a tee, as in:

```
diff -l story1 story2 | tee diff.file
```

output will both appear on the screen and be written to the file.

```
LaserWriter cartridges,2
Blue pencils,15
Red pencils,26
Paper clips,16
Post-it notes,30
Thin-rule pads,6
Scotch tape,12
Stapler,2
Staples,15
Blue felt-tip pens,6
Black felt-tip pens,10
Blue medium-point pens,12
Black medium-point pens,2
```

Figure 3.4 A file containing office supply inventory data.

The `diff` command is documented in *A/UX Command Reference (A–L)*. See the section *User Commands (1)*; the commands are in alphabetical order.

Counting Words

The `wc` command counts the number of characters, words, and lines in a text file. For example, assume that the data in Figure 3.4 appear in a file named `inventory`. The command

```
wc inventory
```

will then produce

```
 16  35  295 inventory
```

The `16` represents the number of lines in the file, `35` the number of words, and `296` the number of characters.

Flag options can be added to restrict the output to one or two of the counts. For example,

```
wc -c inventory
```

```
Jones,John,1256 W. 99th St.,Westview, MA,02211
Baker,Emily,85 Summer St.,Westview,MA,02211
Anderson,Sue,P.O. Box 196,Westview,MA,02222
Cramer,James,1435 Main St.,Westview,MA,02211
Coolidge,Peter,P.O. Box 1022,Westview,MA,02222
Richardson,Marilyn,P.O. Box 14,Westview,MA,02222
Smithson,Emily,3910 Sunset Dr.,Westview,MA,02211
```

Figure 3.5 A sample address file.

will count just the number of characters and produces

```
295 inventory
```

By the same token, `-l` will count just the number of lines and `-w` just the number of words. The options can also be combined: `-wc`, for example, will count the words and characters but not the number of lines.

The `wc` command is documented in *A/UX Command Reference (M–Z and Games)*. See the section *User Commands(1)*; the commands are in alphabetical order.

Cutting and Pasting

Among the more useful things that A/UX allows you to do is pull files apart and put them together again. The `cut` command extracts columns from a file; the `paste` command puts them together again.

Cutting Files Apart

Assume, for example, that you will be working with the address file in Figure 3.5. Notice that the names begin with the last name, followed by a comma (the field separator) and the first name;. The `cut` and `paste` commands can be used to create a file containing only the names, with the first name preceding the last.

`Cut` extracts entire columns of data from a file either by character position e.g., 12th through 25th character) or by field (e.g., second and

third fields, where fields are separated by commas). To cut by character position, use the syntax:

```
cut -c<starting column>-<ending column> <file name>
```

as in:

```
cut -c12-24 address.file
```

The above command will remove the 12th through 24th characters of each line and write them on the standard output. To capture the output in a file, use output redirection.

Cutting by field requires two options, one to tell A/UX what the separator character is and another to indicate the fields to be cut. The general format is therefore:

```
cut -d<separator character> -f<field numbers>
```

For example, to cut the second and fourth fields from the address file the command is written:

```
cut -d, -f2,4
```

The first step in rearranging the address file is to create two temporary files, one that contains only first names and one that contains only last names. This is achieved with two `cut` commands:

```
cut -d, -f1 >last.names
cut -d, -f2 >first.names
```

The results of each of these commands can be seen in Figure 3.6 and Figure 3.7.

The `cut` command is documented in *A/UX Command Reference (A–L)*. See the section *User Commands (1)*; the commands are in alphabetical order.

```
Jones
Baker
Anderson
Cramer
Coolidge
Richardson
Smithson
```

Figure 3.6 The file `last.names`.

```
John
Emily
Sue
James
Peter
Marilyn
Emily
```

Figure 3.7 The file `first.names`.

Pasting Files Together

To create the final output file, `first.names` and `last.names` should be placed side by side in a new file. That can be accomplished with `paste`. `Paste` lines up the contents of two or more files. Creating the reformatted names file might be performed with:

```
paste first.names last.names >reversed.names
```

Used in this way, each first name will be followed by a tab character and then the last name, providing even–aligned columns. Although such an arrangement is useful for tables, it isn't the way in which names are generally printed.

A more desirable output can be seen in Figure 3.8. This is achieved by telling A/UX to use a character other than the default tab to separate the columns with the `-d` option:

```
paste -d" " first.names last.names >reversed.names
```

```
John Jones
Emily  Baker
Sue Anderson
James Cramer
Peter Coolidge
Marilyn Richardson
Emily Smithson
```

Figure 3.8 The file `reversed.names`.

Because the new separator character is a blank, it must be enclosed in double quotes. Otherwise, A/UX will be unable to recognize it as a part of the command (i.e., it will appear as any other blank that separates options and file names).

The `paste` command is documented in *A/UX Command Reference (M–Z and Games)*. See the section *User Commands (1)*; the commands are in alphabetical order.

Sorting Files

A/UX's `sort` command will sort and merge text files. Assume that the `inventory` file is modified slightly (a field for the units in which an item is purchased has been added) as in Figure 3.9.

To sort the file, issue the command:

```
sort inventory >sorted.file
```

Output will be written to `sorted.file` rather than the standard output. Its contents can be seen in Figure 3.10. When used without any options, `sort` uses each line in the file as the sort key.

If `sort` is issued with more than one input file name, the command will merge the input files into a single sorted output file. Assume that the lines in Figure 3.11 are entered into the file `new.items`. The command:

```
sort inventory new.items >sorted.file
```

will write `sorted.file`, whose contents appear in Figure 3.12.

```
LaserWriter cartridges,each,2
Blue pencils,box,15
Red pencils,box,26
Paper clips,box,16
Post-it notes,pad,30
Thin-rule pads,each,6
Scotch tape,roll,12
Stapler,each,2
Staples,box,15
Blue felt-tip pens,box,6
Black felt-tip pens,box,10
Blue medium-point pens,box,12
Black medium-point pens,box,2
```

Figure 3.9 The expanded inventory file.

```
Black felt-tip pens,box,10
Black medium-point pens,box,2
Blue felt-tip pens,box,6
Blue medium-point pens,box,12
Blue pencils,box,15
LaserWriter cartridges,each,2
Paper clips,box,16
Post-it notes,pad,30
Red pencils,box,26
Scotch tape,roll,12
Stapler,each,2
Staples,box,15
Thin-rule pads,each,6
```

Figure 3.10 The sorted inventory file.

```
LaserWriter paper,ream,30
3-ring binders,each,10
3-ring dividers,package,10
3-hole punch,each,
```

Figure 3.11 The file `new.items`.

```
3-hole punch, each,1
3-ring binders, each,10
3-ring dividers,package,10
Black felt-tip pens,box,10
Black medium-point pens,box,2
Blue felt-tip pens,box,6
Blue medium-point pens,box,12
LaserWriter cartridges,each,2
LaserWriter paper, ream,30
Paper clips,box,16
Post-it notes,pad,30
Red pencils,box,26
Scotch tape,roll,12
Stapler,each,2
Staples,box,15
Thin-ruled pads,each,6
```

Figure 3.12 Output of the command `sort inventory new.items`.

Sort takes a number of flag options that affect how the sort/merge is performed. Two of the more commonly used are:

1. `-f`: "Fold" lowercase letters to uppercase (i.e., ignore case differences when sorting).

2. `-r`: Reverse the sort order (i.e., descending rather than ascending order).

In addition, sorting can be performed using a sort key that is less than an entire line. This type of sorting assumes that you are working with a data file, like `inventory`, that is broken into fields. By default, A/UX assumes that fields are separated by either blanks or tabs. In that case, the sort command might be written

```
sort +1 -2 inventory
```

The `+1` refers to the starting position of the sort key (actually the second field, since field numbering begins with zero); `-2` indicates the ending position. This particular command will, therefore, sort by the second field in a file whose fields are separated by blanks or tabs.

```
Black felt-tip pens,box,10
Black medium-point pens,box,2
Blue felt-tip pens,box,6
Blue medium-point pens,box,12
Blue pencils,box,15
Red pencils,box,26
Paper clips,box,16
Staples,box,15
3-hole punch,each,1
3-ring binders,each,10
LaserWriter cartridges,each,2
Stapler,each,2
Thin-rule pads,each,6
3-ring dividers,package,10
Post-it notes,pad,30
LaserWriter paper,ream,30
Scotch tape,roll,12
```

Figure 3.13 Output of the command `sort -t +1 -2 sorted.file`.

The `inventory` file, however, uses commas as field separators. To tell `sort` to use a different separator, use the `-t` option. The command

```
sort -t, +1 -2 sorted.file >new.inventory
```

will produce the output in Figure 3.13.

The `sort` command is documented in *A/UX Command Reference (M–Z and Games)*. See the section *User Commands (1)*; the commands are in alphabetical order.

Joining Files

The *join* operation is well known to people who work regularly with relational database systems. It is a method for combining two data files based on matching values in a field common to both files. Consider, for example, the two files that appear in Figure 3.14. Each data file contains two fields. The field delimiter (i.e., separator) is a comma. The file `inventory1` con-

```
#2 pencils,17
Black felt-tip pens,10
Black medium-point pens,2
Blue felt-tip pens,6
Blue medium-point pens,12
Blue pencils,15
LaserWriter cartridges,2
Paper clips,16
Post-it notes,30
Red medium-point pens,1
Red pencils,25
Scotch tape,12
Stapler,2
Staples,15
Thick-rule pads,6
Thin-rule pads,6
```

inventory 1

```
#2 pencils,box
Black felt-tip pens,box
Black medium-point pens,box
Blue felt-tip pens,box
Blue medium-point pens,box
Blue pencils,box
LaserWriter cartridges,each
Paper clips,box
Post-it notes,pad
Red medium-point pens,box
Red pencils,box
Scotch tape,roll
Stapler,each
Staples,roll
Thick-rule pads,each
Thin-rule pads,each
```

inventory2

Figure 3.14 The files inventory1 and inventory2.

tains the name of an item and the quantity of that item in the supply closet. The file inventory2 contains the name of the item and the unit in which it is purchased. The purpose of a join operation will be to combine the two files into a file like that in Figure 3.15.

Before two files can be joined, they must first be sorted on the field that will be used to perform the join. Notice that both inventory1 and inventory2 have been sorted on the first field.

During the join operation, A/UX will process the files line by line, looking for matches in the first field. If a value of the matching field exists in one file but not the other, no line will appear in the output. For example, if inventory1 contains the line:

```
#2.5 pencils,2
```

but the line does not appear in inventory2, the result of a join will not include a line for #2.5 pencils.

The join command has the general format:

```
join -j<field on which to join> -t <delimiter> -o <fields to include>
     <first file name> <second file name>
```

```
#2 pencils,17,box
Black felt-tip pens,10,box
Black medium-point pens,2,box
Blue felt-tip pens,6,box
Blue medium-point pens,12,box
Blue pencils,15,box
LaserWriter cartridges,2,each
Paper clips,16,box
Post-it notes,30,pad
Red medium-point pens,1,box
Red pencils,25,box
Scotch tape,12,roll
Stapler,2,each
Staples,15,box
Thick-rule pads,6,each
Thin-rule pads,6,each
```

Figure 3.15 The joined file `all.inventory`.

The field on which the join is made and the fields that are included in the result are specified in the format `file_number.field_number`. By default, files are joined on the first field of both files. To use the second field of file 2 instead, include `2.2` in the command line.

The `join` command to produce the file `all.inventory` is issued as:

```
join -t, -o 1.1 1.2 2.2 inventory1 inventory2 >all.inventory
```

The `-t` option is followed by a comma, the character used to separate the fields in both files. Because the files are joined on the first field, there is no need to include a `-j` option. The fields copied to the output file are `1.1` (the first field of `inventory1`), `1.2` (the second field of `inventory1`), and `2.2` (the second field of `inventory2`).

```
3-hole punch,each,1
3-ring binders,each,10
3-ring dividers,package,10
Black felt-tip pens,box,10
Black medium-point pens,box,2
Blue felt-tip pens,box,6
Blue felt-tip pen,box,6
Blue medium-point pens,box,12
Blue pencils,box,15
LaserWriter cartridges,each,2
LaserWriter paper,ream,30
Paper clips,box,16
Paper clips,box,16
Post-it notes,pad,30
Red pencils,box,26
Red pencils,box,26
Red pencils,box,26
Scotch tape,roll,12
Stapler,each,2
Staples,box,15
Thin-rule pads,each,6
Thin-rule pads,each,6
```

Figure 3.16 The inventory data file modified to contain duplicate lines.

Removing Duplicate Lines

One of the hazards of large data files is duplicate lines. A/UX provides the `uniq` command to remove duplicates. Assume, for example, that the inventory data file has been modified as in Figure 3.16. Notice that the lines describing blue felt-tip pens, paper clips, and thin-rule pads appear twice; the line describing red pencils appears three times.

To remove the duplicate lines, type

```
uniq inventory uniq.inventory
```

The first file name is the file from which `uniq` will remove duplicates; the second file name is the output file. In this case, the output file will appear identical to Figure 3.12.

Uniq works by comparing adjacent lines in the input file. That means that the input file must be sorted *before* running uniq. When sorting, use the entire line as the sort key rather than restricting it in any way.

The uniq command is documented in *A/UX Command Reference (M–Z and Games)*. See the section *User Commands (1)*; the commands are in alphabetical order.

Splitting Files

It sometimes becomes necessary to split files into one or more pieces. For example, files that are going to be posted to USENET, the world-wide network of Unix computers,[1] should be no longer than about 600 lines. A/UX provides two commands that split files—split and csplit. Split breaks a file into pieces by counting lines; csplit splits a file based on the contents of the file.

Splitting a File Into Even-sized Chunks

The general format for split is:

```
split -<number of lines/file> <input file> <output file name stub>
```

For example, if the 2,600–line file named sample.prog should be broken into 600–line segments, the command is written:

```
split -600 sample.prog my.prog
```

A/UX will create five output files:

---

1. USENET is discussed in Chapters 6 and 14.

`my.progaa` (600 lines)
`my.progab` (600 lines)
`my.progac` (600 lines)
`my.progad` (600 lines)
`my.progae` (200 lines)

`Split` takes the output file stub supplied in the command line and adds a suffix to create a unique file name. The suffixes begin with `aa` and end with `zz`. Split will therefore produce up to 676 output files.

The `split` command is documented in *A/UX Command Reference (M–Z and Games)*. See the section *User Commands (1)*; the commands are in alphabetical order.

Splitting a File By Its Contents

`Csplit` divides a file based on actual text in the file. Assume, for example, that a file (`many.chapters`) contains three chapters of a document. You would like to place each chapter in a separate file. The `csplit` command might be written:

```
csplit -f chapter many.chapters /Chapter2/ /Chapter3/
```

A/UX will produce three output files:

`chapter00` (from the start of the file to the line containing "Chapter 2")
`chapter01` (from the line containing "Chapter 2" to the line before the line containing "Chapter 3")
`chapter02` (from the line containing "Chapter 3" to the end of the file)

The `-f` option provides the output file name stub. A/UX appends sequential numbers to the stub to create unique output file names. Numbering begins at 00 and goes through 99; `csplit` will therefore produce a maximum of 100 output files.

Following the `-f` option on the command line is the name of the input file. In turn, it is followed by arguments that define where the output files should begin. The first output file contains text from the beginning of the file up to (but not including) the first argument; the second output file contains text beginning with the line containing the first argument and up to (but not including) the line containing the second argument. The last output file contains text beginning with the last argument through the end of the file. If there are *n* arguments, `csplit` will produce *n+1* output files.

An argument surrounded by slashes (/) instructs `csplit` to search the file for the characters between the slashes. However, if the argument is surrounded by percent signs (%), then `csplit` will search for the section so defined but not created as an output file. The percent signs can therefore be used to instruct `csplit` to skip some portion of the input file.

If an argument is a number, then `csplit` will create an output file that contains text from the current line up to (but not including) the line number specified in the argument. This is different from the way `split` works. `Split` counts lines; csplit works with absolute line numbering within the file.

However, `csplit` can be made to work like `split` by telling it to repeatedly create output files of the same size. For example, to use `csplit` to break the 2,600–line file into 600 line segments, the command would be written:

```
csplit -k -f prog sample.prog 600 {99}
```

The 99 in curly braces instructs csplit to repeat the argument 99 times. However, this file has less than 59,400 lines. Csplit will consider this an error and, by default, will erase all files that it has created. This is prevented by including the `-k` option, which prevents the deletion of output files in case of an error.

The `csplit` command is documented in *A/UX Command Reference (A–L)*. See the section *User Commands (1)*; the commands are in alphabetical order.

Pattern Searching

Assume that you have written a novel that is 30 chapters long. Your editor isn't happy with the name of one of the minor characters and wants it changed from George to Gregory. However, you can't remember in which chapters George appears. The solution is to use the `grep` command. `Grep` will search one or more files for text and display the lines and/or file names where the text appears.

In general, `grep` takes the format:

```
grep <expression to find> <files to search>
```

For example, to search the first two chapters of the novel for the character George, the command might be written:

```
grep 'George' chapter1 chapter2
```

Assuming that `chapter1` contains two references to George and `chapter2` contains three, the output will be:

```
chapter1:and George was there as well. His hair wasn't as grey as
Jack remembered, but
chapter1:forever. Nonetheless George was a good friend to have in a
pinch, especially if you
Chpater2:Are you kidding? George, that's nuts!"
chapter2:whenever he went to the garage. It was just like George to
forget the beer.
chapter2:didn't do it!" George squeaked.
```

`Grep` displays the name of the file and then the line in which the search text was found.

To ensure that the shell doesn't become confused by characters that have special meaning to it, the search text in the above command was surrounded by single quotes. Although the quotes aren't required for search text containing only letters, they are if the text includes $, *, [, ^, (,), or \.

`Grep` takes a number of flag options:

- `-v` Display those lines *not equal* to the search text.
- `-c` Display a count of the number of lines containing the search text
- `-n` Precede each line in the output with the line's number in the file.
- `-l` Display only the names of the files in which the search text is found (useful only where there is more than one file name in the command).
- `-i` Conduct a search that is not case sensitive.

Searching for the character George in the chapters of the novel could be more informative if one or more of these options were used. For example, if all you need is the names of the files in which George appears, the command could be written:

```
grep -l 'George' chapter*
```

and would produce

```
chapter1
chapter2
chapter12
chapter17
chapter25
chapter26
```

The changes would be easier to make, however, if `grep` reported the line numbers on which the references occurred. Therefore, the form of the command that would be most useful in this particular situation might be:

```
grep -n 'George' chapter* >George.lines
```

Because this command has the potential for a great deal of output, the output is redirected to a file where it can be stored until needed.

The `grep` command is documented in *A/UX Command Reference (A–L)*. See the section *User Commands (1)*; the commands are in alphabetical order.

Checking Spelling and Style

Although A/UX doesn't pretend to provide all the features that you might expect to find in a word processor, it does provide a simple spelling checker and a utility to analyze the writing style in a document.

The Spelling Checker

A/UX has a spelling checker, `spell`, that will check the spelling of words in a text files against a file containing a list of correct spellings. Words that do not appear in the spelling list, or cannot be derived from words in the spelling list, are displayed on the standard output. Unlike the spelling checkers that are integrated into word processors, `spell` will not show misspelled words in context.

As an example, consider the following portion of a letter (saved in a file named `sample.letter`):

```
Dear Mr. Johnson,

Throughout the past ytear we have benn wroking on an exciting new
product. It's called "Punch It!". This tool will punch holes in the
case of 3 1/2" disks so that disks labeled for 720K (MS-DOS) and 800K
(Macintosh) can be used in high desnity (1.44 M) drives.
```

To check the spelling in this file, type

```
spell sample.letter
```

A/UX will respond by displaying

```
benn
desnity
wroking
ytear
```

Note that the misspelled words have been sorted in alphabetical order; no information is given as to their location within the source file.

It is highly likely that the spelling list used by `spell` will not contain all of the correctly spelled words that you will use in your documents. A/UX therefore provides utilities to create a custom list of words that should be checked as well as the default dictionary file.

Creating a custom spelling list is a three–step process. First, create a text file containing the words that should be in a custom spelling list. Second, convert the text file into a sorted list of codes with `hashmake`:

```
/usr/lib/spell/hashmake <word.list | sort -u >temp
```

By default, `hashmake` takes its input from the standard input (i.e., the terminal keyboard). The command therefore redirects input by including `<word.list>`, telling `hashmake` to use `word.list` as its source. The result is then piped into `sort`, which creates a unique ordered list of the codes.

To complete the process, use `spellin` to compress the file created by `hashmake`. `Spellin`, which takes its input from the standard input unless told otherwise, needs to know how many codes are in the file to be processed. The command, therefore, has the general format

```
spellin n
```

where *n* is the number of codes in the file. The easiest way to get that number is to count the number of lines in the file created by `hashmake`. For example,

```
cat temp | wc -l
```

will do the trick. However, the result of the above command must be *part* of the `spellin` command, not piped to it. The trick is to surround the command with back-quotes (the back-quote is on the same key as the tilde [~]):

```
`cat temp | wc -l`
```

The `cat` command displays the contents of the file `temp`; the output is piped into `wc`, which then counts the number of lines it receives. The back-quotes surrounding the two commands instruct A/UX to compute the

result of whatever is within the back-quotes and placed that result on the command line. The complete `spellin` command can therefore be written:

```
/usr/lib/spell/spellin 'cat temp | wc -l' <temp >custom.list
```

Note that input is redirected to the `temp` file and output to a new file named `custom.list`.

To use a custom spelling list, add it to the `spell` command line, prefaced with a plus sign (+), as in:

```
spell +custom.file sample.letter
```

Analyzing Document Style

In addition to its spelling checker, A/UX will also analyze the style of a document. To do so, use the `style` command. For example, to check the style of the sample letter type:

```
style sample.letter
```

The output appears in Figure 3.17.

> **The commands `spell`, `hashmake`, and `spellin` are documented in *A/UX Command Reference (M–Z and Games)*. See the section *User Commands (1)*. All three appear on the `spell` command's pages; the commands in the manual are in alphabetical order.**

Managing a Bibliography

A/UX provides a set of utilities that will help you build, maintain, and search a bibliography. The bibliography is a text file with a special format that will be discussed shortly. It can be created with a text editor (e.g., `vi`) or with the command `addbib`, which presents a set of prompts for entering bibliographic information.

```
    sample.letter
readability grades:
    (Kincaid) 5.3 (auot) 6.7 (Coleman-Liau) 6.8 (Flesch) 6.2 (87.8)
sentence info:
    no. sent 3  no. wds 52
    av sent lang 17.3  av word leng 4.13
    no. questions 0  no. imperatives 0
    no. nonfunc wds 34 65.4%  av leng 4.76
    short sent (<12) 33% (1)  long sent (>27) 33% (1)
    longest sent 31 wds at sent 3; shortest sent 5 wds at sent 2
sentence types:
    simple 67% (2)  complex 33% (1)
    compound 0% (0)  compound-complex 0% (0)
word usage:
    verb types as % of total verbs
    tobe 50% (2)  aux 50% (2)  inf 0% (0)
    passives as % of non-inf verbs 50% (2)
    types a % of total
    prep 9.6% (5)  conj 1.9% (1)  adv 1.9% (1)
    noun 32.7% (17)  adj 23.1% (12)  pron 5.8% (3)
    nominalizations 0% (0)
sentence beginnings:
    subject opener: noun (0)  pron (0)  pos (0)  adj (2)  art (0)  tot 67%
    prep 0% (0)  adv 0% (0)
    verb 0% (0) sub-conj 0% (0) conj 0% (0)
    expletives 33% (1)
```

Figure 3.17 Output of the command `style sample`.

Creating a Bibliography File

A portion of a bibliographic data file can be seen in Figure 3.18. Each entry begins with a percent sign (%) followed by a letter that identifies the type of entry. For example, an `A` prefaces an author line while a `J` prefaces the name of the magazine or journal in which an article appears. Although there are 21 types of entries, only those that are actually needed by an entry need be used.

The entries in a bibliography can be any of the following:

```
%A Author of book or article
%A Resse Jones
%T Following Protocol
%J MacUser
%P 114-123
%D May, 1989
%K AppleTalk, telecommunications protocols, protocols

%A Robert R. Wiggins
%T The Art of Persuasion and MORE II
%J MacUser
%P 127-135
%D May, 1989
%K outliners, presentation graphics

%A Pamela Sue Burdman
%T Word Processing with Character
%J MacUser
%P 137-146
%D May, 1989
%K word processing, word processors, Chinese
```

Figure 3.18 A portion of a bibliographic data file.

%B	Name of book in which an article appears
%C	City where published
%D	Date published
%E	Editor of book or book in which an article appears
%F	Footnote number (used by A/UX's advanced text formatting tools)
%G	Government publication order number
%H	Header to be printed before the bibliographic entry
%I	Issuer (publisher)
%J	Journal or magazine in which an article appears
%K	Keywords describing article or book that will be used to search for the item
%L	Label option (used by A/UX's advanced text formatting tools)
%N	Number of magazine within a volume

%O	"Other" commentary, printed at the end of a bibliographic entry
%P	Page numbers
%Q	Corporate or foreign author
%R	Report, paper, or thesis (an unpublished work)
%S	Series title
%T	Title of book or article
%V	Volume of magazine or journal
%X	Abstract (summary of book or article)

Only the %A (author) line can be repeated within a single bibliographic entry. However, a given type of entry may occupy more than one line in the file. To continue to a second line, end the preceding line with a backslash (\).

The key to creating a bibliography that can be searched effectively is assigning the keywords on line %K. It is up to the person creating the bibliography file to determine the terms that will be used to describe books and articles. Unless keywords are assigned consistently, it will be difficult to retrieve books and articles that correspond to the same topic.

The bibliography file can be created by using a text editor and typing the needed lines. Alternatively, `addbib` will provide a set of prompts and write the file. To use it, type

```
addbib <name of bibliography file>
```

as in

```
addbib Mac.articles
```

A/UX will display prompts for the most commonly used types of entries, creating a dialog similar to that seen in Figure 3.19. Entries that are not applicable can be skipped by pressing a RETURN at the prompt.

If the prompts displayed by `addbib` do not include entries that you need, create a custom prompt file. The prompt file has the format

```
<prompt string>     <entry letter>
```

```
    Author: Joshua Brown
    Title; Under Your Computer's Hood
    Journal:
    Volume:
    Pages:
    Publisher: Westfield Computer Press
    City: New York, NY
    Date: 1989
    Other:
    Keywords: computer architecture, microprocessors
    Abstract (ctrl-d to end)
This is one of the finest books describing basic computer architec-
ture and how microprocessors work.

Continue?
```

Figure 3.19 An `addbib` dialog.

as in

```
Editor    E
```

The prompt string and the entry letter must be separated by a TAB, not by spaces.

To use the custom prompt file, add the `-p` option to `addbib`:

```
addbib -p prompt.file Mac.magazines
```

A/UX will use the prompts in the file `prompt.file` to create the bibliography data file `Mac.magazines`.

> The `addbib` command is documented in *A/UX Command Reference (A–L)*. See the section *User Commands (1)*; the commands are in alphabetical order.

Indexing a Bibliography File

Searching a bibliography data file is performed with the `lookbib` command. However, before a search can be executed, the file must be indexed. In addition, you may first wish to sort it to change the order of the output.

To sort a bibliography data file, first decide which entry letters should be used as the sort key (up to four can be used). Then use the `sortbib` command:

```
sortbib -sAT Mac.magazines >sorted.bib
```

The command line above will sort the `Mac.magazines` bibliography file by the author and title entries and write the result to `sorted.bib`. `Sortbib` is fairly smart about sorting author entries; it assumes that the last word of the entry is the author's last name.

The `sortbib` command is documented in *A/UX Command Reference (M–Z and Games.* See the section *User Commands (1)*; the commands are in alphabetical order.

Once the file has been sorted, it can be indexed with:

```
indxbib <name of data file>
```

as in

```
indxbib sorted.bib
```

`Indxbib` produces three output files:

```
sorted.bib.ia
sorted.bib.ib
sorted.bib.ic
```

These three index files are used by `lookbib`, the command that actually searches the bibliography data file.

The `indxbib` command is documented in *A/UX Command Reference (A–L)* as part of the `lookbib` command. See the section *User Commands (1)*; the commands are in alphabetical order.

Searching the Bibliography

To search for bibliographic entries by keywords, type

```
lookbib <name of data file>
```

as in

```
lookbib sorted.bib
```

A/UX will respond by displaying a > prompt. Type the keywords for which `lookbib` should search and press RETURN. If `lookbib` can find bibliographic entries that match the keywords, it will display those entries on the screen. Otherwise, it will respond with another >. Type CTRL-D to exit from `lookbib`.

The `lookbib` command is documented in *A/UX Command Reference (A–L)*. See the section *User Commands (1)*: the commands are in alphabetical order.

Chapter 4

Creating, Editing, and Printing Text Files

A/UX provides many ways to create and edit text files, ranging from the very simple (the `cat` command), to a line editor (`ed`) and a full screen editor (`vi`). Most UNIX users prefer to use a full screen editor such as `vi`. However, there are times when both `cat` and `ed` are useful. In particular, `ed` is the only text editor available from the stand-alone shell (see Chapter 11) and must, therefore, be used when modifying system files before A/UX is launched.

This chapter concludes with a introduction to printing text file's on an A/UX system's default printer. This type of printer is often directly connected to the A/UX machine using a serial port; it is not necessarily connected using AppleTalk.

Cat

Chapter 1 uses the `cat` command to display the lines of a text file on the terminal screen. However, the action of the command is actually to *concatenate* lines to the current output file (remember that UNIX views every output destination as a file). When used with output redirection, `cat` will write text to a file.

Assume, for example, that you issue the command:

```
cat >more.inventory
```

Once you have pressed the RETURN or ENTER key, A/UX responds by moving the cursor to the left edge of the next line; no prompt appears. Type the contents of the first line of the file and press RETURN. Continue to type lines, ending each with a press of the RETURN key. When all the lines have been entered, signal the end-of-input by typing `CTRL-D` on a new line (i.e., the `CTRL-D` should be the only thing on the line).

With `cat`, there are very few editing features available. If you catch a typing error on a line before pressing `RETURN`, use the `BACKSPACE` key to erase characters and retype the line correctly. However, once you have pressed `RETURN`, there is no way to go back and edit existing lines. To do so, you will need to use some other text editor (e.g., `ed` or `vi`).

The cat command is documented in *A/UX Command Reference (A–L)*. See the section *User Commands (1)*; the commands are in alphabetical order.

Ed

Ed is a *line editor*. A line editor views a text file as a collection of numbered lines, each of which ends with a carriage return. (Unlike a word processor, a line editor cannot do word wrap.) The line editor maintains a line pointer to indicate the current line. Editing therefore affects either the line numbers specified in a command or the line on which the line pointer is resting.

Because a line editor relies on line numbers to locate the target of editing commands, full screen editing keys (e.g., the arrow keys) cannot be used to move around the file. Instead, line editors require commands that move the line pointer. The only editing key that can be used is the BACKSPACE, which will delete characters to the left of the cursor when used before RETURN is pressed. For this reason, line editors are generally only used to make quick modifications on very small files or when a terminal cannot support full screen editing (e.g., a hard copy terminal). Most of the time, you will want to use a full screen editor like vi.

Commands are issued to ed in the same way that commands are issued to the shell: Each command is typed on a separate line and terminated with a carriage return. If ed cannot understand a command, it will respond with a question mark (?). To see the reason for the most recent question mark, type h. To automatically see the explanation for all question marks, use H to turn on error message printing; using H again will turn off the automatic printing.

A/UX's line editor, ed, is documented in two places. A command summary appears in *A/UX Command Reference (A–L)*, where it can be found in alphabetical sequence in the *User Commands (1)* section. However, a more tutorial explanation can be found in the first section of *A/UX Text Editing Tools*.

Entering and Leaving Ed

To invoke `ed` to create a new file, type:

```
ed
```

The cursor will be placed at the left–hand edge of the screen on the next line:

```
$ ed <cr>
_
```

The line editor's buffer (the place in main memory where it stores the contents of a file while it is being edited) is empty.

To invoke `ed` to work on an existing file, type:

```
ed <name of file to be edited>
```

as in:

```
ed inventory
```

If the file exists, `ed` will read the file into its buffer and display the number of lines in the file:

```
$ ed inventory <cr>
17
_
```

If the `ed` command is issued with the name of a file that does not exist, A/UX will not indicate that an error has occurred. Instead, it will use the file name from the command line the first time the file is saved. (See the next section for instructions on how to save a file.)

To exit `ed` and return to the dollar sign prompt, type a `q` followed by a carriage return. The `q` command does not save the file being edited; if `q` is issued before changes are saved, they will be lost.

Saving the File

The contents of `ed`'s buffer is written to disk with the `w` command. If used by itself, `w` will write the entire contents of the buffer to an existing file. If the contents of the buffer have not yet been saved, or if they are to be saved to a file name other than the one from which they were read, follow `w` with the name of the file:

```
w <name of file>
```

as in:

```
w inventory2
```

To save only a portion of the buffer, specify the range of lines that are to be saved, using the format:

```
<starting line #>, <ending line #> w
```

For example, to save the first 20 lines of the buffer type:

```
1,20 w
```

If necessary, a file name can be added to the command:

```
1,20 w inventory2
```

Moving the Line Pointer

To move the line pointer, type the number of the line to which the line pointer should be moved. `Ed` will display the line on the screen as well as moving the line pointer.

To move the line pointer back one line (i.e., to the preceding line), type either a caret (^ {shift-6]) or a minus sign (-). Placing more than one of either on a line moves back in the file as many lines as there are characters. For example,

```
^^^^^
```

will move the line pointer five lines back.

There are two shortcuts for specifying line numbers. A period (.) represents the current line; a dollar sign ($) stands for the last line in the buffer. The dollar sign can be used to move the line pointer without actually having to know the total number of lines in the buffer.

Looking at the Contents of the Buffer

The p command will list lines in the buffer on the screen. If used without any arguments, p displays only the current line. However, p can be given a range of lines using the format:

```
<first line to print>, <last line to print>p
```

For example, to see the first 25 lines in the buffer, type:

```
1,25p
```

The two line number shortcuts described above can be used with p. For example, to see all of the lines from the current line to the end of the buffer, the command is:

```
.,$p
```

In addition to using absolute line numbers, p will accept line numbers that are specified relative to the current line. For example,

```
.+1p
```

will print the line after the current line, and

```
.-1p
```

will print the line before the current line.

Entering Text

When ed is invoked, anything entered from the keyboard is interpreted as a command to the line editor. Therefore, ed must be instructed to interpret input as new text rather than as a command. The a command will signal ed to add lines to the buffer *after* the current line; the *i* command will insert lines *before* the current line.

In either case, text is entered by typing from the keyboard, following each line with a carriage return. To stop entering text and return to entering commands, type a period (.) in the leftmost column of the last line. The period must be the only character on the line; it will not be entered into the buffer.

For example, a text entry session into the inventory file might appear as:

```
a
Paper clips, 16 boxes
No. 2 lead pencils, 5 boxes
Blue pencils, 1 box
Red pencils, 2 boxes
Thin-ruled pads, 25
Wide-ruled pads, 12
Scotch tape, 18 rolls
.
```

Everything except the period on the last line will be added to the file.

As mentioned in Chapter 2, several characters have a special meaning to A/UX. Those that are important to consider when entering text are:

1. @: Instructs A/UX to ignore the entire line.
2. #: Instructs A/UX to ignore the character to the left.
3. \: Instructs A/UX to ignore the special meaning of the following character and insert it into text instead.

To enter either a @ or # into text, precede it with \, as in:

```
\@
\#
```

To enter the backslash, type it twice:

```
\\
```

Inserting Text From Another File

In addition to entering text directly from the keyboard, text can be copied from an existing file with the `r` command:

```
r <file name>
```

Text will be appended to the end of the buffer.

To insert text at some position other than the end of the buffer, precede the `r` with a line number, as in:

```
15r more.inventory
```

To place text after the current line, use a period:

```
.r add.goods
```

If the file name following `r` is replaced with an exclamation point (!) and an A/UX command, the output of the command will be inserted into `ed`'s buffer. For example, to place a columnar listing of the files in the current directory into the file after the current line, type:

```
.r !ls -C
```

Changing Text

Because `ed` is a line editor, changes cannot be made using standard Macintosh editing techniques, or even by using DEL and BACKSPACE along with the arrow keys to move the cursor. Instead, the one general

technique is to move the line pointer to the line that is to be edited and then issue the s command to change text in that line.

Searching and Replacing Text

The format of the s command is:

```
s/<text to find>/<text to replace it with>/
```

The slashes are *delimiters*, used to separate the text to be found from the text that is to replace it. If the slash is to be part of either the text to be found or the replacement text, then select another character as the delimiter. Any character except a blank or a tab can be used.

Assume, for example, that the line following is the current line:

```
LaserJet toner cartridges, 7
```

The characters "Jet" can be changed to "Writer" with:

```
s/Jet/Writer/
```

Ed searches the current line for the first occurrence of "Jet" and replaces it with "Writer."

To delete characters from a line, use no replacement text, as in

```
s/Jet//
```

Note that there is no space between the two trailing delimiters. If the command were written

```
s/Jet/ /
```

then the characters "Jet" would be replaced with a blank.

If the line being searched contains more than one occurrence of the search text, only the first occurrence will be replaced. If the current line is

```
pen and pencil sets, 15
```

then the command

```
s/pen/Pen
```

will produce

```
Pen and pencil sets, 15
```

To replace every occurrence of the search text, append a `g` to the end of the `s` command, as in:

```
s/pen/Pen/g
```

The result of this command on the line above will be

```
Pen and Pencil sets, 15
```

By default, `s` does not display the result of its actions. However, `p` can be added at the end of the command line to print the current line.

Replacing an Entire Line

The `c` command will delete one or more lines and then accept the input of new lines as replacement. Its general format is:

```
<first line to remove>, <last line to remove>c
```

If line numbers are left omitted, `c` will delete only the current line.

As an example, assume that the buffer contains the following lines:

```
White 3 x 5 cards, 6 packages
Blue 3 x 5 cards, 2 packages
Pink 3 x 5 cards, 2 packages
Green 3 x 5 cards, 4 packages
```

If the pink and green cards are to be deleted and replaced by white, pink, yellow, and blue 4 x 6 cards, the commands issued to `ed` are:

```
3,4c <cr>
White 4 x 6 cards, 10 packages
Pink 4 x 6 cards, 10 packages
Yellow 4 x 6 cards, 10 packages
Blue 4 x 6 cards, 10 packages
.
```

Note that the input is terminated by a period and that the number of lines inserted does not necessarily have to be the same as the number of lines removed.

Deleting Lines

One or more lines are deleted with the `d` command. It has the general format:

```
<first line to be deleted>, <last line to be deleted>d
```

If the line numbers are omitted, only the current line will be deleted. To delete the fourth through 15th lines in the buffer, use the command:

```
4,15d
```

Simple Text Formatting

For the most part, text files created with `ed` cannot be formatted. However, it is possible to set tab stops, the left margin, and the maximum line length. To do so, a format line is inserted as the first line in the file. A format line has the general format:

```
<: format specifications :>
```

Format specifications are separated from one another by spaces.

By default, each press of the TAB key during text entry moves the cursor eight spaces. The default can be overridden by placing the letter `t` followed by the columns where tab stops should be set within the format line. For example, to set tab stops at 5, 10, 15, and 20 characters across the line, use a format line like:

```
<:t5,10,15,20:>
```

To set evenly spaced tabs across an entire line, following the `t` with a minus sign and the tab interval, as in:

```
<:t-5:>
```

Left margins are set by following the letter `m` with the number of spaces that should be placed at the beginning of each line. Assuming that tab stops are to be set every five spaces and that the left margin is to be ten, the format line appears as:

```
<:t-5 m10:>
```

The maximum line length is set by following the letter `s` with the number of characters that will be allowed on a line. If the line length is to be 60 characters, the format line will appear as:

```
<:t-5 m10 s60:>
```

The effect of the above format line is to create a file with both left and right margins of ten spaces.

Unless told otherwise, `ed` will assume that the format line in the first line of the file affects the entire file. However, if an `e` appears in the format line, the format line will be in effect only until another format line appears in the file. In this way, a variety of margin and tab settings can be applied to one file.

File formatting for use with `ed` is documented in *A/UX Programmer's Reference*. See the section *File Formats (4)*; see the *fspec* entry (the entries are in alphabetical order).

Vi

`Vi` is the full screen editor shipped with all UNIX systems. It displays an entire screen of text and supports the use of full screen cursor movement keys such as the arrow keys, PAGE UP, and PAGE DOWN. Keep in mind, however, that `vi` is a text editor, not a word processor. Each line in a document ends with a carriage return; there is no word wrap. As a text editor, `vi` supports the entry and modification of text; it does provide text formatting. (You must use `troff` or `nroff` to format text files for output.)

`Vi` also has a line editor mode (`ex`). `Ex` is very similar to `ed`, and in most circumstances `vi` users stay away from it. However, a number of `user commands` are available only through `ex`. Such commands are preceded with a colon (:), which temporarily places `vi` in line editing mode. When the colon is typed, `vi` places the colon on the bottom line of the screen. The remaining characters in the command also appear on that line.

To properly interpret presses of cursor movement keys, `vi` needs to know the type of terminal being used. The current terminal is stored in the system variable TERM. In most cases, the terminal will be a Macintosh II. Issuing the command:

```
echo $TERM
```

will produce

```
mac2
```

If you are using a Macintosh II (or some variety thereof) and TERM contains something other than `mac2`, type:

```
TERM=mac2
```

If you have logged in to A/UX using a modem and some type of computer other than a Macintosh II, then your telecommunications software will probably support emulation of a VT100 terminal. In that case, set TERM by typing:

```
TERM=vt100
```

If you are using some other kind of terminal, check with your system administrator to find out exactly what character string corresponds to the terminal definition. (A/UX comes with a variety of terminal definition files, but their names may not correspond to the name of the terminal exactly.)

The `vi` text editor is documented in three places. An introduction appears in *Getting Started with A/UX*. Tutorial materials can be found in *A/UX Text Editing Tools*. A command summary is included in *A/UX Command Reference (A–L and Games)*. In the latter, see the section *User Commands (1)*; the commands are in alphabetical order.

Modes

`Vi` has two modes, a *command* mode (the mode in which `vi` opens) and an *insert* mode. When working in command mode, key presses are interpreted as commands to `vi`. All of the commands described in the following sections of this chapter must be issued in command mode.

In insert mode, characters are inserted into the document being edited. There are a number of ways to enter insert mode (discussed in the section on entering text). To return to command mode, press ESC.

Entering and Leaving Vi

To enter `vi`, use the following command syntax:

```
vi <name of file to edit>
```

as in

```
vi inventory
```

If the file name included in the command line represents an existing file, the file will be opened and presented for editing. If the file name does not exist, `vi` will assume that you wish to create a new file.

```
Blue pencils, 6 boxes
Red pencils, 2 boxes
Staples, 15 boxes
Narrow-ruled pads, 30
Wide-ruled pads, 12
Scotch tape, 5 boxes
Message cubes, 5
~
~
~
~
~
~
~
~
~
~
~
~
~
~
~
~
~
```

Figure 4.1 The initial `vi` screen.

The `vi` command can also be issued without a file name. In that case, `vi` will assume that a new file is being created. The file name must be supplied when the file is saved for the first time.

The `vi` screen (Figure 4.1) displays as many lines of a file as will fit. If the file is less than the maximum number of lines on the screen or if a new file is being created, `vi` fills each empty line with a tilde (~). The tildes are not part of the file, but indicate that lines are empty rather than containing blanks or carriage returns.

Under some circumstances, you may wish to look at a file but not modify it. In that case, enter `vi` with the `view` command, as in:

```
view sensitive.data
```

The file will be opened in *readonly* mode, permitting reading but not writing.

There are two ways to leave `vi`. Assuming that the file on which you are working has been previously name, pressing ZZ will save the file, exit `vi`, and return to the shell prompt. (`ZZ` will not work if the file has been opened with `view`, since `view` opens a readonly file.) To exit without saving the file, type:

```
:q
```

The colon places `vi` temporarily in line editing mode. The `q` is a line editing command that exits without saving. (For additional ways to save a file, see the next section of this chapter.)

Saving Files

As described above, a previously named file can be saved by typing `ZZ`. The `ZZ` command will also exit `vi`, returning to the shell prompt. Because `ZZ` is issued without a preceding colon, it is a `vi` command, not a line editor (`ex`) command.

A file that has not yet been named is saved by typing

```
:w <file name>
```

as in,

```
:w logs
```

This same syntax can also be used to save a previously named file under a different name.

Some system files (e.g., /etc/passwd, the file that is used to set up user accounts) have no write permissions, even for the owner of the file. However, the superuser can override the file permissions and write to those files by typing

```
:w!
```

The `:w!` command will also write readonly files (i.e., those that have been opened with `view` rather than `vi`).

Moving the Cursor (Scrolling)

`vi` provides a wide range of commands that will move the cursor to a new position in the file being edited. Movement may be by character, word, sentence, paragraph, line, or screen. The following commands must all be entered in command mode:

- Moving one character at a time.
  - `^` Move to the first nonwhite (nonblank) character.
  - `0` Move to the beginning of the current line.
  - `$` Move to the end of the current line.
  - `h`, `SPACEBAR`, *or* `”` Move one character to the right.
  - `l`, `CTRL-H`, *or* `u` Move one character to the left.
- Moving one word at a time.
  - `w` Move one word forward.
  - `b` Move one word back.
  - `e` Move to the end of the current word.
  - `W` Move one word forward. (With this command, a word is defined as a string of characters with a blank at the beginning and a blank at the end. It will, therefore, skip words that end with punctuation marks.)
  - `B` Move one word back, skipping words that end with punctuation marks.
  - `E` Move to the end of the next word, skipping words that end with punctuation marks.
- Moving one sentence at a time.
  - `)` Move to next sentence.
  - `(` Move to previous sentence.

- Moving one paragraph at a time.
  - `}` Move to next paragraph.
  - `{` Move to previous paragraph.

- Moving one or more lines at a time.
  - `H` Move to the top line on the screen.
  - `L` Move to the bottom line on the screen.
  - `M` Move to the middle line on the screen.
  - `RETURN` *or*
  - `+` Move to first nonwhite (nonblank) character on the next line.
  - `-` Move the the first nonwhite (nonblank) character on the previous line.
  - O *or*
  - `j` Move down one line.
  - = *or*
  - `k` Move up one line.
  - `G` Move to the end of the file.
  - *n*`G` Move to line number *n*, where *n* is some line within the file.

- Moving one or more screens at a time.

`CTRL-D`	Scroll down one-half screen.
`CTRL-U`	Scroll up one-half screen.
`CTRL-F`	Scroll one screen forward.
n`CTRL-F`	Scroll *n* screens forward, where *n* is an integer.
`CTRL-B`	Scroll one screen back.
n`CTRL-B`	Scroll *n* screens back, where *n* is an integer.

In addition to the above commands, `vi` will position the cursor based on matches with existing text in the file:

- Matching one character (*x*).
  - `f`*x* Search forward in the file and position the cursor under the first occurrence of *x*.
  - `F`*x* Search backward in the file and position the cursor under the first occurrence of *x*.

`tx` Search forward in the file and position the cursor to the left of the first occurrence of *x*.
`Tx` Search backward in the file and position the cursor to the right of *x*.
`;` Repeat last f, F, t, or T.

- Matching a string of characters (*string*).
  `/string` Search forward in the file, moving the cursor to the next line that contains *string*.
  `?string` Search backward in the file, moving the cursor to the closest previous line containing *string*.
  `n` Repeat last / or ?.
  `N` Reverse the last / or ?.

Entering Text

`vi` has seven commands to enter the insert mode, six of which insert characters to the left of the cursor and one which replaces existing characters:

1. `a`: Add (append) characters after the cursor.
2. `i`: Insert characters before the cursor.
3. `A`: Add (append) characters at the end of the current line.
4. `I`: Insert characters before the first nonblank character on the current line.
5. `o`: Insert a blank line below the line where the cursor is placed and enter insert mode.
6. `O`: Insert a blank line above the line where the cursor is placed and enter insert mode.
7. `R`: Replace existing characters beginning at the current cursor position (word processors often refer to this as *overtype* mode).

To enter text, first place `vi` in the insert mode. Then type the text that is to be added to the file. It is not necessary to type a carriage return at the end of every line on the screen. However, unlike a word processor, `vi` cannot do word wrap. If a word will not fit completely on a line, it will be broken in the middle:

```
advisable that we return the samples immediately, esp
ecially since we do not intend to order the merchandi
se.
```

In most cases, it is more convenient to enter a carriage return at the end of each line, just as you would if you were using a typewriter. If editing shortens lines, they can be joined (removing the trailing carriage return) with the `vi` command `J`.

During text entry, there are a few editing commands that can be used:

1. `BACKSPACE` or `CTRL-H`: Erases the character to the left of the cursor.
2. `DEL`: Erases the character under and to the right of the cursor.
3. `@` (the default *kill* character): Erases the current line.

Inserting Text From Another File

Text stored in another file can be inserted into a `vi` document by typing:

```
:r <name of file>
```

`Vi` will place the entire contents of the file named in the `r` command into the file being edited, beginning on the line below the current cursor position.

Editing Text

To edit text, exit from the insert mode by pressing ESC. Then use any of the scrolling commands described earlier to place the cursor at the line, word, or character that is to be modified. Existing text may be deleted or replaced.

Changing Text

`Vi`'s change command, `c`, will delete a section of text and place `vi` in the insert mode so that text may be added. After typing the new text, press ESC to return to the command mode.

The amount of text that is deleted depends on what cursor movement letter follows `c`, as in:

`cj`	Delete one character to the right and enter the insert mode.
`ck`	Delete one character to the left and enter the insert mode.
`cw`	Delete the next word and enter the insert mode.
`cb`	Delete the previous word and enter the insert mode.

In addition, the following `c` commands are also useful:

`cc`	Delete the current line and enter the insert mode.
`C` *or* `c$`	Delete from the cursor to the end of the line and enter the insert mode.

As an alternative to using `c`, remember that `R` will place `vi` in the insert mode where new characters will replace existing characters.

Deleting Text

Deleting text is very similar to changing text. The `d` command affects whatever amount of text is specified by the cursor movement letter that follows `d`. For example,

`dj`	Delete one character to the right of the cursor.
`dk`	Delete one character to the left of the cursor.
`dw`	Delete the next word.
`db`	Delete the previous word.
`dd`	Delete the current line.
`D` *or* `d$`	Delete from the cursor to the end of the line.
`x`	Delete the character under the cursor.

When text is deleted, `vi` places it in a buffer, similar in concept to the Macintosh Operating System's Clipboard. However, `vi` can handle up to 27 buffers, the unnamed default buffer and 26 others labeled a through z. To place text in a buffer other than the default buffer, precede the delete command with a double quote and the name of the buffer. For example, to delete the next paragraph and place it in buffer *p*, enter the command:

```
"pd}
```

Copying and Pasting Text

Placing text in a buffer without deleting the text from the file is known as *yanking* the text. This is similar to the Macintosh Operating System's copy operation. Like `c` and `d`, the yank command (`y`) operates on whatever amount of text is specified by the cursor movement command that follows it:

`y)`	Copy the following sentence to the default buffer.
`"by}`	Copy the next paragraph to buffer *b*.
`yw`	Copy the next word to the default buffer.
`"gyb`	Copy the previous word to buffer *g*.
`yy`	Copy the current line to the default buffer.
`"pyy`	Copy the current line to buffer *p*.

Copying text from a buffer into the document uses the `p` (put) command. Similar to the Macintosh Operating System's paste operation, the `p` command can be issued in several different ways:

`p`	Copy text from the default buffer and place it in the document beginning on the line below the cursor.
`P`	Copy text from the default buffer and place it in the document above the cursor.
`"bp`	Copy text from some buffer and place it in the document beginning on the line below the cursor.

Printing Text Files

Any A/UX file that contains text (i.e., not binary) can be sent to a printer. In most cases, printing requires to steps–formatting the file or files for output (the `pr` command) and actually sending the formatted file to the printer (`lp` or `lpr`). The `lp` command is the System V version of the command; `lpr` is the BSD version.

Formatting for Printed Output

In its simplest form, `pr` has the general form:

```
pr <file to format>
```

The output will be sent to the standard output. However, since the intention of the command is to create a formatted file that can then be sent to a printer, `pr`'s output is commonly redirected to a file. For example,

```
pr user.logs >log.output
```

will format the file `user.logs` and write the result to `log.output`.

`Pr`'s default formatting breaks the input file into pages and places a page number, the current date and time, and the name of the file at the top of each page. Tabs are expanded to eight spaces; any format strings in the file are ignored. However, these defaults can be changed and augmented by using one or more of `pr`'s flag options:

+*k* Set the page number (e.g., `+5` begins page numbering at page 5 rather than the default of page 1).

-d Print double–spaced output.

-e*k* Expand tabs to a multiple of *k* spaces (e.g., `-e5` will place five spaces in the output for each tab character in the input file, overriding the default eight).

`-nk` Print the file with line numbers that take up *k+1* spaces. (e.g., `-n3` will preface each line with a four digit line number).

`-lk` Set the number of lines per page to *k* (the default is 66).

`-h` Specify a header other than the file name (e.g., `-h "January User Logs"` will replace the file name `user.logs`).

The `user.logs` file might therefore be printed with the command:

```
pr user.logs -d -e5 -h "January User Logs" >log.output
```

The file will be printed double spaced, with each tab inserting five spaces and a header of "January User Logs." The output will be written to the file `log.output`.

Sending Files to the Printer

The `lp` command sends a request to `lpsched` to print a text file. (Note: Although text files are often formatted with `pr` before being sent to the printer, they need not be.) When issued in the form

```
lp <name of file to print>
```

the command will send the file named in the command to the system's default printer. A/UX will respond with a print request number:

```
lp logs.output
request id is pr1-87 (1 file)
```

In this particular number, `pr1` identifies the printer to which the request was sent; `87` is the actual request number. The user is returned to the shell's prompt immediately, without waiting for the file to be printed. Printing is, by default, a background activity; the & to send printing to the background is unnecessary.

A/UX printers are shared by everyone using the same machine. They may even be shared by other users on the same network who are using other computers. For that reason, a printer may not always be available when a request is made to print a file. In that case, the print request is placed at the end of the print queue and waits until all previous print requests have been processed.

If you wish to print on a file other than the default printer, first ask the system administrator for the destination designation of the printer (e.g., `pr1` is often the default destination; other designations vary from one installation to another). Then use the format

```
lp -d<destination> <file to be printed>
```

When a file is queued for printing, it is linked rather than copied into the /usr/spool/lp directory. For that reason, you should not delete files until they have physically been printed.

Managing Printing Requests

To see all of the files that you have queued for printing, use the `lpstat` command without any options. You will see output similar to:

```
pr1-87   jon    175    May 10   12:39
pr1-88   jon    306    May 10   13:22
pr1-93   jon    856    May 10   14:01
```

The leftmost column contains the print request ID; the second column from the left contains the name of the user that issued the request. The remaining columns contain the size in bytes of the file and the date and time the request was issued.

If you decide that one or more of the queued requests should not be printed, cancel it with the `cancel` command:

```
cancel <printer request ID number>
```

For example,

```
cancel pr1-88
```

will cancel the second print request identified by the `lpstat` command above. A/UX will acknowledge the cancellation by displaying

```
request "pr1-87" cancelled
```

Chapter 5

Formatting Text Files

UNIX text editors provide only a minimum of formatting. Nonetheless, UNIX systems do contain programs that will format files for both screen and printer output. A/UX provides `nroff` (used to format documents for printing on line-oriented devices like line printers), `troff` (used for device-independent formatting), and `psroff` (a shell script that uses `troff` to generate PostScript code that can be sent to a PostScript printer). The way in which files are prepared for all three text formatters, however, is generally the same.

A/UX's text formatters are documented in *A/UX Text Processing Tools*. In addition, reference for each of the formatters appears under the command name in *A/UX Command Reference (M–Z and Games)*. See the section *User Commands (1)*; the commands are in alphabetical order.

To prepare a document for formatting, first use a text editor such as `vi` to enter the contents of the document. Then add formatting commands and *macros*. Formatting commands begin with a period at the left edge of a line. The commands are made up of two lowercase characters; in some cases, the characters are followed by arguments. A formatting command ends with a carriage return.

The term "macro" refers to a sequence of commands that performs a formatting function. Each macro has a name. To invoke the commands that comprise the macro, a period followed by the macro name (one or two *uppercase* characters) is placed on a line by itself within the document. The period must be at the far left of the line.

A/UX comes with several macro packages. These include the `mm` (Memorandum Macros, used formatting documents), `man` (macros for formatting manual pages), `mptx` (macros for formatting a permuted index like the index in *A/UX Command Reference*), and `mv` (macros for formatting graphs and slides). Although the documentation also describes the `ms` macro package, it is not included as part of A/UX 1.1.

Macro packages assemble groups of formatting commands that are applicable to a specific type of document such as margins, tab stops, and header styles. For that reason, most files that are formatted make very little use of the formatting commands themselves but instead use macros from one of the macro packages. It is also possible to write customized macros and create macro packages.

In addition to macros, the text formatters recognize *strings*. A string is a variable that is expanded into text when the document is processed by a text formatter. Strings can be used, for example, to insert the current date, create special characters (e.g., a bullet), or define footnotes.

The macro packages are documented in *A/UX Programmers Reference*. See the section *Miscellaneous Facilities (5)*; the contents of this section are in alphabetical order.

Running a Text Formatter

In Listing 5.1 you will find the contents of a text file that has been prepared for processing with either `nroff`, `troff`, or `psroff`. (This particular file is the documentation for a public domain Unix program called `month`. `Month` is an appointment scheduler that lets users check each others schedules to make it easier to schedule group meetings.)

When processed by `psroff`, the file appears on paper as in Listing 5.2. When processed by `nroff` or `troff` and displayed on the screen, the file appears the same but without the boldface or italics.

To create the PostScript output the command is issued as:

```
psroff month.1
```

`Psroff` runs `troff` and intercepts the output, adding PostScript commands before automatically spooling the result for printing. If you don't want to automatically spool the output, it can be redirected to the standard output with the `-t` option, as in:

```
psroff -t month.1
```

To save the PostScript code, redirect the output of the above command to a file:

```
psroff -t month.1
```

The `nroff` and `troff` commands use virtually the same command line. Although the examples that follow use `troff`, the syntax applies to `nroff` as well. To process the file in Appendix 5.A and view on the screen the command can be written:

```
troff -man month.1 | more
```

Because `troff` normally sends its output to the standard output, the command pipes the output to `more` so that it can be viewed one screen at a time. Alternatively, the output can be redirected to a file:

```
troff -man month.1 >month.doc
```

The `-m` option is used to identify the macro package that `troff` should use. `Troff` takes the characters following `-m` and appends them to `/usr/lib/tmac/tmac` to create the complete path name of the macro package.

How Text Formatters Work

A text formatter is not the same as a word processor, even a word processor that uses commands preceded by periods to specify formatting (e.g., WordStar). Word processors identify the ends of paragraphs by searching for carriage returns. However, because text formatters work on files created by text editors that cannot perform word wrap and because the formatting commands for type styles must appear on separate lines, the end of a paragraph cannot be signaled by a carriage return.

A text formatter, therefore, begins a new paragraph every time it sees the `.br` (break) command or a blank line in the text. Listing 5.1, for example, contains a `.br` at the end of every section of text that should be formatted as a single paragraph. Notice that the contents of a paragraph are not typed continuously without carriage returns as they would be for a word processor. In most cases, a single paragraph is interrupted by a number of formatting commands.

By default, text processors will full justify text (i.e., both left and right margins are kept even, just as they are in this book). If the text is set in a monospaced font (every character occupying the same amount of space),

the text processor will add blank spaces as needed to keep the margins straight.

Just as the ends of paragraphs are not indicated by carriage returns, blank lines are also not inserted into a document by adding carriage returns. As mentioned above, a blank line will force a break (i.e., it is the equivalent of the `.br` command). Instead, blank lines in an output document are created by the `.sp` command. When used without an argument, `.sp` inserts one blank line. If followed by a number, as in:

```
.sp 3
```

the formatting command inserts multiple blank lines. Each of the lines without text in Listing 5.2 was created in that way. Although you may not like the layout of Listing 5.2 (you may wish there were more blank lines to separate paragraphs), what appears in the formatted document is exactly what was specified by the formatting codes in the source document.

Formatting Commands

Although most document setting are contained in the macro packages, there may be times when you wish to override them and use `nroff/troff/psroff` formatting commands to override what appears in the macros. The `.br` and `.sp` commands are examples of formatting commands that are commonly used. In addition, you may find the following commands useful:

1. `.ll` (line length): Follow `.ll` with the length of the printed line, as in:

   ```
   .ll 7.5i
   ```

   The `i` indicates that the units are inches (use `c` for centimeters, `p` for points).
2. `.bp` (begin page): Eject the page being printed and begin at the top of a new page.

3. `pi` (page length): Follow `.pi` with a number that indicates the length of the page, as in:

```
.pi 11i
```

4. `.pn` (set page number): Follow `.pn` with a new starting page number. If omitted, page numbering always begins with 1.
5. `.ad` (adjust): follow `.ad` with a letter that indicates how text should be justified (the default is full justification). The arguments are:
   a. `l`: left justify only
   b. `r`: right justify only
   c. `c`: center
   d. `b` or `n`: full justification
6. `ls` (line spacing): Follow `.ls` with a number to indicate the line spacing. For example:

```
.ls 2
```

   will produce double–spaced text.
7. `in` (indent): Follow `.in` with a measurement to indicate how far each line should be indented from the left margin. For example, to indent a hanging quote 0.5", use:

```
.in 0.5i
```

8. `ti` (temporary indent): Follow `.ti` with a measurement to indicate an indentation for just the following line. (An example of a temporary indent appears on the seventh line of the last page of Listing 5.1)
9. `ta` (tab stops): Follow `.ta` with a series of measurements where tab stops should be set. For example, Listing 5.1 sets a special tab stop to line up the example at the end of the document with the command:

```
.ta 2.5i
```

This inserts a single tab stop 2.5" from the left margin. Additional tab stops can be specified on the same command line by separating each measurement with a space.

For complete documentation of `nroff` and `troff` formatting commands, see Chapter 3 of *A/UX Text Processing Tools.*

Using Macros

As discussed earlier, a macro package gathers together `nroff`/`troff`/`psroff` commands. Each macro package defines a text processing environment. When working with a text formatter, the most common strategy is, therefore, to pick the macro package that most closely matches the way in which you would like your document formatted. Formatting commands can be used at any time to override any settings in the macro package that may not meet your needs.

The easiest way to decide on a macro package is to consult the *A/UX Programmers Reference* manual. The macros, default setting, and strings provided by each macro package are documented in *Miscellaneous Facilities (5)* under the name of the macro package. Because Listing 5.1 represents documentation for a UNIX program, the authors selected the `man` macro package, which is designed to produce the format of entries in UNIX reference manuals.

The `man` macro package provides the following default settings:

1. page size: 8.5" x 11" (text area is 6.5" x 10")
2. default type size: 10 point
3. default line spacing: 12 point

In addition, `man` defines three strings:

1. `\*R` `[` - `troff` or (Reg.) - `nroff`
2. `\*S` Revert to default type size
3. `\*(TM` `]`

The use of macros in Listing 5.1 is typical of the way in which macros are used to format a document. The `.SH` macros defines a subhead; the text of the subhead follows the macro as an argument. By default, the paragraphs following a subhead in Listing 5.2 are indented from the left margin. For example, notice that the lines following the subheadings `NAME` and `SYNOPSIS` are indented. However, the lines following `OPTIONS` are not. If you look closely at Listing 5.1, you will notice that each option is preceded by the macro `.TP`. This macro creates a hanging indent (i.e., the first line of a paragraph begins to the left of the paragraph's left margin).

The document is Listing 5.2 contains a great deal of boldface and italic text. Text that is to be set in boldface is placed on a separate line following the `.B` macro. For example:

```
.B \-D interval
```

produces:

-D interval

in the printed text. Because the hyphen has a special meaning to A/UX commands, it must be preceded by a backslash when included in the document. The backslash serves its usual purpose of "escaping" the character that follows, removing its special meaning to A/UX.

Notice also that boldface character often appear in the middle of formatted lines in the output document. However, they appear on separate lines with the `.B` macro in the source document. As mentioned earlier, UNIX text formatters do not define the ends of paragraphs with carriage returns.

To set type in italics, Listing 5.1 uses the `.I` macro. Like the boldface macro, the text that should be set in italics appears on the same line as the macro, as in:

```
.I appt (1)
```

As complex as Listing 5.1 might appear, the `.SH`, `.TP`, `.B`, and `.I` are all that are used to format the document. They are combined with the formatting commands `.br.`, `.sp`, `.ti`, and `.ta` to provide complete document

formatting. When you are ready to format your text file, consult the documentation for the macros packages (either printed or online) to determine which macro package comes closest to providing the layout you will need and to find detailed information on the available macros.

Escape Sequences

An alternative method for indicating boldface and italics can be found in the next to the last paragraph of Listing 5.1. It uses escape sequences to specify where a typeface should begin and where it should end. For example, the escape sequence `\fB` means to begin printing in boldface; the escape sequence `\fR` tells the text processor to return to plain text. The advantage to an escape sequence is that it can be embedded in the text, without having to use a macro and place the text on a separate line.

In addition to specifying type styles, escape sequences can be used to:

1. Add comment lines to a source document (\").
2. Print character accents (\' [acute]; \` [grave]).
3. Create a space that will not be expanded when the text processor is performing full justification (`\SPACE`).
4. Insert a minus sign or hyphen (\-).

For complete documentation of the text formatter escape sequence, see pages 3-51 and 3-52 of *A/UX Text Processing Tools*.

Listing 5.1: month.1

```
.SH NAME
month \- a visual calendar and time/event organizer
.SH SYNOPSIS
.B month
[
.B \-ACLNdv
] [
.B \-D interval
]
.br
.B month
[
.B \-B
[
.B month/
]
.B day
[
.B /year date2 date3
] ]
.br
.B month
[
.B \-m user1
[
.B user2 .....
] [
.B month/
]
.B day
[
.B /year
] [
.B hours:
]
.B minutes
]
.br
.SH OPTIONS
.TP
.B \-A
Output the
.I month
database in a format compatible with
.I appt (1).
.TP
.BI \-B " days"
Allows the printing of an event schedule for that day or days.
The default is today.
.TP
```

```
.B \-C
Output the
.I month
data file in a format compatible with
.I calendar (1).
.TP
.B \-d
Create background daemon that will wake up at 15 minute intervals
during the current login session,
check your event database, and print a message to your
terminal with a bell if it finds an event that is 15 minutes, or less, away.
It will do this on invocation, then
every 15-minutes until killed or you log out.
.TP
.BI \-D " interval"
Create background daemon (same as \-d option) that wakes up every
.I interval
minutes during the current login session.
.TP
.B \-L
Output the lunar picture of what the moon will
look like at 11:00PM of the current day.
.TP
.BI \-m " users times"
Allows one to see if others users are free to meet for a given
period of time.
.TP
.B \-N
Output the current day's events in a format compatable with
.I nag (1).
.TP
.B \-v
Output the version ID of
.I month
being run.
.SH DESCRIPTION
.TP
.B Overview
.br
.sp 1
.I Month
displays a calendar of the current month of the current year,
with the current day highlighted.
It then allows the user to browse to any month/day/year,
and to schedule and recall events for a day or for some regular
repeating series of days.
Note that the UPPER/lower case of commands are significant.
.br
.TP
.B Screen Areas
.br
.sp 1
There are four distinct areas of the screen:  the
.I days
```

```
area where the days of the month are listed in calendar format, the
.I months
area where the months of the year are listed, the
.I years
area where a sequence of years are listed, and the
.I schedule
area, which may be blank and occupies lines 19-24 on the terminal
(lines below 24 are not used).
.br
.TP
.B Commands
.br
.I On-line help
.br
.sp 1
You may type '?' almost any time to get addition help.
.br
.sp 1
.I Quitting
.br
.sp 1
You may type 'Q' almost any time to quit.  This will update
the event database if any changes have been made.
The event database is a file called
.B .month
in your home directory.
.I <CNTL-c>
can be used any time for an immediate abort and no event database update.
When you quit, you will be informed of the update status of your event
database.
.br
.sp 1
.I Cursor motion
.br
.sp 1
The
.B h, l, k,
and
.B j
keys are used to move the cursor left, right, up and down respectively
within a screen area.
Sometimes, as explained later,
.B j
and
.B k
will not work, and a
.I <TAB>
or
.I <CR>
provides movement between fields in a circular fashion.
.br
.sp 1
.I Selection
.br
```

```
.sp 1
.I <CR>
and
.I <LF>
are used to select items/commands at the cursor position.
.br
.sp 1
.I Direct entry of numbers
.br
.sp 1
The user may type the number of a desired month, day, or year
whenever the cursor is appropriately positioned.
This is true in all screen areas.
.I <ESC>
can be used to abort any function.
.br
.sp 1
.I Scrolling numbers
.br
.sp 1
In the schedule area, numbers may be scrolled forwards and
backwards with the
.I <SPACE>
and
.I <BACKSPACE>
keys respectively.
This is the only way to change hours and minutes.
.br
.sp 1
.I Time browsing
.br
.sp 1
The keys 'm', 'd' and 'y' are used to move into the months area, the
days area or the years area respectively.  This is only when
time browsing in these three panes.  To get to a particular
month or year, move to the appropriate area and onto the
desired month or year, and select it via
.I <CR>.
Years may be
scrolled a year at a time by using the scroll areas marked
by '<<' and '>>'.  Attempting to move passed these areas will
scroll by one year, selecting them scrolls by ten years.
The last month of the previous year, or the first month of
next year, may be obtained by selecting the area above
January or below December respectively.
The cursor is the positioned for immediate return via a later selection.
.br
.sp 1
The keys
.B n
and
.B p
can be used to go to the next or previous month,
day, or year, depending on the screen area you are in.
```

```
.br
.sp 1
The
.B M
key will mark a specific date.  You will be prompted for
an identifier that is a single digit between '0' and '9'.
Once a mark has been set at a certain date, you may jump to
that date from any other date with the command below.
.br
.sp 1
The
.B G
key controls movement to a previously set mark.
You will be prompted for the mark's identifying digit.
.br
.sp 1
The key
.B ';'
provides access directly to the last date you viewed that
was in a different month than currently displayed.
Use the same command again to return to where you were originally.
.br
.sp 1
The
.B T
key goes directly to the actual, real current date.
This is the date initially displayed on startup.
.br
.sp 1
The key
.B '/'
allows direct access to a date to be fully specified by the user.
A prompt is given and the user should respond with
a date in the form m/d/y, such as 5/6/86.  Years less than
100 are assumed to be in this century, hence, 5/6/80 is the same as
5/6/1986.
.TP
.B Overviewing a day
.br
.sp 1
The
.B O
key will fill the schedule area with a read only view
of your day according to your event database.
Four six-hour grids appear showing the hours of the day
that have been pre-scheduled.
The cursor must be placed on the day to be viewed with this function.
.br
.sp 1
The
.B B
key will print, in sorted order, events for the currently selected day.
.br
.sp 1
```

```
.TP
.B Overviewing a month
.br
.sp 1
The
.B A
key will mark all the days on the calendar that have
at least one event posted.  This feature is especially
useful before scanning; described next.
.TP
.B Scanning events
.br
.sp 1
The
.B S
key will cause a sequential list of events for the current day
to be displayed in the schedule area.  The events for any given
day may be scanned, deleted, or modified.
After displaying each one, the prompt "
.B [n,p,d,e,q]
" is put up and will respond to these character commands:
.br
.sp 1
.I 'n':
go to next event
.br
.I 'p':
go to previous event
.br
.I 'd':
delete this event
.br
.I 'e':
edit this event as during a posting described below
.br
.I 'q':
quit the scan and return to calendar
.br
.I <ESC>:
same as 'q'
.br
.TP
.B Every event scan
.sp 1
.I 'E'
will display, one at a time, absolutely every event
in your event database.
After displaying each one, the prompt "
.B [n,p,d,e,q]
" is put up and will respond to these character commands:
.br
.sp 1
.I 'n':
go to next event
```

```
.br
.I 'p':
go to previous event
.br
.I 'd':
delete this event
.br
.I 'e':
edit this event as during a posting described below
.br
.I 'q':
quit the scan and return to calendar
.br
.I <ESC>:
same as 'q'
.br
.TP
.B Posting an event
.sp 1
.I 'P'
is the command used to post an event.  The
cursor is placed into the schedule area with a host of
information displayed.
.sp 1
To abort  at any point, use
.I <ESC>.
.sp 1
The cursor first appears on the first line of the schedule area.
This line gives the starting date for the event, and when it shall occur.
The user may move through the highlighted starting date field
(using the
.B h
and
.B l
keys) and change the month, day or year by scrolling with
.I <SPACE>
and
.I <BACKSPACE>,
or by direct input.
.br
.sp
The other fields in this first line may also be moved onto and selected
in a similar fashion (but without direct entry).
.br
.sp
.I <TAB>
will move the cursor to the next line that contains the
time that the event occurs.
Again, the
.B h,
.B l,
.I <SPACE>,
and
.I <BACKSPACE>
```

```
keys manipulate the hours and minutes fields.
The AM/PM indicator changes as the hours scroll across 12:00 boundaries.
.br
.sp
.I <TAB>
will move the cursor to the next line that gives the duration of the event,
and it is edited in the same fashion.
.br
.sp
.I <TAB>
moves the cursor to the next line that is a one line description of the
event, to be typed whenever the cursor is placed here.
.I <TAB>
moves the cursor to the last line in the schedule area and
allows the user to select ACCEPT or CANCEL.
The
.B h
and
.B l
keys toggle between ACCEPT and CANCEL.
Pressing
.I <RETURN>
when the cursor is in the ACCEPT field will put the event
into the user's event database, after verification.
CANCEL aborts the process.
.br
.sp
The
.I <TAB>
key can be used to circulate through the fields.
.TP
.B Event scheduling
.sp 1
When and how often will an event occur?  This information
is contained in the first line of the schedule area.  The
date entered there is the starting date for the event,
that is, the event will not be recalled until that date.
This date is best entered by browsing to it, placing the
cursor in the days area on the desired day, and then
type 'P' to post the event, in which case the desired date
automatically appears as the default, but may be edited.
.br
.sp
In the following examples, only the fields that need to be
selected are mentioned, all others should be turned off.
(not highlighted)  Examples:
.ta 2.5i
.br
.sp 1
.I March 5, 1990 (once only):
.B 3/5/1990
.br
.sp 1
.I Every Tuesday and Wednesday:
```

```
.B m/d/y every TueWed
.br
.sp 1
.I The 7th of each month:
.B m/7/y monthly
.br
.sp 1
.I Each July 4th:
.B 7/4/y yearly
.br
.sp 1
.I The 2nd and last Sunday of
.I each month:
.B m/d/y monthly every 2nd last Sun
.br
.sp 1
.I The 1st and last Friday of
.I each year:
.B \ \ m/d/y yearly every 1st last Fri
.br
.sp 1
.I Every other Thursday:
.B m/d/y every 2nd Thu
.br
.sp 1
Note, this will include the 1st, 3rd, 5th, 7th, etc.
Thursday,
.I starting
from the specified m/d/y
.TP
.B Miscellaneous
.sp 1
The
.B L
key stands for lunar, and causes a picture of what the moon will
look like at 11:00PM on the day on which the cursor is placed.
.I <CNTL-L>
or
.I <CNTL-R>
will redraw the screen.
.br
.sp 1
The
.B F
key is used for storing event descriptions to a file.
The user is prompted for whether he would like to store ALL the events
in his database or just those for the current day.
The user is then prompted for a file name, and if that file exists already,
the user is given a chance to abort the operation or continue.
.SH EXAMPLES
.br
.sp 1
cp \ $HOME/.apptrc \ $HOME/.appt\ ;\ month -A \ >> \ $HOME/.appt
.sp
```

```
.br
month -N > \ $HOME/.nag\ ;\ nag
.sp
.br
month -m bob carol ted alice 19 1:30
.sp
.ti -1i
.SH AUTHORS
Jeff Bauer,
David Connet,
Robert Dextor,
Frank McGee,
Marc Ries,
Brad Smith,
Tom Stoehn
and others.
.SH FILES
$HOME/.month
.SH SEE ALSO
appt (1), calendar (1), and nag (1).
.SH DIAGNOSTICS
month: unknown option \fIarg\fR
.br
Usage: month [-A -B args -C -d -D arg -L -m args -N -v]
.br
Can't open \fIuser's\fR .month file.
.SH CAVEATS/BUGS
Few attempts have been made to prevent the user from browsing
through negatively numbered years or years with more than four
digits in them, the latter causing the years area to get messed up,
but remains functional.
Rarely, events with a starting date before the year 1753,
will not be recalled correctly.With the
.B -A
flag, any date that does not have a time that pertains
to it (i.e. birthdays, holidays, ...), set the starting time to 12:00 AM.
.I Month
requires a starting time whereas
.I appt
does not.The \fB-m\fR option assumes that \fImonth\fR is setuid and owned
by
"\fBroot\fR".  On sites where this is not possible or wanted, the
usefulness of the \fB-m\fR option will be diminished or non-existent,
depending upon the accessibility of user's month databases.The \fB-A\fR
and \fB-C\fR options do not currently provide total
and/or accurate output for complicated combinations of
repeating events.
.SH DATE
8/3/87
options do not currently provide total
and/or accurate output for complicated combinations of
repeating events.
.SH DATE
```

Listing 5.2: month.doc

NAME
month - a visual calendar and time/event organizer
SYNOPSIS
month [**-ACLNdv**] [**-D interval**]
month [**-B** [**month/**] **day** [**/year date2 date3**]]
month [**-m user1** [**user2 .....**] [**month/**] **day** [**/year**] [**hours**:] **minutes**]
OPTIONS
-A Output the *month* database in a format compatible with *appt(1)*
-B days
Allows the printing of an event schedule for that day or days. The default is today.
-C Output the *month* data file in a format compatible with *calendar(1)*.
-d Create background daemon that will wake up at 15 minute intervals during the current login session, check your eventdatabase, and print a message to your terminal with a bell if it finds an event that is 15 minutes, or less, away. It will do this on invocation,then every 15-minutes until killed or you log out.
-D interval
Create background daemon (same as -d option) that wakes up every *interval* minutes during the current login session.
-L Output the lunar picture of what the moon will look like at 11:00PM of the current day.
-m users_times
Allows one to see if others users are free to meet for a given period of time.
-N Output the current day's events in a format compatable with *nag(_1)*.
-v Output the version ID of *month* being run.
DESCRIPTION
Overview

Month displays a calendar of the current month of the current year, with the current day highlighted. It then allows the user to browse to any month/day/year, and to schedule and recall events for a day or for some regular repeating series of days. Note that the UPPER/lower case of commands are significant.

Screen Areas

There are four distinct areas of the screen: the *days* area where the days of the month are listed in calendar format,the *months* area where the months of the year are listed, the *years* area where a sequence of

years are listed, and the *schedule* area, which may be blank and occupies lines 19-24 on the terminal (lines below 24 are not used).

Commands

On-line help

You may type '?' almost any time to get addition help.

Quitting

You may type 'Q' almost any time to quit. This will update the event database if any changes have been made. The event database is a file called **.month** in your home directory. *<CNTL-c>* can be used any time for an immediate abort and no event database update. When you quit, you will be informed of the update status of your event database.

Cursor motion

The **h, l, k,** and **j** keys are used to move the cursor left,right, up and down respectively within a screen area. Sometimes, as explained later, **j** and **k** will not work, and a *<TAB>* or *<CR>* provides movement between fields in a circular fashion.

Selection

<CR> and *<LF>* are used to select items/commands at the cursor position.

Direct entry of numbers

The user may type the number of a desired month, day, or year whenever the cursor is appropriately positioned.This is true in all screen areas. *<ESC>* can be used to abort any function.

Scrolling numbers

In the schedule area,numbers may be scrolled forwards and backwards with the *<SPACE>* and *<BACKSPACE>* keys respectively.This is the only way to change hours and minutes.

Time browsing

The keys 'm', 'd' and 'y' are used to move into the months area, the days area or the years area respectively. This is only when time browsing in these three panes. To get to a particular month or year, move to the appropriate area and onto the desired month or year, and select it via *<CR>*. Years may be scrolled a year at a time by using the scroll areas marked by '<<' and '>>'. Attempting to move passed these areas will scroll by one year, selecting them scrolls by ten years. The last month of the previous year, or the first month of next year, may be obtained by selecting the area above January or below December respectively.The cursor is the positioned for immediate return via a later selection.

The keys **n** and *p* can be used to go to the next or previous month, day, or year, depending on the screen area you are in.

The **M** key will mark a specific date. You will be prompted for an identifier that is a single digit between '0' and '9'. Once a mark has been set at a certain date, you may jump to that date from any other date with the command below.

The **G** key controls movement to a previously set mark. You will be prompted for the mark's identifying digit.

The key ';' provides access directly to the last date you viewed that was in a different month than currently displayed. Use the same command again to return to where you were originally.

The **T** key goes directly to the actual, real current date.This is the date initially displayed on startup.

The key '**/**' allows direct access to a date to be fully specified by the user. A prompt is given and the user should respond with a date in the form m/d/y, such as 5/6/86. Years less than 100 are assumed to be in this century, hence, 5/6/80 is the same as 5/6/1986.

Overviewing a day

The **O** key will fill the schedule area with a read only view of your day according to your event database. Four six-hour grids appear showing the hours of the day that have been pre-scheduled. The cursor must be placed on the day to be viewed with this function.

The **B** key will print, in sorted order, events for the currently selected day.

Overviewing a month

The **A** key will mark all the days on the calendar that have at least one event posted. This feature is especially useful before scanning; described next.

Scanning events

The **S** key will cause a sequential list of events for the current day to be displayed in the schedule area. The events for any given day may be scanned, deleted, or modified. After displaying each one,the prompt "**[n,p,d,e,q]**" is put up and will respond to these character commands:

'n': go to next event
'p': go to previous event
'd': delete this event
'e': edit this event as during a posting described below
'q': quit the scan and return to calendar
<ESC>: same as 'q'

Every event scan

'E' will display, one at a time, absolutely every event in your event database. After displaying each one, the prompt "**[n,p,d,e,q]**" is put

up and will respond to these character commands:

'n': go to next event
'p': go to previous event
'd': delete this event
'e': edit this event as during a posting described below
'q': quit the scan and return to calendar
<ESC>: same as 'q'

Posting an event

'P' is the command used to post an event. The cursor is placed into the schedule area with a host of information displayed.

To abort at any point, use *<ESC>.*

The cursor first appears on the first line of the schedule area.This line gives the starting date for the event, and when it shall occur. The user may move through the highlighted starting date field (using the **h** and **l** keys) and change the month,day or year by scrolling with *<SPACE>* and *<BACKSPACE>*, or by direct input.

The other fields in this first line may also be moved onto and selected in a similar fashion (but without direct entry).

<TAB> will move the cursor to the next line that contains the time that the event occurs. Again, the **h, l,** *<SPACE>*, and *<BACKSPACE>* keys manipulate the hours and minutes fields. The AM/PM indicator changes as the hours scroll across 12:00 boundaries.

<TAB> will move the cursor to the next line that gives the duration of the event, and it is edited in the same fashion.

<TAB> moves the cursor to the next line that is a one line description of the event, to be typed whenever the cursor is placed here.

<TAB> moves the cursor to the last line in the schedule area and allows the user to select ACCEPT or CANCEL. The **h** and **l** keys toggle between ACCEPT and CANCEL. Pressing *<RETURN>* when the cursor is in the ACCEPT field will put the event into the user's event database, after verification. CANCEL aborts the process.

The *<TAB>* key can be used to circulate through the fields.

Event scheduling

When and how often will an event occur? This information is contained in the first line of the schedule area. The date entered there is the starting date for the event, that is, the event will not be recalled until that date. This date is best entered by browsing to it, placing the cursor in the days area on the desired day, and then type 'P' to post the event, in which case the desired date automatically appears as the default, but may be edited.

In the following examples, only the fields that need to be selected are mentioned, all others should be turned off. (not highlighted)

Examples:

March_5, 1990 (once only): **3/5/1990**

Every Tuesday and Wednesday: **m/d/y every TueWed**

The 7th of each month: **m/7/y monthly**

Each July 4th: **7/4/y yearly**

The 2nd and last Sunday of each month: **m/d/y monthly every2nd last**

The 1st and last Friday of each year: **m/d/y yearly every 1st last Fri**

Every other Thursday: **m/d/y every 2nd Thu**

Note,this will include the 1st, 3rd, 5th, 7th, etc. Thursday, *starting* from the specified m/d/y

Miscellaneous

The **L** key stands for lunar, and causes a picture of what the moon will look like at 11:00PM on the day on which the cursor is placed. *<CNTL-L>* or *<CNTL-R>* will redraw the screen.

The **F** key is used for storing event descriptions to a file. The user is prompted for whether he would like to store ALL the events in his database or just those for the current day. The user is then prompted for a file name, and if that file exists already, the user is given a chance to abort the operation or continue.

EXAMPLES

```
cp  $HOME/.apptrc  $HOME/.appt ; month -A  >>  $HOME/.appt

month -N >  $HOME/.nag ; nag

month -m bob carol ted alice 19 1:30
```

AITHORS
Jeff Bauer, David Connet, Robert Dextor, Frank McGee, Marc Ries, Brad Smith, Tom Stoehn and others.
FILES
$HOME/.month
SEE ALSO
appt (1), calendar (1), and nag (1).
DIAGNOSTICS
month: unknown option _a_r_g
Usage: month [-A -B args -C -d -D arg -L -m args -N -v]
Can't open *user's* .month file.
CAVEATS/BUGS
Few attempts have been made to prevent the user from browsing through

negatively numbered years or years with more than four digits in them, the latter causing the years area to get messed up, but remains functional. Rarely, events with a starting date before the year 1753, will not be recalled correctly. With the **-A** flag, any date that does not have a time that pertains to it (i.e. birthdays, holidays, ...), set the starting time to 12:00 AM. **Month** requires a starting time whereas *appt* does not. The *-m* option assumes that *month* is setuid and owned by "**root**". On sites where this is not possible or wanted, the usefulness of the *-m* option will be diminished or non-existent, depending upon the accessibility of user's month databases. The **-A** and **-C** options do not currently provide total and/or accurate output for complicated combinations of repeating events.
DATE
8/3/87 options do not currently provide total and/or accurate output for complicated combinations of repeating events.
DATE

Chapter 6

Communications

The UNIX operating system is very strong in its support for communications. From an A/UX system, a user can communicate with other users who are currently logged in, send electronic mail, and transfer files between computers. In addition, A/UX will allow you to call and log in to another computer using a modem.

Data Communications Concepts

The remainder of this chapter assumes some familiarity with the basics of data communications. If you are familiar with the terms *port*, *serial line*, *modem*, and *baud*, then you can safely skip this section.

Communications between an A/UX system and another computer can be establish using either a direct line or over standard telephone lines. Regardless of the type of line, data leave the Macintosh on which A/UX is running via a *serial port*.

A *port* is an interface between a computer and an external device. Ports communicate with printers, disk drives, plotters, telecommunications hardware, and tape drives. Ports may be built in to the computer or they may be added with expansion boards.

A *serial* port transmits data one binary digit (bit) at a time; a *parallel* port transmits data one word (eight, 16, or 32 bits, depending on the computer) at a time. The Macintosh on which A/UX is running is shipped with two serial ports. A/UX sees them as `/dev/tty0` and `/dev/tty1`. The first is generally used for telecommuications, the second for a direct connection to a printer. Additional serial ports can be added by placing expansion boards in one or more of the Macintosh's NuBus slots.

The Telephone Line Dilemma

The data that computers transmit are *digital*. In other words, the data are made up of discrete bits (the binary digits zeros and ones). However, the signals transmitted by standard telephone lines are *analog* (a continuous wave form). Computers are therefore faced with a problem when they need to send data over telephone lines.

If the A/UX Macintosh is connected to other computers by a cable coming directly from its serial port, then the connection is via a *direct serial line*. Serial lines are designed to carry digital signals. In an ideal world, all connections between computers could be made with digital lines. However, digital lines must be installed or leased by computer owners. Their expense makes it infeasible to provide digital lines for connections that are far apart and/or used infrequently. Because telephone lines already exist to connect most parts of the world, it is convenient and cost effective "to use those analog lines".

Using analog lines to transmit digital data requires devices known as *modems*. One modem is connected between the local computer's serial port and a telephone line; a second modem is connected between the remote computer's serial port and a telephone line. Each modem sends out a high-pitched tone known as a *carrier tone*. To transmit a one, a modem raises the frequency of its carrier tone; to transmit a zero, it lowers the frequency. This is called *modulating* the carrier tone. The modem receiving the transmission strips the zeros and ones off the carrier tone to assemble the digital signal (*demodulation*). The term modem is, therefore, a contraction of modulation and demodulation.

The speed at which a telecommunications line transmits is measured in *baud*. Baud is generally equal to bits per second. The console (the monitor connected to the Macintosh running A/UX) communicates at 9,600 baud. The modems used with personal computers commonly transmit at 1,200 or 2,400 baud. The speed of sending and receiving modems must be the same. Therefore, the speed at which a data call can be made depends on the capabilities of the modems at both ends of the call.

Communications Terminology

There are a number of terms that apply to the environment in which data communications take place. For example, when you establish communication with another computer, your computer is known as the *local* computer. The system with which you are communicating is the *remote* computer.

Much data communications activity involves the transfer of files between computers. Copying a file from a remote system to a local system is called *downloading* a file. The reverse action–copying a file from a local system to a remote system–is known as *uploading* a file.

Real-time Communications

Two A/UX commands—`write` and `wall`—support communication between users who are logged in at the same time. `Write` permits a dialog between two users; `wall` sends a message to all logged–in users.

Talking to Another User

If you want to conduct a conversation with another user who is logged in, type:

```
write <user name>
```

For example, if a user named `jon` wishes to carry on a conversation with the user named `jan`, the command is written:

```
write jon
```

`Jan` will see the following on his or her terminal:

```
Message from jon
```

A/UX will beep the speaker on `jon`'s terminal to indicate that communication has been established.

After hearing the two beeps, jon can begin typing a message to jan. Each line of text ends with a press of the RETURN key; the BACKSPACE key is the only editing key available. When `jon` has finished his message, `jan` can respond.

Because it can take a few seconds for a line that a user is writing to appear on the receiver's screen, it can be difficult for the receiver to tell that the sender has finished and is waiting for a reply. UNIX users have, therefore, adopted the practice of typing `(o)` when a sender is ready to receive a reply.

To terminate a `write` session, type a `CTRL-D` on a line by itself. By convention, when the first party in a conversation is finished, he or she types `(oo)`; the second user types the `CTRL-D`.

The `write` command is documented in *A/UX Command Reference (M–Z and Games)*. See the section *User Commands (1)*; the commands are in alphabetical order.

If you do not wish to be interrupted by messages from other users, use the `mesg` command to prevent their receipt. Type:

```
mesg n
```

to disallow messages. Type:

```
mesg y
```

to allow them again.

Once `mesg` has been set to `n`, any user attempting to `write` to your terminal will receive the message:

```
Permission denied
```

If you initiate a conversation with `mesg` set to `n`, A/UX will respond:

```
Warning: cannot respond, set mesg -y
```

The `mesg` command is documented in *A/UX Command Reference (M–Z and Games)*. See the section *User Commands (1)*; the commands are in alphabetical order.

Talking to All Users

To broadcast a message to every user logged into the system, use the `write` command. Type `write` and then press `RETURN`. Type the message with a `RETURN` at the end of the line. End the message with a `CTRL-D` on a line by itself.

`Write` will send its message only to those users who have `mesg` set to `y`. However, if `write` is used by the superuser, it will override the `mesg` setting.

The `write` command is documented in *A/UX System Administration Reference*. See the section *Maintenance Commands (1)*; the commands are in alphabetical order.

UNIX Networks

The term *network* means more than one thing to a UNIX user. It may refer to a group of UNIX systems with which the user shares a *local area network* (LAN).[1] It is highly likely that the computer on which you are running A/UX shares a local area network with other A/UX machines and, perhaps, machines from other manufacturers. The most common local area network software for A/UX is called *B-NET*. Using B-NET to log in to a remote system and to transfer files is discussed later in this chapter.

A UNIX network may also be a group of computers running the Unix operating system that communicate over telephone lines. These *wide area networks* may be formal (e.g., they connect computers that belong to the same company) or they may be informal (e.g., they connect computers that agree to exchange messages whenever needed, but where few formal telecommunications links exist).

One informal network that connects computers around the world is known as USENET. Systems that become USENET *nodes* agree to forward messages as needed. Most USENET links use standard telephone lines, although some dedicated lines do exist.

USENET's major service is *NetNews*. The "news" organizes the questions and replies of USENET users into "newsgroups." Groups exist for various types of computer systems, social issues, and recreational topics. News articles are transmitted in a batch and retained on a system for some fixed interval (e.g., three days or a week). Users can then read the news

---

1. A local area network is a group of computers and other shared devices (e.g., printers and modems) that are connected over a relatively small area, such as a department, an office building, or a college campus.

articles and post their own articles whenever they are logged in. In addition to the news, USENET systems transmit electronic mail.[2]

USENET is only one of the informal networks in which UNIX systems commonly participate. A/UX computers may also be part of Internet or BITNET. Internet began as ARPANET, a network of major American research universities and U.S. Government installations. BITNET is used primarily by colleges and universities; many nodes are computers that run operating systems other than UNIX. These networks are not completely isolated. It is possible, for example, for a message that originates on a USENET machine to reach a destination on a BITNET machine.

System Names

If informal networks are to work, there must be a unique method of identifying the systems that comprise the network. Each Unix system, therefore, has a name. To see the name of your system, type:

```
uuname -l
```

To see the names of all systems known to yours, use the command without any options.

The `uuname` command is documented as part of the `uucp` command in *A/UX Command Reference (M–Z and Games)*. See page 3 of the `uucp` command in the section *User Commands (1)*; the commands are in alphabetical order.

Addresses

Most of the time, network messages do not travel directly from the originating system to their destination. Instead, they pass through intervening systems. For example, if a system in Waltham, Mass., needs to send a message to a system in Cambridge, Mass., the message may be able

2. If you are interested in reading and sending USENET news, first ask your system administrator if one of the systems on your network is a USENET node. If not, the system administrator must agree to support news (it does require some administrative effort). Then he or she must find a system willing to "feed" the news to yours; the news software is public domain and in all likelihood can be obtained from the system that will be your feed.

to go directly from destination to source.[3] However, if the message is to go to Berkeley, Calif., it might first be sent to a system in Cambridge. From there it might be transmitted to a system in Columbus, Ohio, then to a system in Denver, Colo., and finally to the system in Berkeley. All of the systems through which a message must pass to reach its destination comprise a *mail path*. The user account name and the name of the system on which it resides are an *electronic mail address*.

There are two major formats for electronic mail addresses. The *Internet* format is written:

```
<user account name> @ <system name>
```

For example, if the account named `jon` is on a system named `gryphon`, then the Internet electronic mail address is:

```
jon@gryphon
```

Keep in mind that `@` has special meaning to the Bourne shell (it is the default "kill" character; it will instruct A/UX to ignore the entire line). To type an Internet address, `@` must be preceded with a backslash (\). The backslash instructs A/UX to ignore the special meaning of the following character. Therefore, when typing the above address, the key presses are:

```
jon\@gryphon
```

The backslash is only a message to A/UX and is not recorded as a part of the address.

The second format for electronic mail addresses is the *uucp* format. (`Uucp` (UNIX-to-UNIX copy) is a set of UNIX utilities that manage file transfers between UNIX systems.[4]) Although some UNIX systems cannot use the Internet format, all of them will accept the `uucp` format.

---

3. Two systems can communicate directly only if they have previously agreed to transfer messages to one another. Details can be found in Chapter 14.

4. Regardless of which format is used for the electronic mail address, `uucp` will manage the file transfer.

Uucp addresses have the general format:

```
<system name> ! <user account name>
```

The jon account's address is therefore:

```
gryphon!jon
```

The exclamation point is read "bang," as in "jon bang gryphon."

The remainder of the mail path (the systems through which a message must travel) consists of system names separated by exclamation points.

To be technically correct, whenever a message is sent, the sender must supply the complete mail path. However, many UNIX computers contain a database of mail paths. The utility path alias will attempt to figure out the best mail path to a destination system. If your system has the mail path database, then you don't need to worry about figuring out the complete mail path. Even if the mail path database is not available, it is often enough to only route the message as far as a *backbone* system.

Backbone systems are systems that form the central core of the network. Some of these may be linked by leased lines, rather than relying on standard telephone lines for communications. Backbone sites do have the mail path database and can almost always figure out themselves how to reach a destination system. For example, assume that someone working on the system named gryphon (in Waltham, Mass.) wants to send a message to someone at starnine in Berkeley, Calif. The nearest USENET backbone site is husc6 at Harvard University in Cambridge. The address to reach starnine might be:

stech!husc6!starnine!andrea[5]

---

5. The systems mentioned in this example are real systems: gryphon is the author's system; stech belongs to Scholastech, a nonprofit group that works with computing in higher education; husc6 is one of several UNIX systems at Harvard University; starnine belongs to StarNine, the company that developed hfx.

In this example, gryphon has no direct communication with husc6. Instead, it transmits its message to a system named stech, which in turn forwards the message to husc6. Husc6, the backbone site, does have the mail path database and will, therefore, figure out how to route the message so that it will ultimately reach starnine.

Automatic Dialing and the L.sys File

To make a connection with a remote system, A/UX needs to know something about how to place the call. If the call is to be placed automatically, A/UX must know:

1. The serial port through which the connection should be made. The port whose file is /dev/tty0 is commonly used for a modem.
2. The speed (in baud) at which the connection is to be made.
3. If the call involves modem and telephone lines, the telephone number to be dialed.
4. The sequence of commands to issue to log in to the remote system.

All of this information is stored in a file named /usr/lib/L.sys.

A typical L.sys entry for dialing out using a modem looks like:

```
stech ANY tty0 2400 "" "" ATDT5551234^M BREAK ogin:-BREAK-ogin:--ogin nuucp
```

The leftmost column is the name of the system to which the entry applies. It is followed by the times when calls can be placed (ANY means that the call can be made on any day at any time), the port through which the connection is to be made, and the transmission speed. The next column contains a place holder for the telephone number of the remote system. The last entry is the name of the account to which the call will log in.

Between the telephone number and the login account name are instructions describing anything the computer must transmit to the remote system and the prompt at which the login account name should be entered. In the example above, the calling system must send the modem dialing commands and then two BREAKs to `stech` (`stech`'s modem answers at 1,200 baud and the BREAKs are required to force the modem to cycle to 2,400 baud). The characters `ogin` (part of `login`) signal the sending system to issue the login account name.

The contents of an `L.sys` entry are very dependent on the circumstances under which the remote system is called. For more details on creating these entries, see Chapter 14.

Electronic Mail

The term *electronic mail* refers to private messages that are sent to other users. The recipient may be a user on the same system (the mail address is the user name) or on a remote system (the mail address is a complete mail path).

A/UX stores mail for each user in the `/usr/mail` directory. Each user who has ever received mail will have a file (a *mailbox*) in that directory. As new mail is received, it is appended to the appropriate user's file. When you log in, A/UX checks your mailbox; if you have mail, you will see:

```
You have mail
```

In addition, if new mail arrives while you are logged in, A/UX will display the `You have mail` message as soon as you return to the shell's prompt.

Electronic mail is managed with the `mail` command. By default, typing `mail` does not actually run the `mail` program. Instead, it runs an alternative program called `mailx`. Although mail is supplied with A/UX, `mailx` is more flexible.

The `mailx` command is documented in two places. The *A/UX Communications User's Guide* contains a tutorial (see Chapter 2). Complete command documentation appears in *A/UX Command Reference (M–Z and Games)*. See the section *User Commands (1)*; the commands are in alphabetical order.

Reading Mail

To read your mail, type `mail` at the shell's prompt. A/UX will respond by listing the messages that are in your mailbox. A user named `jon` would see:

```
A/UX release 1.0 Type ? for help.
"/usr/mail/jon":  3 messages 3 new
>N   1    jan       Thu May 18 14:04    11/308    Meeting
 N   2    sysop     Thu May 18 10:25    12/315    Planned shutdown
 N   3    mail      Thu May 18 10:12    13/312    Returned mail

?
```

The second line displays the mailbox from which the messages have been read. (As you will see shortly, it is possible to read mail that has been stored in a different file.) It also reports the total number of messages and classifies them as new, unread (previously received but not viewed), or old (previously viewed but retained in mailbox).

The following lines list mail that needs to be dealt with in some way. Each message is marked with its status (N=new, U=unread, O=old) and a number. The *current message* is marked with a >. In addition, the listing also contains the source of each message, the date and time it was received, and the contents of its "Subject" field. After the messages, `mail` will print its prompt, a question mark.

To read a message, type its number at the question mark and press RETURN or ENTER. (Pressing RETURN or ENTER without typing anything will display the current message; pressing RETURN or ENTER displays the next message.) A sample message display appears in Figure 6.1. The body of the message is preceded by a rather lengthy header that indicates the mail path the message took from source to destination. (The message in Figure 6.1 came from another user on the recipient's system; therefore, it represents the shortest possible header.)

Disposing of Messages

Once a message has been read, it must be disposed of in some way. If you quit `mail` without explicitly doing anything to the message, it will be de-

```
Message 1:
From jan Thu May 18 14:04 EDT 1989
Received by: gryphon.apple (5.59/SMI-3.2)
          idAA00030; Thu, 18 May 89 14:04:04 EDT
Date: Thu, 18 May 89 14:04:04 EDT
From: jan
Message-ID: <8905181804.AA00030@gryphon.apple>
To: jon
Subject: Meeting
Status: RO

I talked with Emily. She is available on the 20th at 10 a.m. and the
21st at 10:30 a.m. Which one of those would be more convenient for
you? I can do either. Send me mail and let me know ASAP.

Jan
```

Figure 6.1 A sample mail message.

leted from your mailbox and saved in a file named `mbox` in your home directory. Messages that have been read are appended to `mbox`; it has the same format as the mailbox file in /usr/mail. The other options for disposing of messages are:

1. Save the message in a separate file: To save the file in a file other than the default `mbox`, type:

   ```
   save <message number> <file name>
   ```

   as in:

   ```
   save 2 reminder
   ```

   The `save` command can be abbreviated as `s`.
2. Delete the message: To delete the message without saving it anywhere, type:

   ```
   delete <message number>
   ```

   as in:

```
delete 3
```

The `delete` command can be abbreviated as `d`.

3. Retain the message in the mailbox: To retain the message in the default mailbox, type:

```
hold <message number>
```

or

```
preserve <message number>
```

as in:

hold 1

Messages can be undeleted if the decision to undelete is made before you quit `mail`. To undelete, type:

```
undelete <message number>
```

as in:

```
undelete 1
```

Reading Mail From a File Other Than the Mailbox

Mail can be read from a file other than the default mailbox by invoking `mail` with its `-f` option. For example, to see the messages that have been archived in the `mbox` file, type:

```
mail -f mbox
```

If the command is issued without a file name, it will default to the `mbox` file.

Quitting Mail

When you are ready to leave `mail` and return to the shell's prompt, type `quit` or `q` at the dollar sign. The `quit` command will dispose of deleted messages, store message that have been read but not held in `mbox`, and leave all unread messages in the mailbox. If you wish to leave mail without making any changes to the mailbox, leave with `exit` or `x`.

Referencing Messages

Although `mail` displays one message at a time for reading, many `mail` commands, including those discussed above, will accept a range of message numbers. These are known as *message lists*. Message lists can be constructed in either of the following ways:

1. Range of message numbers: The starting and ending message numbers are separated by a hyphen (i.e., `1-3`). Absolute message numbers can be replaced with:
   a. `-` (hyphen): first message
   b. `.` (period): current message
   c. `$` (dollar sign): last message

2. All messages from one source: The message number is replaced by the name of a user from whom messages have been received (i.e., `sysop` will reference all messages from that user name).

3. All messages: An asterisk used in place of a message number refers to all messages.

Sending Mail

Mail is sent under two circumstances. The message may be a reply to mail that you have received or it may be a message that you are originating. The procedures for creating the mail is similar in both cases. Regardless of how a message is created, it is not sent immediately to the next system in the mail path. Instead, it is spooled to a special area on disk so that it can be transferred as a background activity,

The directory /usr/spool contains a subdirectory, uucp, that contains one subdirectory for each system with which the sending system exchanges electronic mail. Mail messages waiting to be transmitted are stored in these directories. For example, the system stech can call amcad and husc6 directly; a system named allegra calls stech nightly to transfer mail (allegra *polls* stech). The following directories will therefore exist:

```
/usr/spool/uucp/amcad
/usr/spool/uucp/husc6
/usr/spool/uucp/allegra
```

Originating New Mail

To send a message, type:

```
mail <mail path of recipient>
```

at either the shell's prompt or mail's prompt. For example, if jon wants to reach andrea at starnine, the command is:

```
mail stech!husc6!starnine!andrea
```

A/UX will respond with a prompt for the subject of the message:

```
Subject:
```

Type a short statement of the message's subject or press RETURN or ENTER to leave the subject blank.

A/UX will move the cursor to the left edge of the next line. There are then three ways to create the text of the message:

1. Type the message, ending each line with a RETURN. The only editing available is the BACKSPACE key to erase characters on the current line. During this process, there are some commands that make the process easier:
   a. ~p: Print the complete text of the message.

   b. ~r <file name>: Append the file named in the command to the message.
   c. ~m <message list>: append the message whose number appears in the command to the message. (This is particularly useful if you are replying to a message and want to include it in the reply.)
2. Invoke ed by typing ~e (a tilde followed an e) and pressing RETURN or ENTER. Use ed to create the message text. Exit ed by writing the file. Mail will display

```
(continue)
```

3. Invoke vi by typing ~v (a tilde followed by a v) and pressing RETURN or ENTER. Use vi to create the message text. Exit vi by saving the file. Mail will display

```
(continue)
```

When the message is complete, type CTRL-D to send it. If you decide not to send the message, type a CTRL-C (A/UX's default interrupt character) rather than a CTRL-D. The text of the message will be saved in a file named dead.letter in your home directory.

As you may have noticed, mail often uses the tilde (~) to distinguish commands from characters that should be part of a message. If, for some reason, you need to include a tilde as the first character of a line in a message, type two tildes (i.e., ~~). Only one will actually become a part of the message.

Replying to a Message

To reply to mail that you have received, type:

```
reply <message list>
```

as in:

```
reply 1
```

If you wish to reply to the current message, a message number is not required after the command.

A/UX will respond with a header in the following format:

```
To: <return mail path>
Subject: Re: <subject of message to which reply is made>
```

For example, `jon`'s reply to `jan`'s message about meeting dates would generate:

```
To: jan
Subject: Re: Meeting
```

Mail then moves the cursor to the left edge of the next line. The reply can then be created and sent in the same way as a new message.

The `reply` command will mail your response not only to the message's author but to every other user who received the message as well. To restrict the response to just the author, use the `Reply` command instead. (The difference between the two is the case of the first letter.) The `reply` command can be abbreviated as `r`; `Reply` is abbreviated `R`.

Mailing Files

Although `mail` was not designed as a file transfer facility, it can nonetheless be used to transfer both text and binary files.

Mailing a Text File

If combined with input redirection, the `mail` command can be used to transfer any text file. For example, if `jon` wanted to share the C source code in the file `aux.dimmer` with `andrea` at `starnine`, the file could be transmitted with:

```
mail stech!husc6!starnine!andrea <aux.dimmer
```

When used in this way, `mail` will transfer the file, much in the same way that `uucp` (discussed in the next section) will transfer files. However,

there is a major difference. Mail always spools files for later transmission; by default, uucp transfers files immediately, not releasing the user's terminal until the transfer is complete.

Mailing a Binary File

Mail, or more specifically the uucp routines that underlie it, can only transfer text files. Therefore, if you need to transfer a binary file (e.g., a compiled program), the file must first be transformed into an encoded text file with the uuencode program.

By default, uuencode takes its input from the standard input and sends its output to the standard output. Practically, however, the input is usually from a file and the output is piped to mail. The destination for the file is a directory named decode:

```
uuencode <source file> <mail path> | mail <mail path!decode>
```

For example, if jon wants to send the compiled version of kermit (a public domain communications program supplied with A/UX) to brenda at katz, another A/UX system sharing the same local area network, the command would be: written

```
uuencode kermit katz!brenda!kermit | mail katz!decode
```

The above syntax assumes that the receiving system is automatically set to decode the incoming file with uudecode and place it in brenda's home directory.

If the receiving system will not automatically decode incoming encoded mail, then the file should be sent using the following command line:

```
uuencode kermit katz!brenda!kermit | mail katz!brenda
```

The file will appear in brenda's mailbox in its encoded form. It can then be decoded manually by typing:

```
uudecode kermit
```

Although uuencode and uudecode make it possible to transmit binary files, keep in mind that it doesn't make sense to do so unless the receiving system is the same kind as the sending system. This is because binary files are generally executable programs and systems that have different CPUs and/or different versions of UNIX will not be able to execute programs for other CPUs and/or UNIX versions.

The uuencode and uudecode commands are documented together under uuencode in *A/US Command Reference (M–Z and Games)*. See the section *User Commands (1)*: the commands are in alphabetical order.

Uucp

Uucp is one of several utilities that can be used to transfer files between UNIX systems. The recipient of a uucp transfer does not need to be another A/UX system; it only needs to be running UNIX.

Using uucp is documented in two places. The *A/UX Communications User's Guide* contains a tutorial (see Chapter 4). A complete command summary can be found in *A/UX Command Reference*. See the section *User Commands (1)*; the commands are in alphabetical order.

Organizing Uucp

Uucp file transfers follow the same paths from one computer to another as electronic mail. (This is because mail is sent by uucp and not the other way around.) As a file moves from one system to another, each sending computer must be able to log on and write a file on the receiving system.

Most systems that are capable of uucp file transfers have one login–nuucp–that is used by any system wishing to exchange files using uucp. Open systems will have no password on the nuucp account, allowing any system that knows the correct phone number to gain access. More restrictive systems will place a password on nuucp and issue that password only to systems that are to be allowed uucp access.

Regardless of whether nuucp has a password, uucp file transfers are generally only permitted into and out of a single directory, /usr/spool/uucppublic. This directory is nuucp's home directory; whenever a

computer logs in as the user named uucp, it will be placed in that directory. Nuucp will have access to no directories other than uucppublic and the mail subdirectories discussed earlier. As a further restriction, a calling system will have access only to its own mail directory.

Uucppublic contains one subdirectory for each user who has ever sent or received files using uucp. For example, if jon at gryphon has used uucp, then there will be a directory name /user/spool/uucppublic/jon.

A system administrator may decide to allow uucp to read and write from additional directories. Uucp will still log in to nuucp, but the path names of target files can then include directories other than /usr/spool/uucppublic.

How the Transfer is Processed

Issuing a uucp file transfer command initiates a series of actions:

1. Uucp examines the destination mail path and extracts the name of the first system in the path.
2. Uucp searches the file /usr/lib/L.sys for an entry matching the first system name.
   a. If the system does not appear in L.sys, uucp will print an error message and return the user to the shell's prompt without further processing.
3. Uucp uses information in L.sys to place a call to the system.
   a. Uucp determines which piece of hardware will be used to connect to the telecommunications lines (e.g., a modem).
   b. Uucp accesses the serial port to which the device is connected.
   c. Uucp places the call. If the device is a modem, uucp takes the phone number of the system to be called from L.sys.
4. Once the connection to the remote system is completed, uucp copies the file being transferred from disk through the serial port to the telecommunications line.

Transferring a File Using Uucp

The general syntax for a `uucp` file transfer is either:

```
uucp <path name of file to send> <mail path to receiving system>
```

or

```
uucp <mail path to file on remote system> <path name to store incoming file>
```

The first syntax will transfer a file from the user's system (the *local* system) to another UNIX computer. The second will copy a file from a remote system and store it on the local system.

For example, the command

```
uucp/usr/spool/uucppublic/jon/aux.dimmerstech!husc6!starnine!uucppublic/andrea/aux.dimmer
```

will transmit the file `aux.dimmer` (stored in the current directory) to `starnine`'s public directory. To retrieve a file stored on `starnine`, the command is:

```
uucpstech!husc6!starnine!uucppublic!andrea!ds.script/usr/spool/uucppublic/jon/ds.script
```

At the end of a successful transfer, `uucp` will send a mail message notifying the sender.

A Path Name Shortcut

As you can see from the examples above, the path names for `uucp` transfers can be very long and complex. There is, however, a convenient shorthand that can be used to cut down on the typing. The tilde (~) will substitute for `nuucp's` login directory. If the login directory is /usr/spool/uucppublic, then the command to transfer a file from `gryphon` to `starnine` can be written:

```
uucp ~jon/aux.dimmer stech!husc6!starnine!~andrea/aux.dimmer
```

Keep in mind that the tilde translates to whatever nuucp's login directory happens to be. If the login name on the remote system is something other than nuucp, then the tilde represents the path name to the login directory.

Foreground Versus Background Transfers

As mentioned earlier, uucp normally retains control of a user's terminal during the entire file transfer. If, however, you would like the file transfer to take place in the background, use an ampersand (&) at the end of the command. For example,

```
uucp ~jon/aux.dimmer stech!husc6!starnine!~andrea/aux.dimmer &
```

will initiate the transfer of the file aux.dimmer and then release the user's terminal.

Monitoring Uucp Status

There are two commands that monitor the status of uucp transfers, uulog and uustat. Uustat can also be used to perform a variety of maintenance activities on files that are queued for transfer.

Viewing Uucp History

A/UX keeps a log of uucp activity (mail and uucp) in the file /usr/spool/uucp/LOGFILE. This file is usually cleaned out once a day in the early hours of the morning. Querying the log file with uulog will, therefore, reflect activity only since the last time the file was cleaned.

When used without options, uulog displays the entire contents of the log file. For example, a portion of the log from gryphon can be seen in Figure 6.2. The first two lines log allegra's call to gryphon; this call was unsuccessful. The next eight entries are for conversations with amcad. Notice that two files are transferred from amcad to gryphon. The final entries are for conversations with stech. The files that are transferred are USENET news articles and therefore have file names assigned by uucp.

The output from uulog can be restricted by adding arguments to restrict the systems and/or users about which log data are displayed. To see data about conversations with only one system, type:

```
uucp allegra  (5/18-3:09:24,12843,0) OK (startup)
uucp allegra  (5/18-3:09:25,12843,0) CAUGHT (SIGNAL 2
)uucp amcad  (5/18-0:19:53,12415,0) SUCCEEDED (call to amcad )
uucp amcad  (5/18-0:20:04,12415,0) OK (startup)
uucp amcad  (5/18-0:20:16,12415,0) REMOTE REQUESTED (amcad!/usr2/sources/bin/
undo.h)
uucp amcad  (5/18-0:20:19,12415,1) REMOTE REQUESTED (amcad!/usr2/sources/bin/
undo.c)
uucp amcad  (5/18-0:20:25,12415,2) OK (conversation complete tty01 127)
uucp amcad  (5/18-0:21:55,12430,0) SUCCEEDED (call to amcad )
uucp amcad  (5/18-0:22:07,12430,0) OK (startup)
uucp amcad  (5/18-0:22:11,12430,0) OK (conversation complete tty01 23)
uucp stech  (5/18-0:11:57,12387,0) FAILED (LOGIN FAILED)
uucp stech  (5/18-0:12:46,12387,0) FAILED (LOGIN FAILED)
uucp stech  (5/18-0:13:35,12387,0) FAILED (LOGIN FAILED)
uucp stech  (5/18-0:14:24,12387,0) FAILED (LOGIN FAILED)
uucp stech  (5/18-0:14:24,12387,0) CONN FAILED (CALLER SCRIPT FAILED)
uucp stech  (5/18-1:43:34,12608,0) FAILED (LOGIN FAILED)
uucp stech  (5/18-1:43:56,12608,0) SUCCEEDED (call to stech )
uucp stech  (5/18-1:44:07,12608,0) OK (startup)uucp stech
(5/18-1:44:19,12608,0) REMOTE REQUESTED (stech!D.stechBq2e2 -->
gryphon!D.gryphonCa331)
uucp stech  (5/18-1:48:27,12608,1) REMOTE REQUESTED (stech!D.stechXq2e0 -->
gryphon!D.gryphonCa332)
```

Figure 6.2 Sample output from `uulog`.

```
uulog -s<system name>
```

as in:

```
uulog -samcad
```

To see `uucp` activity generated by a specific user, type:

```
uulog -u<user name>
```

as in:

```
uulog -usysop
```

The `uulog` command is documented on page 3 of `the uucp` documentation in *A/UX Command Reference (M–Z and Games)*. See the section *User Commands (1)*; the commands are in alphabetical order.

Checking Status and Canceling Jobs

More detailed information about `uucp` activity can be obtained from `uustat`. `Uustat` can also be used to remove files that have been queued for transfer and to prevent files that have been queued from being deleted because they have been queued too long (*rejuvenating* the files)[6].

When used without options, `uustat` displays the status of every file that the user has queued for `uucp` transfer, including electronic mail messages:

```
0012 jon husc6 05/27-07:44 05/27-07:44 JOB IS QUEUED
0013 jon husc6 05/27-07:50 05/27-07:52 CANNOT COPY TO LOCAL DIRECTORY
0014 jon husc6 05/27-08:22 05/27-08:22 JOB IS QUEUED
```

Each line begins with a *job number* that is used to identify files when they are canceled or rejuvenated. The job number is followed by the name of the user that queued the file and the name of the system to which the file is being sent. The fourth column from the left represents the time that the job was queued; the fifth column is the time at which the status was determined.

The line ends with the status of the job. In most cases, the status will be either `JOB IS QUEUED` or JOB IS COMPLETE. However, you may also see any of the status messages in Table 6.1.

The function of `uustat` can be expanded by using one or more of the following arguments:

1. `-j`*job#*   Display the status for job number *job#*

---

6. The utility program `uuclean` will delete `uucp` jobs that cannot be successfully transmitted within a predetermined period of time (usually about three days).

Table 6.1
Status Message for uucp

Status	Notes
THE COPY FAILED, BUT THE REASON CANNOT BE DETERMINED	Uucp was unable to write the file on the remote system; the reason for the failure is unknown.
PERMISSION TO ACCESS LOCAL FILE IS DENIED	The permissions set for a file to be transmitted from the current system to a remote system are set in such a way that uucp cannot read the file.
PERMISSION TO ACCESS REMOTE FILE IS DENIED	The permission set for a file that is to be copied from a remote system are set in such a way that uucp cannot read the file.
BAD uucp COMMAND IS GENERATED	
REMOTE SYSTEM CANNOT CREATE TEMPORARY FILE	In most cases, this status is the result of insufficient disk space on i-nodes on the remote system.
CANNOT COPY TO REMOTE DIRECTORY	Uucp does not have write permission to the target directory on the remote machine.
CANNOT COPY TO LOCAL DIRECTORY	Uuucp does not have writer permission to the target directory on the local machine
LOCAL SYSTEM CAN NOT CREATE TEMPORARY FILE	In most cases, this status is the result of insufficient disk space or i-nodes on the local system.
CANNOT EXECUTE uucp	
COPY (PARTIALLY) SUCCEEDED	An error occurred during transmission, resulting in a partial file transfer.
COPY FINISHED, JOB DELETED	This message also appears as JOB COMPLETED.
JOB IS QUEUED	
JOB KILLED (INCOMPLETE)	A command to delete the job was issued while the file was being transmitted. Some of the file was transmitted before the job was killed.
JOB KILLED (COMPLETE)	The job was deleted before transmission began.

2. `-kjob#` Kill (delete) the job with job number *job#*. Unless you are the superuser, you can kill only those jobs that you have queued.
3. `-rjob#` Reset the time that the job with job number was queued to the current time. This will permit the job to remain in the queue for another period of the length set by `uuclean`.
4. `-uuser` Display status information about all jobs queued by *user*
5. `-ssys` Display status information about all jobs queued for transmission to system *sys*.

For example, the command

```
uustat -ujan -sstech
```

will display the status of all `uucp` requests that `jan` has queued for `stech`.

The `uustat` command is documented in *A/UX Command Reference (M–Z and Games)*. See the section *User Commands (1)*; the commands are in alphabetical order.

Cu

`Cu` (call up) is a utility that will make a connection with a remote system over telephone lines using modems or through a direct serial line connection. If the remote system is a UNIX system, `cu` can be used to transfer files. If the remote system is running some other operating system, `cu` does not support file transfer.

The `cu` command is documented in two places. For a tutorial, see Chapter 5 of the *A/UX Communications Users Guide*. For complete reference, see *A/UX Command Reference (A–L)*. See the section *User Commands (1)*; the commands are in alphabetical order.

There are two ways to establish a connection using `cu`. If the system you are calling has an entry in the `L.sys` file, then typing:

```
cu <system name>
```

will instruct A/UX to dial the system. It will use the port, phone number, and transmission speed from the `L.sys` entry. For example, to place a call to `stech` using the `L.sys` entry described earlier in this chapter, type:

```
cu stech
```

If the system you wish to call does not have an `L.sys` entry (e.g., the system runs an operating system other than UNIX) or if the calling parameters are different from those in `L.sys`, `cu` can be used with flag options to specify the parameters on the command line. These include:

1. `-l` the file that corresponds to the telecommunications port
2. `-s` the transmission speed

To call information service such as CompuServe, the `cu` command might be written:

```
cu -l /dev/tty0 -s1200
```

When the connection with the modem is made, `cu` responds with:

```
Connected
```

At that point, enter the modem dialing commands. Assuming that you are using a Hayes-compatible modem, the conversation, with the modem's responses in italic, might appear as:

```
AT
OK
AT
OK
ATDT 5550987
Connect 1200
```

Keep in mind that when a connection is placed in this way, the user must complete the login sequence manually. A/UX will place the call and report that a connection has been made, but nothing else.

Cu Commands

Once a connection has been established, almost every command that you issue will be transmitted to the remote system. A/UX will assume that any command line preceded by a tilde (~) is intended for your local machine. The following commands are often useful:

1. `~.` Hang up the phone (end the connection).
2. `~!` Interact with the shell on the local machine. Issuing an end-of-file (CTRL-D) returns to interaction with the remote system.
3. `~!`*cmd* Issue a command (*cmd*) on the local system.
4. `~$`*cmd* Issue a command (*cmd*) on the local system.Transmit its results to the remote system.
5. `~%cd` Change the current directory on the local system. (Don't do this with `~!cd`.)

File Transfer

If the remote system in a conversation initiated by `cu` is another system, then `cu` can be used for file transfer. To upload a file (transfer a file from the local system to the remote system), use the `~"%put` command:

```
~%put <source file name> <destination file name>
```

For example, if the file `aux.dimmer` should be transmitted to a remote system and stored on that system under the name `dimmer.c`, the `put` command is typed:

```
~%put aux.dimmer dimmer.c
```

To download a file (copy a file from the remote system to the local system), use the ~"%take command:

```
~%take <source file name> <destination file name>
```

A file named inventory can be copied from a remote system and stored on a local system under the same file name by:

```
~%take inventory
```

If, as in the example above, the destination file name is omitted, cu will use the source file name.

Output Redirection

Cu normally displays commands sent to a remote system on the remote system's terminal screen (its standard output). If the remote system is running UNIX, output can be redirected to a file, just as it is when a user interacts directly with the shell on his or her local system.

To begin output redirection, type:

```
~> : <file name>
```

For example, the command:

```
~> :session.log
```

will store succeeding transmissions in the file session.log on the remote system.

To append lines to an existing file, use the >> notation, as in:

```
~>> :multi.log
```

Output redirection will continue until you issue:

```
~>
```

B-NET

B-NET refers to a group of commands that provide access to UNIX systems connected to each other via a local area network. These commands assume that the network uses direct serial lines.

A B-NET tutorial can be found in *A/UX Communications User's Guide*. See chapter 3.

Logging In to a Remote System

The `rlogin` command allows you to log in to a remote, or *host*, system from a local system. In its simplest form, the command is issued as:

```
rlogin <host name>
```

For example, assume that a system named `dragon` is sharing a local area network with `gryphon`. A user first logs in to `gryphon` in the normal manner. Then, to log in to `dragon` while remaining logged in to `gryphon` the user types:

```
rlogin dragon
```

A/UX will connect to the host, using the account name under which the user is logged in on the local system.

The host computer maintains a file named `/etc/hosts.equiv` that contains the names of other systems with which it shares account names. In other words, before a `gryphon` user can use `rlogin` to connect to `dragon`, `dragon`'s `/etc/hosts.equiv` file must contain an entry for `gryphon`. In addition, a user who wishes to use `rlogin` to access `dragon` must have an account on `dragon` with the same name as his or her account on `gryphon`. Because the account names are equivalent, no password is required for the login (the password was supplied when the user logged in to his or her local system).

If you wish to log in to an account on a remote host that is not the same as the account to which you have logged in on the local system, use `rlogin`'s `-l` option, as in:

```
rlogin dragon -l marty
```

The above command will connect to `dragon` and then attempt to log in to the account named `marty`. In this case, a password may or may not be required.

A password will not be required if the account to which you are attempting to log in has an entry for your local system account name in a file named `.rhosts`. The `.rhosts` file is placed in the home directory for each account that will permit remote logins by accounts with names that don't match. For example, if `jon` should be able to log in to `marty` on `dragon` from his account on `gryphon`, then the `/users/marty/.rhosts` file will contain the line:

```
gryphon jon
```

However, if the above line does not appear in `marty`'s `.rhost` file, then `jon`'s attempt to log in to `marty` will generate a request for a password. `Jon` must then supply the correct password for the `marty` account before the remote login will be accepted.

Once the remote login is completed, you will see the prompt for the host account's default shell. Interact with that shell just as would a shell on your local machine.

The `rlogin` command is documented in *A/UX Command Reference (M–Z and Games)*. See the section *User Commands (1)*; the commands are in alphabetical order.

Ending a Remote Session

To end a session with a remote host, do not log out in the normal manner. Instead, type `~.` to both log out and disconnect from the host. (Note that this is the same as the disconnect sequence used with `cu`).

Toggling Remote and Local Systems

If you have changed your default shell on your local system to the C or Korn shell, then you can temporarily disconnect from the remote system

to work with the local system by typing ~CTRL-Z. However, if are working with the Bourne shell (A/UX's default shell), then ~CTRL-Z won't work.

The solution is to use shl to create at least two shell layers before issuing the rlogin command. One layer can then be used to log in to the remote system while another remains with the local system. CTRL-Z will then return to shl's >>> prompt, at which point you can switch to another shell as needed. (Details on using shl appear at the end of Chapter 1.)

File Transfer

To copy files between a local and a remote machine, use the rcp (remote copy) command. The general form of the command is:

```
rcp <source file name> <destination file name>
```

If a user logged in to gryphon wishes to transfer a file to dragon, the command might be written:

```
rcp inventory dragon:inventory
```

Notice that the destination system name is separated from the file name by a colon. This is different from uucp notation, which uses an exclamation point.

There is no requirement that either the source or destination files must be on the source machine. Assume, for example, that a user logged in to gryphon wishes to copy a file from chimera to dragon. A command to process the request could be issued as:

```
rcp dragon:sales.force chimera:/sales/list
```

Rcp does not prompt for passwords. Therefore, the account name issuing the copy request must be known to the system or systems in the rcp command. In other words, the destination account must either be the same as the account issuing the rcp request or the requesting account must appear in the destination account's .rhosts file.

If the account name on the local system is not the same as the account name on the remote system, the rcp command must contain the account name under which you wish to log in. If a user logged in to `gryphon` wishes to copy a file from `dragon` under the account name of `marty`, the command is written:

```
rcp marty@dragon:blanker.c grphyon:blanker.c
```

This form of the command uses the Internet address format to specify the account name on the remote machine.

The `rcp` command is documented in *A/UX Command Reference (M–Z and Games)*. See the section *User Commands (1)*; the commands are in alphabetical order.

Part II
Focusing on A/UX

Chapter 7

A/UX Tools

Every time you issue a command to A/UX, you are running a program. In addition to A/UX's commands, you may also wish to run programs written for the Macintosh Operating System. This chapter discusses the transfer of files (data file and programs) between the Macintosh Operating System and A/UX and the procedure for running Macintosh programs under A/UX. It also looks at an A/UX utility that will allow you to have more than one window on the screen at a time, each containing its own A/UX program.

Transferring Files

Although many Macintosh Operating System (Macintosh OS) programs will run under A/UX, the two operating systems do not coexist easily. A/UX will not recognize Macintosh Operating System disks. By the same token, the Macintosh Operating System ignores any A/UX disk partitions. For that reason, you must use a special utility program—`hfx`—to transfer files between the two. Unlike most A/UX utilities, `hfx` is a true Macintosh application, supporting Macintosh menus, buttons, dialog boxes, and scrollable lists.

`Hfx` will transfer files between any A/UX file system and disks formatted for the Macintosh Operating System. It will recognize floppy disks and hard disks. However, if a hard disk contains more than one soft partition (a partition allocated through software), it may only see the first. Although files can be transferred *from* any disk to A/UX, files should only be copied from A/UX to a floppy disk. This is because there is some chance that transferring to a hard disk will corrupt files.[1]

`Hfx` is stored in `/usr/toolboxbin`. To run it, type:

1. The `hfx` utility is actually available from two sources. It is shipped with A/UX 1.1 but is also part of the *StarNine Utilities*. Apple bought `hfx` from StarNine. Although the two implementations are almost identical, the StarNine version will permit transfer to a Macintosh hard disk (possible, but never recommended). The StarNine version also is available when running `term`, the windowing utility discussed later in this chapter. If you are using the version shipped with A/UX, it must be used as a stand-alone program. In other words, it cannot be used if any other ToolBox application is running (e.g., `term`).

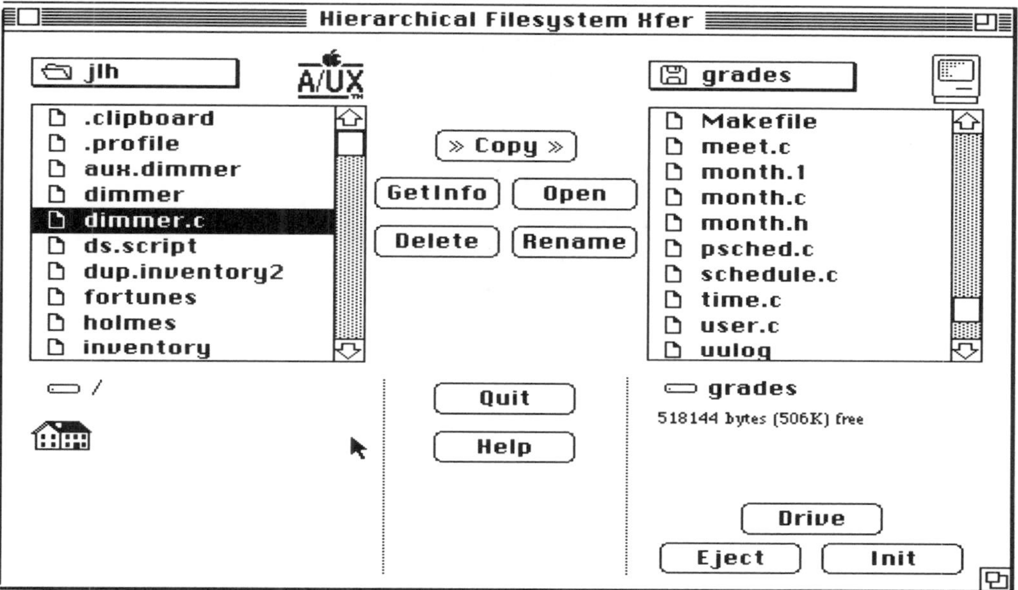

Figure 7.1 The `hfx` dialog box.

```
/usr/toolboxbin/hfx
```

You will see the screen in Figure 7.1. The scrollable list on the left contains the files and subdirectories of the current A/UX directory; its name appears above the list as a Macintosh folder icon.

Changing the A/UX Directory

To change directories, use the same technique you would use to change folders in a Macintosh OS Get File or Put File dialog box. To open a subdirectory, double-click on the subdirectory's name with the mouse pointer. To move up one or more levels in the directory hierarchy, place the mouse pointer over the folder icon and depress the mouse button. Move the mouse pointer to the name of the directory that should be the new current directory and release the mouse button.

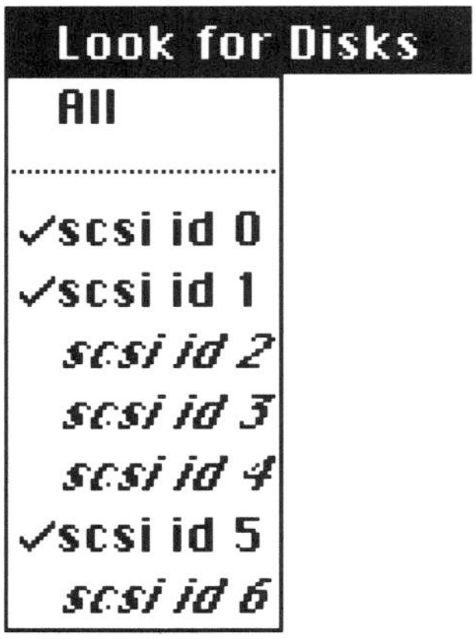

Look for Disks
All
✓scsi id 0
✓scsi id 1
scsi id 2
scsi id 3
scsi id 4
✓scsi id 5
scsi id 6

Figure 7.2 The `Look for Disks` menu.

Accessing Macintosh Disks and Files

The scrollable list on the right of the screen in Figure 7.1 displays the contents of a Macintosh OS volume. A volume corresponds to either a floppy disk or a partition on a hard disk. When it is launched, `hfx` will not automatically recognize any attached disks other than the floppy disk drive and the Macintosh OS partition on the A/UX drive. To get hfx to recognize other disk drives (*mounting* the drives), use the `Look for Disks` menu (Figure 7.2).

`Look for Disks` searches for disk drives attached to the Macintosh's SCSI bus. To force `hfx` to mount the disk, you must select the drive's SCSI ID number from the `Look for Disks` menu. Although it may be tempting to simply select the `All` option if you aren't sure of the SCSI ID, try to resist doing so. If some device other than a disk drive is attached to the SCSI bus (e.g., an Apple tape drive or a SCSI printer), using the `All` option will unmount the device, probably making your system administrator more than just a little unhappy.

To change the disk whose files are displayed in the right scrollable box, click on the Drive button with the mouse pointer. `Hfx` will cycle

through the drives that have been mounted with each successive click of the mouse button. To change floppy disks, use the Eject button.

Moving a Macintosh File to A/UX

To transfer a file from a Macintosh OS disk to an A/UX disk, select the drive on which the Macintosh file resides and then click on its name in the scrollable list to highlight it. If you wish to transfer more than one file at a time, hold down the shift key while clicking on additional file names. Once one file name is highlighted, the Copy button will be enabled (i.e., no longer dimmed); its arrows will point to the list of A/UX files on the left.

Begin the transfer by clicking on the Copy button. `Hfx` will display the dialog box in Figure 7.3. Use the edit box at the top to enter the path name of the directory in which the file should be stored. By default, `hfx` will use the path name of the directory whose files are listed in the left scrollable list. In the box below, enter the name under which the file should be stored. `Hfx` will use the Macintosh OS file name as a default. If the file name contains characters not allowed in A/UX file names (e.g., spaces,],)), they will be replaced with underscores.

The check box to the right of the file name should, in most cases, be left unchecked. Check it only if you know that carriage returns should be replaced by newline characters. (A carriage return issues a newline and a line feed, bringing the cursor to the left edge of the file on the line below; a newline returns to the left edge without dropping to the next line.)

The remainder of the dialog box sets the A/UX file attributes: owner, group, and file access permissions. By default, `hfx` will set the owner to the current account name and the group to the current group. The file will be readable by the owner, the owner's group, and everyone else; it will be writeable only by the owner. To change any of these defaults, enter a new owner and/or group in the appropriate text edit boxes and check or un-check the permission check boxes.

Press ENTER or click on the OK button to process the transfer. As with any other Macintosh dialog box, choosing the Cancel button will abort the operation.

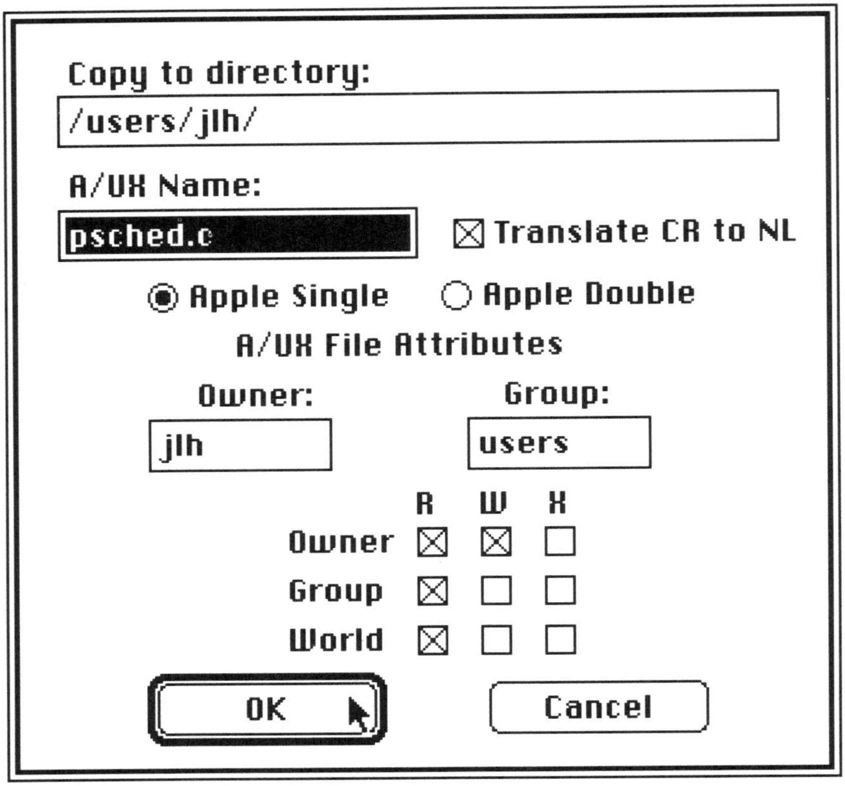

Copy to directory:
/users/jlh/
A/UX Name:
psched.c
Translate CR to NL
Apple Single
Apple Double
A/UX File Attributes
Owner:
jlh
Group:
users
R W X
Owner
Group
World
OK
Cancel

Figure 7.3 The dialog box to copy a file from the Macintosh OS to A/UX.

Moving an A/UX File to the Macintosh

To move an A/UX file to a Macintosh OS floppy disk, click on the file name in the left scrollable list. If you wish to select more than one file, hold down the shift key while clicking on additional file names. As soon as one file name is highlighted, the Copy button will be enabled, its arrows pointing to the right. Click onthe copy button to display the dialog box in Figure 7.4.

By default, `hfx` will assign the file its A/UX file name. The file can be stored on the Macintosh disk with another name by editing the edit box at

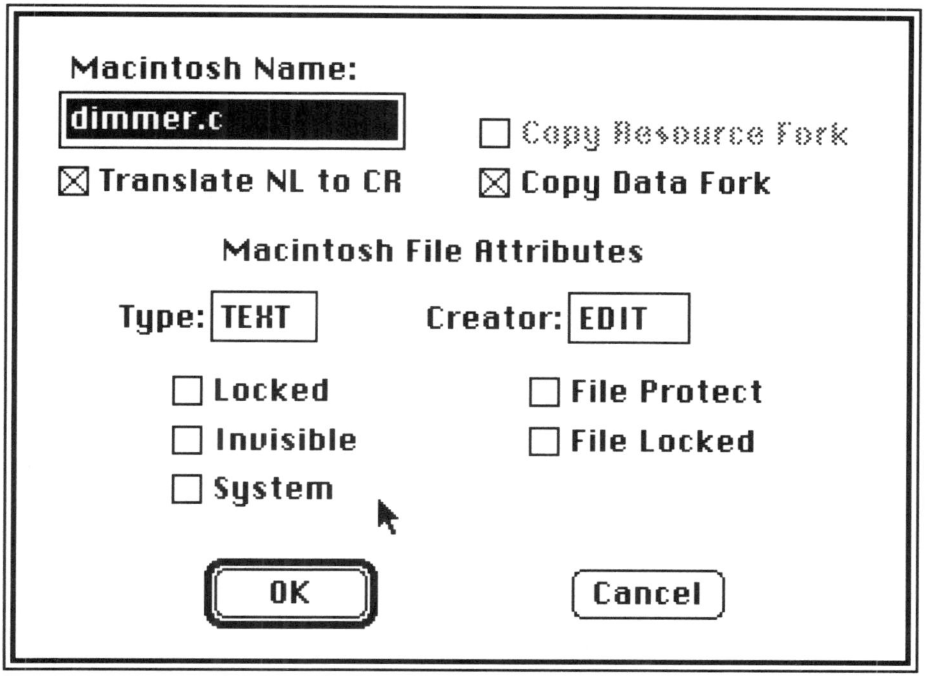

Figure 7.4 The dialog box to transfer an A/UX file to the Macintosh OS.

the top left of the dialog box. In most cases, the check box below (Translate NL to CR) can be left checked.

Setting the Macintosh file attributes requires a bit of knowledge of Macintosh files. The "creator" of a file is a four–character code that corresponds to the application that created the file. In the case of documents, the creator identifies the application that will be launched when you double–click on the document icon from the Finder. `Hfx` assumes that the file that is being transferred is a text file (i.e., not a binary file) and that it was created by the Macintosh text editor EDIT.

The "type" of a Macintosh file is a four–character code that identifies the kind of file. For example, executable files (i.e., programs) have a file type of APPL. ASCII text files (those without word processor formatting

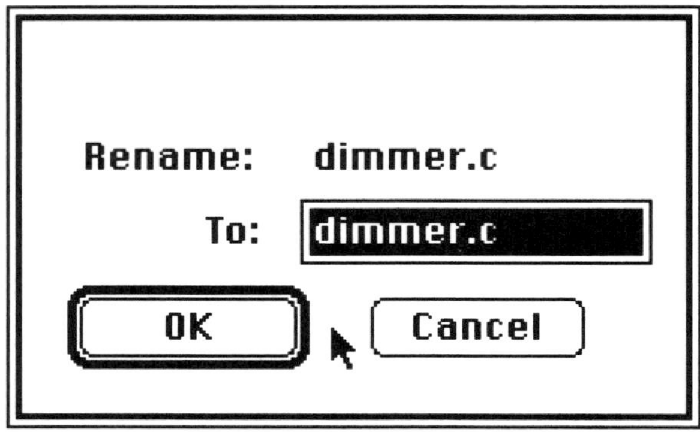

Figure 7.5 Renaming files.

codes) have a type of TEXT. TEXT files can be read by most Macintosh word processing programs, although they must be opened using the program's File menu rather than by double-clicking on the document's icon. In most cases, you should accept the default type and creator.

The check boxes represent special Macintosh file characteristics. For example, the icon for an invisible file does not appear on the desktop; a locked file cannot be deleted. Most of the time, all of these boxes can be left unchecked.

To process the transfer, press ENTER or click on the OK button. As you would expect, the Cancel button aborts the transfer.

Renaming Files

`Hfx` provides an easy way to rename A/UX files. First, highlight the name of the file whose name is to be changed. Then, click on the Rename button to display the dialog box in Figure 7.5. Enter the new name in the edit box and press ENTER (or click the OK button). The Cancel button aborts the operation.

Deleting Files

`Hfx` will also delete files. To do so, select the file name and then click on the Delete button. The alert in Figure 7.6 appears to give you a chance to

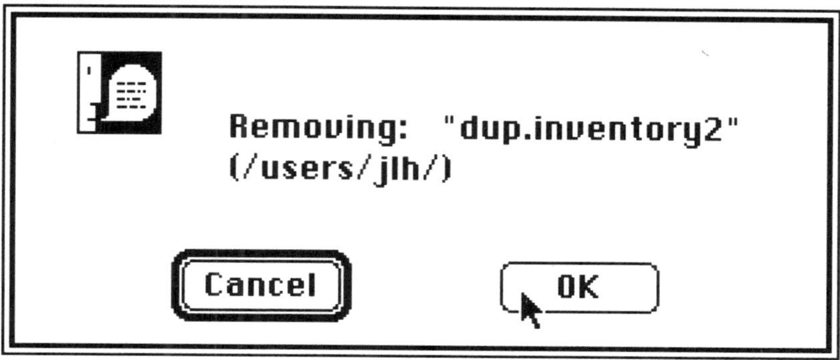

Figure 7.6 An alert box to confirm a file deletion.

change your mind. Pressing ENTER or clicking on the Cancel button will abort the deletion. Click the OK button to go ahead and delete the file.

Viewing File Info

The GetInfo button displays a dialog box like the one in Figure 7.7 containing a file description. The data in these boxes can be useful in determining, for example, whether there is enough space on a floppy disk to copy a file.

Opening Files

The Open button will launch (execute) a Macintosh program that has been transferred from the Macintosh OS to A/UX. However, as you will discover in the next section of this chapter, not all Macintosh OS application programs will run under A/UX. Because an attempt to run a program that is not A/UX compatible may disrupt operations of the entire A/UX system, it is better not to use this button to launch a program that has not been previously certified to run under A/UX.

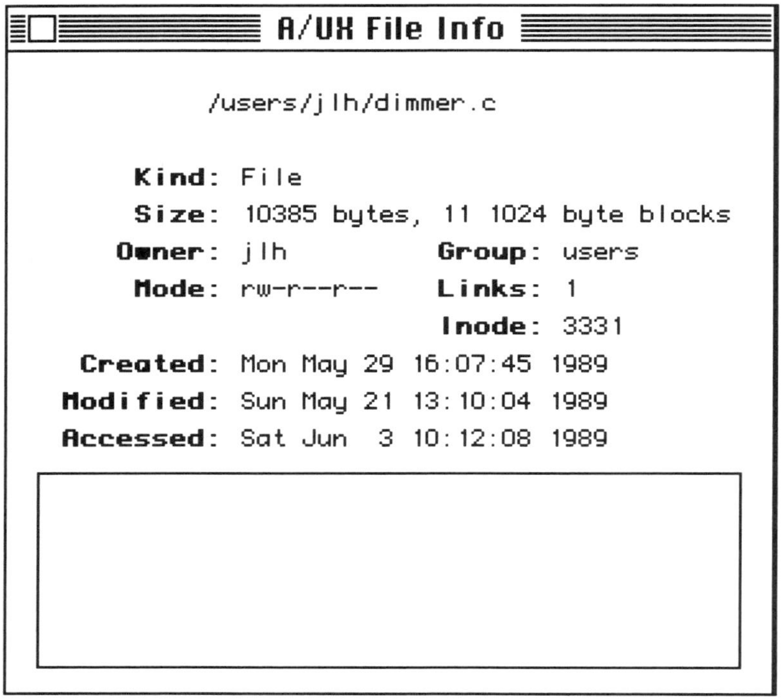

A/UX File Info

/users/jlh/dimmer.c

Kind: File
Size: 10385 bytes, 11 1024 byte blocks
Owner: jlh **Group:** users
Mode: rw-r--r-- **Links:** 1
Inode: 3331
Created: Mon May 29 16:07:45 1989
Modified: Sun May 21 13:10:04 1989
Accessed: Sat Jun 3 10:12:08 1989

Figure 7.7 A File Info box.

Initializing Disks

Like the Macintosh OS, `hfx` will respond if an unformatted or damaged floppy is inserted in the A/UX Macintosh's floppy drive. Inserting an unreadable disk brings up the alert box in Figure 7.8. If the disk has files on it, then it is probably damaged. In that case, click the Cancel button or press ENTER to remove the alert. Then click on the Eject button to eject the disk from the disk drive. If the files on the disk are important, you may wish to use a Macintosh OS disk recovery program in an attempt to salvage the disk's contents.

If you wish to format the disk, click on the OK button. `Hfx` will present the dialog box in Figure 7.9. (This dialog box will also appear if you

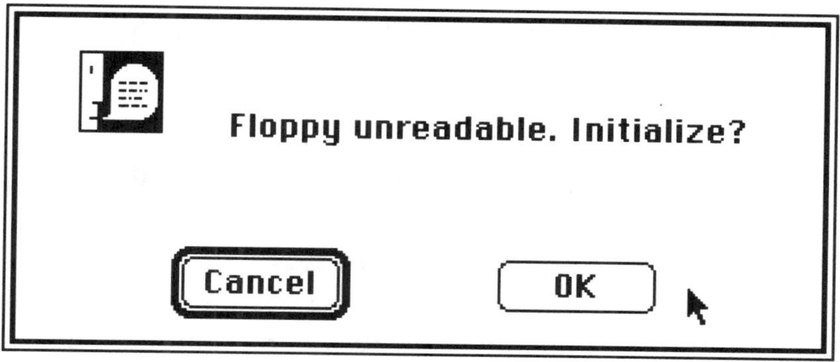

Figure 7.8 An `hfx` alert warning of an unreadable disk.

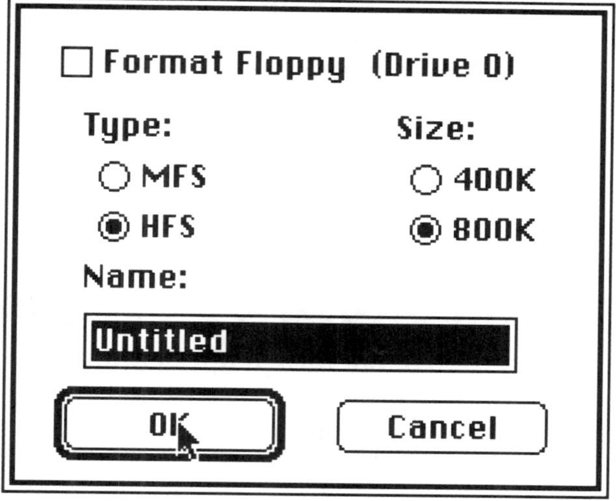

Figure 7.9 A dialog box to format Macintosh OS floppy disks.

click on the Init button in the `hfx` dialog box.) Unless the disk will be used in an older Macintosh (i.e., one prior to the Macintosh Plus), it should be formatted as HFS (hierarchical file system) and 800K. Type a name for the disk in the Name edit box. Press ENTER or click the OK button to begin the formatting. The Cancel button will terminate the process.

The `hfx` utility is documented in Chapter 6 of *Getting Started with A/UX.*

Running Macintosh Operating System Applications

Any Macintosh OS application program that is "32-bit clean" (i.e., adheres to Apple's programming guidelines for 32-bit microprocessors) will run under A/UX 1.1. In practice, however, many application programs have not been written in such a way that they meet all of Apple's rules. For that reason, the behavior of a Macintosh application should be carefully monitored before it is assumed to run properly.

The other thing to keep in mind when running a Macintosh application is that it completely takes over the user terminal. As far as the user running the application is concerned, A/UX's identity as a multitasking system is gone. It is not possible, for example, to run a Macintosh application in one `term` window and an A/UX program in another (`term` is discussed in the next section).

Launching a Macintosh OS Program

There are three ways to launch a Macintosh application. One is to use the Open button from the `hfx` dialog box. As mentioned earlier, this should only be done when the Macintosh application is known to run correctly under A/UX.

If you do not wish to execute `hfx`, a Macintosh application can be launched directly from the shell with the `launch` command. The command has the general format:

```
launch <program name> <document name>
```

For example, to run MacDraw, type:

```
launch MacDraw
```

If a document name is added to the command line, `launch` will open the document, just as the Finder would if the document icon had been double-clicked. A MacDraw document named `objects` will be opened with:

```
launch MacDraw objects
```

Some Macintosh applications rely on the Finder to initialize portions of the Macintosh ToolBox. Those applications will fail if launched under A/UX. If an application you are attempting to run fails, add the -i flag option to the command to instruct A/UX to perform the initialization:

```
launch -i MacDraw objects
```

> The `launch` command is documented in *A/UX Command Reference (A–L)*; see the section *User Commands (1)*; the commands are in alphabetical order. The command is also discussed in Chapter 6 of *Getting Started with A/UX*.

Using `launch` to start an application brings with it the same danger as using `hfs`'s Open button: there is the very real possibility of crashing the system with a badly behaved program. The alternative, at least for testing purposes, is `s9launch`, StarNine's version of the `launch` command that is lurking in `/usr/lib/hfx`. The syntax for using `s9launch` appears when the path name of the command is typed without an arguments or options:

```
USAGE: /usr/lib/hfx/s9launch [-d] [-f] [-h] [-r <program>] [-s
<snapshot file> [-S <seconds>] [-t <minutes>] <macProgram>
    -c:          make continuous snapshots
    -d:          create the snapshot file in APPLEDOUBLE format
    -f:          do not compress snapshot file
    -h:          print this help/usage message
    -r <program>: restart <program> on <macProgram> exit
    -s <file>:    put a snapshot of the screen into <file>
    -S <seconds>: take a snapshot of the screen after <#seconds>
    -t <minutes>: set timer for kill signal to <#minutes>
    <macProgram>: name of Macintosh binary to be executed
```

Of particular interest to testing Macintosh applications is s9launch's -t flag option. This option instructs A/UX to terminate (kill) the Macintosh application after a specified number of minutes. For example,

```
/usr/lib/hfx/s9launch -t 2 MacDraw
```

will launch MacDraw and then terminate the program after two minutes have elapsed. If the program being tested has hung in some way (i.e., frozen so that no further action is possible), A/UX will automatically kill it and free the user's terminal. S9launch is, therefore, the safer way to launch a newly transferred application.

A Macintosh application that is compatible with A/UX will run under A/UX just as it runs under the Macintosh OS. However, printing from that application may not always be possible. Many A/UX systems have Image Writers or LaserWriters connected directly to the A/UX computer, rather than using the AppleTalk network. If your system uses a direct connection, printing from Macintosh applications is not possible. However, if the system has an AppleTalk communications board and a LaserWriter or Image Writer is connected to the network, then printing is performed just as it is from the Macintosh OS.

Working with Multiple Windows

People who are used to working in the Macintosh environment often find A/UX a bit of a disappointment, since there are no windows, no menus, and the mouse might as well not even exist. However, A/UX 1.1 does provide a utility named term that supports multiple A/UX commands running in multiple windows. Term uses Macintosh-style menus and allows the copying and pasting of text between windows.

The term utility is documented in Chapter 6 of *Getting Started with A/UX.*

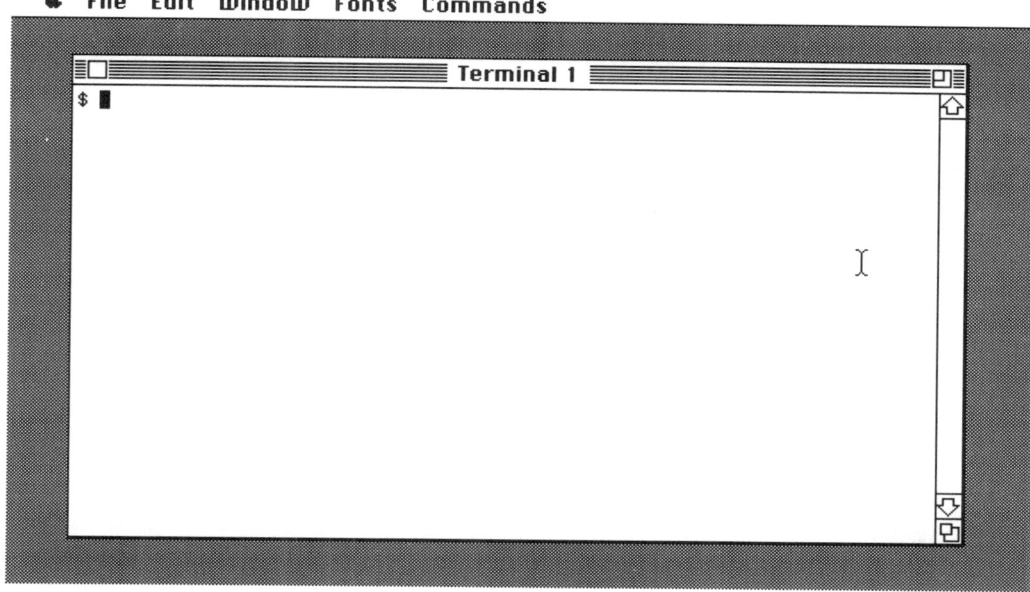

Figure 7.10 The initial `term` window.

To invoke `term`, type:

```
term
```

at the shell's prompt. The initial `term` screen can be seen in Figure 7.10. It includes a Macintosh-style window with vertical scroll bars named Terminal 1 as well as a Macintosh-style menu bar.

Additional Terminal windows, up to a limit of 16, can be added as needed. To create a new window, choose New from the File menu (Figure 7.11) or press Command-N. Each `term` window corresponds to an A/UX shell. A different foreground process can run in each window. Look, for example, at Figure 7.12. The foreground window, Terminal 4, shows the results of a `ps` command. The console, from which `term` was invoked, is running the `term` process. In addition, there are four terminals (`p1`, `p2`, `p3`, and `p4`) that are running `sh`, the Bourne shell. Each of these terminals corresponds to a window on the `term` screen.

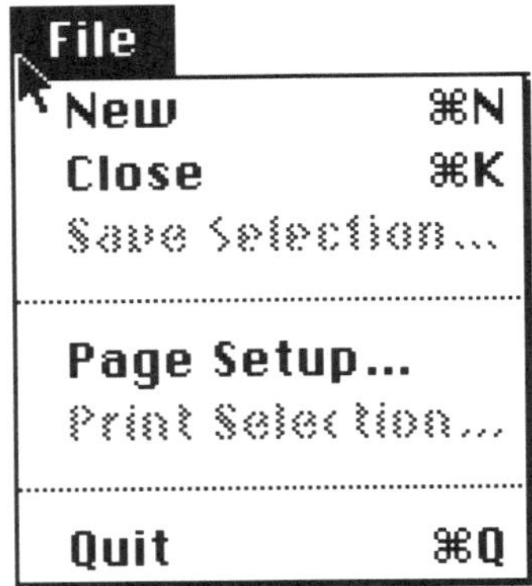

Figure 7.11 The `term` file menu.

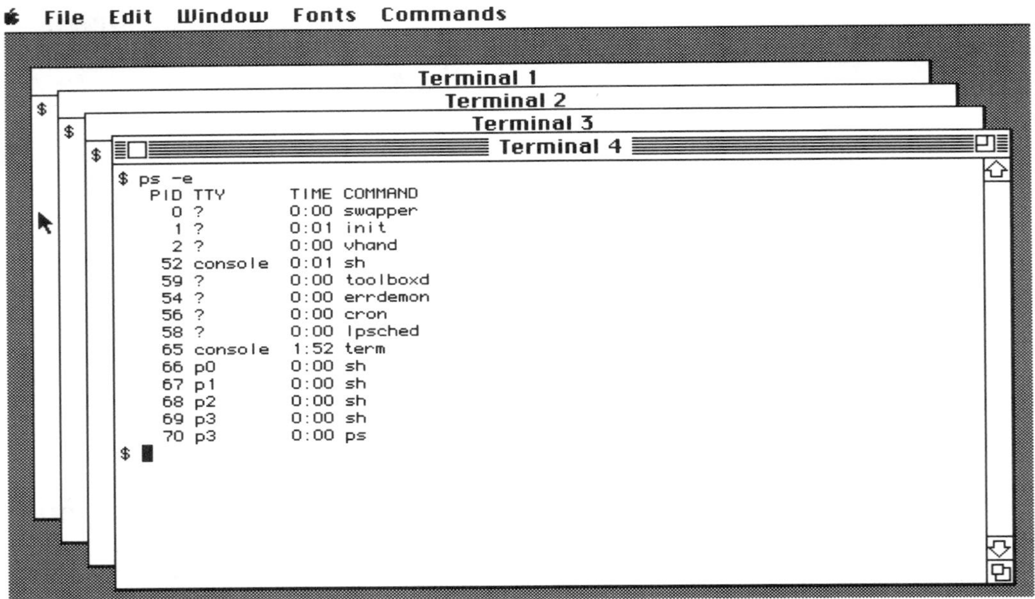

Figure 7.12 The processes created to support four `term` windows.

Window

Tile	⌘T
Tile Horizontal	
Tile Vertical	
Standard Positions	
Standard Size	⌘S
Full Height	⌘F
Zoom Window	⌘/
Hide "Terminal 1"	⌘H
Show All Windows	
Last Window	⌘L
Rotate Windows	⌘R
✓Terminal 1	⌘1
Terminal 2	⌘2
Terminal 3	⌘3
Terminal 4	⌘4

Figure 7.13 The `term` utility's Window menu.

Working with Windows

Although a different process can be running in each `term` window, the user can only interact with one window at a time. This window is the *active* window. The active window is identified by the highlighting in its title bar (horizontal lines appear) and a solid black cursor.

There are a number ways to make a window active. If the window is visible, click on any part of the window with the mouse pointer. Alternatively, select the window's name from the list at the bottom of the window menu or press the command key along with the window's number(Figure 7.13).

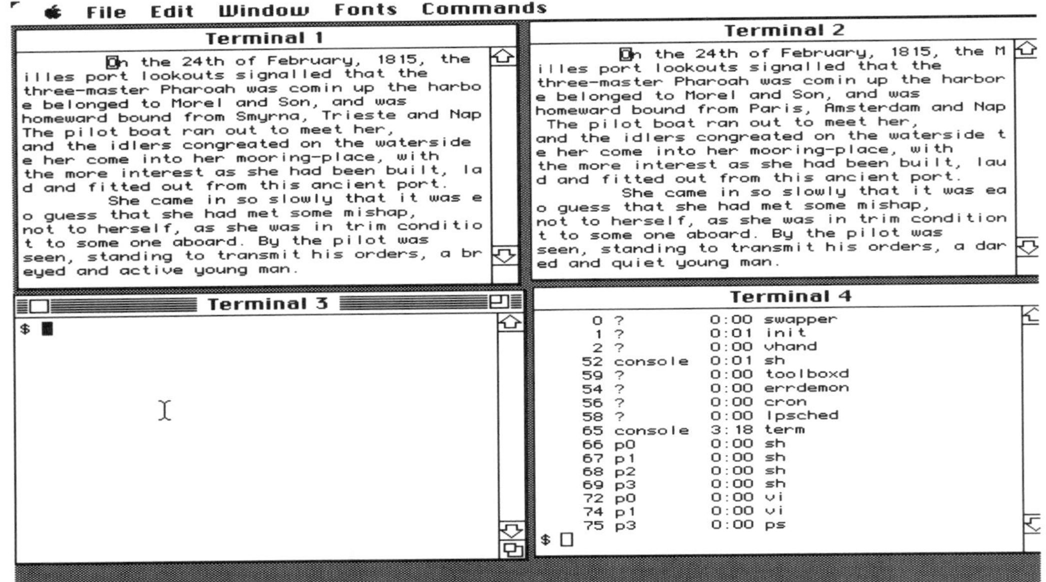

Figure 7.14 Tiled windows.

The Last Window option of the Window menu makes the previous active window the active window; if the new active window is overlapped by other windows, it will be brought to the front. The Rotate Windows option of the Window menu makes the last window the active window; if it is hidden by other windows, it will be brought to the front.

The "standard position" of `term` windows is overlapped, just as they are in Figure 7.12. In addition, windows can be *tiled.* Tiling sizes the windows so all will fit on the screen without overlap. In Figure 7.14, Terminal 1 and Terminal 2 are running `vi`, although each is editing a different document. Terminal 3 is the active window, while Terminal 4 displays the result of the `ps` command. Windows can also be tiled horizontally (Figure 7.15) and vertically (Figure 7.16). All forms of tiling are selected from the Window menu. Note that the Window menu also contains an option to return the windows to their standard, overlapped positions.

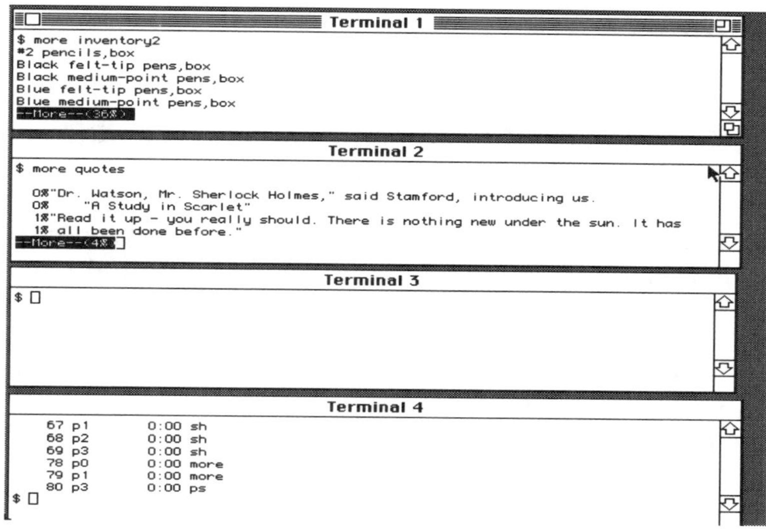

Figure 7.15 Horizontal tiling.

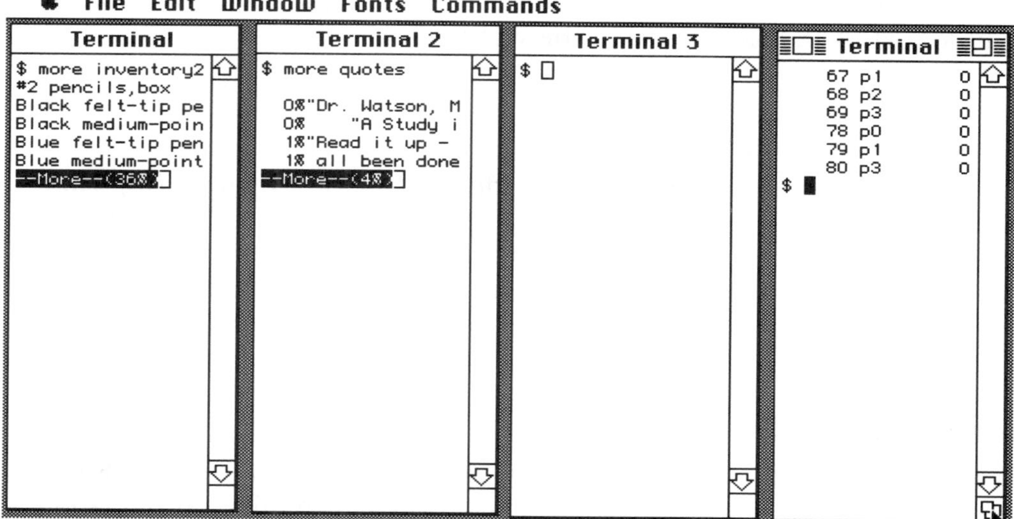

Figure 7.16 Vertical tiling.

Sizing Windows

Windows can be sized in four ways:

1. Drag the size box in the lower right corner of the window, just as you would any other Macintosh window.
2. Zoom the window to full screen size.
   a. Click on the zoom box (at the right of the window's title bar); click again to return the window to its original size.
   b.. Choose Zoom window from the Window menu; choose Standard size to return it to its original size.
   c. Press Command-/ to zoom the window; press Command-S to return it to its original size.
3. Make the window the full height of the screen by choosing Full Height from the Window menu or pressing Command–F.

When you are working with a program like `vi`, the number of characters that will fit on a line is determined by the size of the window when the program is launched. However, if the window is resized, the text will not be adjusted to match the window's new size (i.e., making a window smaller may hide text at the right edge of the window).

Hiding Windows

An active window can be temporarily hidden from view by selecting Hide Window from the Window menu or pressing Command-H. To make the window visible again, choose its name from the Window menu or press the command key and its number. All hidden windows can be made visible at once with the Window menu's Show All Windows command.

Changing the Display Font

To change the font in the active window, make a selection from the Fonts menu (Figure 7.17). The Monaco font is a monospaced (all characters occupying the same width) bit-mapped font. Courier is a monospaced LaserWriter font. You may wish to use Courier if window contents will be printed on a LaserWriter.

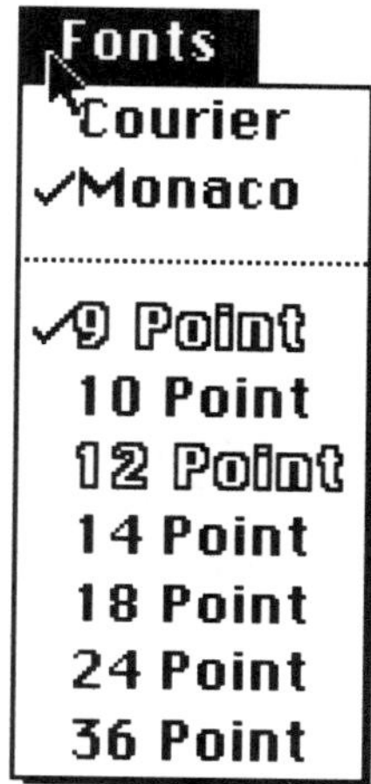

Figure 7.17 The `term` utility's Fonts menu.

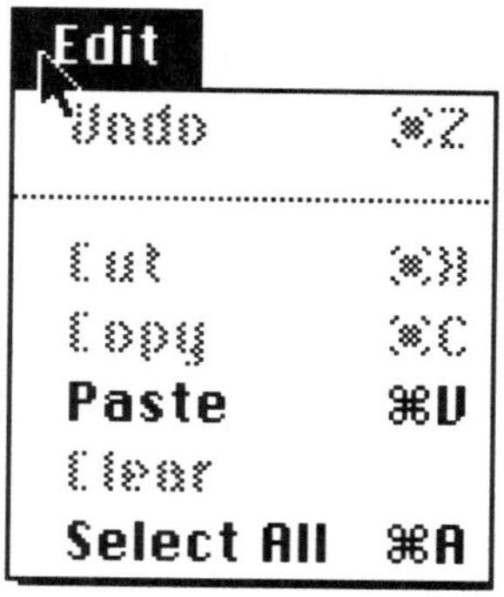

Figure 7.18 The `term` utility's Edit menu.

Editing Operations

The `term` utility supports Macintosh editing operations between windows. Editing commands are available from the Edit menu (Figure 7.18) or with their keyboard equivalents. In most cases, only Copy and Paste are available. In other words, text cannot be Cut from a `term` window. The full range of editing operations are available only with desk accessories that support them.

To copy text onto the Macintosh clipboard, select the text to be copied with the mouse, just as you would select it in any Macintosh OS document. Then choose Copy from the Edit menu or press Command-C. To paste the text into another window, make the target window the active window and click with the crosshair cursor at the place where the next text should appear. Choose Paste from the Edit menu or press Command-V. A/UX interprets pasted text as if it had been typed on the keyboard. A common use for this cut–and–paste feature is to transfer text between two documents that have been opened (e.g., with `vi`) in two `term` windows.

Playing with Selected Text

As well as copying and pasting selected text, `term` will print selected text as well as saving it to a file. As with printing from a Macintosh application, printing is available only if the A/UX Macintosh is connected to AppleTalk (a direct serial connection to a printer is not sufficient).

To print a selection, choose Print from the File menu. Make any necessary changes to the Macintosh print dialog box and press ENTER. To save selected text to a file, choose Save As from the File menu. Enter a file name in the Put File dialog box and press ENTER.

Recording Window Contents

When lines scroll off the top of the standard A/UX screen, they are simply lost. The same is true for `term` windows, unless `term` is instructed to do otherwise. If you would like `term` to retain the contents of a window as it scrolls out of view, make it the active window and select Record Lines Off Top from the Command menu (Figure 7.19).

`Term` will draw vertical scroll bars on the window and retain the lines that scroll off the top in main memory. Use the scroll bars to view the recorded lines at any time. Keep in mind, however, that the recorded lines are not kept after the window is closed. If you need to retain them, select the lines that should be retained and then save them to a file, using the technique described in the previous section.

Figure 7.19 The `term` utility's Commands menu.

After Record Lines Off Top has been chosen, the menu option changes to Don't Record Lines Off Top. Choose that option to stop retaining lines from the active window.

Chapter 8

Bourne Shell Programming

The most precise definition of a UNIX shell is to call it a *command interpreter*. Like the BASIC language interpreters with which you may be familiar, it takes the commands that are issued to it and translates them to machine language, one at a time, executing each command line immediately after it has been translated. Because a shell is actually an interpreter, it supports a programming language. This chapter discusses using the Bourne shell's language to create *shell scripts*, programs that are interpreted (translated to machine language at run time) by the shell as they are executed.

Because shell scripts are interpreted, they execute more slowly than programs that are compiled (translated to machine language before run time). For that reason, shell scripts are generally short. They may be used to customize a user's working environment, to simplify the use of a command with a complicated syntax, or to perform functions that can be done in less than a page or two of program code. Some developers may also create a prototype of a program as a shell script and later rewrite the program in C so that it will run faster and more efficiently.

Shell programming is documented as part of the `sh` command in *A/UX Command Reference (M–Z and Games)*. See the section *User Commands (1)*; the commands are in alphabetical order. In addition, see the chapter on the Bourne shell in *A/UX User Interface*.

Creating a Shell Script

Shell scripts can contain any command that can be issued at the shell's prompt as well as programming language statements. To create a shell script, first use a text editor (e.g., `vi`) to enter the contents of the script. Save it under some meaningful name.

For example, assume that you have become tired of entering the entire command line for the `find` command:

```
find / -name <file name> -exec echo "{}" ";"
```

Instead, you would like to place that command in a shell script so that you could type just one word plus the name of the file you wanted to find. The contents of the simple shell script would be:

```
find / -name $1 -exec echo "{}" ";"
```

This single line is saved as a file named `sfind` (for "simple find").

The name of the file for which `sfind` is to search has been replaced with $1. The dollar sign is a signal to the shell that what follows is a *positional parameter* name and that it should use the contents of the parameter. Positional parameters are variables with names that are numbers, which are passed to the script when it is executed. In this case, the shell is to use the contents of the *first* parameter.

A/UX cannot tell the difference between a file that contains the text of a document and a file that contains a shell script. A script's default permissions will include read and write access only. To make a script executable, use `chmod`[1] :

```
chmod +x sfind
```

Once the script has execute permissions, it can be run like any other A/UX command, by typing its name at the shell's prompt, followed by any necessary options or arguments. The `sfind` script requires one argument–the name of the file to be found. To find the file `dimmer.c`, the command would be written:

```
sfind dimmer.c
```

The output is exactly the same as if the entire command had been typed at the shell's prompt.

Shell scripts can also be run without making the file executable by using the name of the script as an argument to `sh`, as in:

---

1. For details on the `chmod` command, see Chapter 2.

```
sh logs
```

This command will create two processes. The first is `sh`, the daughter shell under which the script will run. The second is a process for the script itself. In this case, the script (`logs`) displays a list of the last ten people who have logged in to the system.

Quotes

The shell uses quotes differently than most programming languages. If a string of characters is surrounded by single quotes, the shell will remove any special meaning the characters might have and treat them as a literal string. For example,

```
>output.file
```

is normally used to redirect output. However, if the shell sees:

```
'>output.file'
```

it will ignore the special meaning of the > and assume that it is the first character in the string.

Double quotes also remove the special meaning of most characters. The major exception is the dollar sign. While the shell will interpret:

```
'$1'
```

as the literal string `$1` it will assume that:

```
"$1"
```

means to use the contents of the script's first parameter.

Back quotes are used to instruct the shell to evaluate whatever expression is between the quotes and to use that value rather than the

expression itself. For example, to obtain the path name of the current directory, a statement within a shell program would include:

```
`pwd`
```

If it sees:

```
pwd
```

or

```
"pwd"
```

the shell will assume that it should manipulate the characters `pwd` rather than executing the command that returns the path name of the current directory.

In addition, the backslash (\) is used to remove the special meaning of a number of characters. For example, the asterisk is normally used as a file name wildcard. However, it is also the multiplication operator. When used within multiplication, it must be preceded by a backslash. For example, to multiply 15 by 99 the expression must be written:

```
15 \* 99
```

The backslash can also be used to indicate that a statement will be continued on the next line of the script. The shell will interpret a backslash as a continuation character when it is the last character on the line (followed by a carriage return). For example, the commands:

```
who | \
grep tty0
```

is equivalent to:

```
who | grep tty0
```

The backslash can also be used as a continuation character at the shell's prompt. (This particular command displays the name of the user who is logged in through the port `tty0`, the default modem port.) When the shell detects a continuation character, it does not process the command immediately, but displays its level two prompt, waiting for further input. For example, if the pipeline above is issued interactively, the screen will appear as:

```
$ who | \
> grep tty0 <cr>
```

The > is the shell's level two prompt. It appears whenever the shell expects additional data to complete a command. As long as the read is successful (i.e., there is a line in the file to be read), the body of the loop will be executed.

Shells and Command Execution

Whenever a program or command is executed by typing its name at the shell's prompt, the shell creates two new processes, one that is the program itself and another that is a copy of the shell itself (a *daughter* shell). If you are working at the shell's prompt, the creation of the daughter shell process under which the program or command will run generally creates no problems. However, there are circumstances where a shell script needs to force execution of a command without spawning a new shell process.

The `exec` command executes a command without creating a daughter shell. For example,

```
exec <inventory
```

replaces the standard input with the file `inventory`. Input will be taken from the file until it is redirected back to the keyboard with:

```
exec </dev/tty
```

By the same token, the standard output can be redirected to a file with:

```
exec >output.file
```

It can be sent back to the screen with:

```
exec >/dev/tty
```

In addition to the `exec` command, any command invoked with a period preceding its name will also execute without spawning a new shell. An example of a command designed to be executed in this manner appears later in this chapter in the section Configuring a Working Environment.

Shell Variables and Assignment Statements

Like any programming language, shell scripts support variables to which values can be assigned. Variable names can be any series of up to 14 characters. As with shell commands, upper- and lowercase letters are different. For example, `path` is not the same as `PATH`.

To avoid confusion, variable names should be different from the names of A/UX commands and shell programming commands. In addition, there are some variables that are reserved for use by the shell. These *environmental parameters* include:

1. `CDPATH`: The file path that A/UX will search when the `cd` command is issued.
2. `HOME`: The user's login directory.
3. `IFS`: The characters that will be used to separate fields (by default, space, tab, and newline).
4. `MAIL`: Contains the name of the file that A/UX should check to determine if there is any mail waiting for the user.
5. `MAILCHECK`: Contains, in seconds, how often A/UX should check for incoming mail (the default is 60 seconds [1 minute] rather than the 600 seconds indicated in the documentation).

7. MAILPATH: If MAIL has not been set, contains a list of files that A/UX should check for incoming mail.
8. PATH: A list of directories that A/UX should search whenever a command is issued.
9. PS1: The shell's level one prompt string ($ by default).
10. PS2: The shell's level two prompt string (> by default).
11. TERM: The type of terminal in use.
12. TZ: The current time zone.

Assigning Values

Values are assigned to variables across an equals sign, just as they are in most high-level programming languages. For example,

```
prompt="Press any key to continue: "
```

will place the string `Press any key to continue:` in the variable `prompt` and

```
SearchPath=/usr/toolboxbin
```

will place the string `/usr/toolboxbin` in the variable `SearchPath`. Note that no spaces are permitted on either side of the equals sign.

In most cases, strings do not need to be surrounded by quotes when they are assigned to variables. However, if the string contains blanks or commas, it should be surrounded by either double or single quotes.

Because strings do not have to be quoted, the shell has a problem distinguishing between strings and variable names when they appear on the right-hand side of an equals sign. For that reason, a variable must be preceded by a dollar sign when the shell should use its contents. For example, the commands:

```
path=/usr/toolboxbin
NewPath=$path
```

first assign the string `/usr/toolboxbin` to the variable `path`. The contents of `path` are then assigned to the variable `NewPath`.

The result of an A/UX command can be assigned to a variable. For example, if the path name of the current directory will be needed throughout the script, it probably makes sense to store it in a variable:

```
CurrentPath=`pwd`
```

Note that the command is surrounded by back quotes to instruct the shell to assign the value returned by the command (rather than the name of the command) to the variable.

Doing Arithmetic

Although the Bourne shell has powerful tools for processing text, it is relatively weak in arithmetic operations. To perform arithmetic, the arithmetic operations must be preceded by the shell command `expr`. `Expr` instructs the shell to evaluate what follows rather than to view it as a string of characters.

Assume, for example, that a shell script needs to count something. The normal way to do this is to initialize a variable with the starting value and then to increment it by one every time something should be counted. The starting value can be assigned across an equals sign:

```
counter=1
```

However, `counter` must be incremented with `expr`:

```
counter=`expr $counter + 1`
```

In addition to using `expr` and surrounding the entire expression, arithmetic operators must be surrounded by at least one blank on each side.

Arithmetic using `expr` is limited to integer operations with the following operators:

1. `+` addition
2. `-` subtraction
3. `\*` multiplication
4. `/` division
5. `%` remainder of an integer division

> Additional documentation for `expr` can be found in *A/UX Command Reference (A–L)*. See the section *User Commands (1)*; the commands are in alphabetical order.

The Power of expr

The `expr` command can be used for more than just arithmetic operations. In particular, `expr` will perform comparisons that return values based on the result on the comparison.

Relationship Operators

When two quantities or strings are compared with the relationship operators (e.g., less than, greater than), `expr` will return a one if the comparison is true and a zero if the comparison is false. Numbers are compared based on their numeric values; strings are compared based on alphabetical order.

Because the greater than and less than operators have special meaning to the shell (they are used to redirect input and output), they must be preceded by the backslash escape character. The operators are written as `=`, `\>`, `\>=`, `\<`, `\<=`, and `!=`. They might be used in the following manner:

`expr 6 \> 5` (returns 1 because the comparison is true)

`a='Baker'`
`b='Zebra'`
`expr $a = $b` (returns 0 because the comparison is false)

`expr $a \< $b` (returns 1 because the comparison is true)

Additional Comparison Operators

`Expr` also accepts three special comparison operators: `\|`, `\&`, and `:`. When two quantities or strings are compared with `\|`, the shell returns the value on the left of the operator if the value is not zero (for a quantity) or null (for a string). Otherwise, it returns the second value. As an example, consider the following:

```
a=''
b='jon'
expr $a \| $b
```

This statements above return the contents of `b` because `a` contains the null string (the quotes assigning a value to `a` have no space between them). One important use of `\|` is to assign a default value to a positional parameter when the user of a shell script has not supplied a value:

```
file.name=`expr $1 \| "output.file"
```

In the above statement, the shell script uses a default name for the output file if the user has not supplied one on the command line.

The `\&` operator returns the value on the left of the operator if neither of the values is zero (for quantities) or null (for strings). If both expressions are either zero or null, it returns a zero. Consider the following examples:

```
a=''
b=0
```
`expr $a \& $b` (returns 0 because both arguments are null and/or zero)

```
a='output.file'
b=''
```
`expr $a \& $b` (returns the `$a` because at least one value is nonnull)

The `:` is the matching operator. Its operation depends on how the values on either side of the operator are expressed. In most cases, the statement returns the number of characters that match. For example:

`expr 'abcdef' : 'defgh'` (returns 3)

Shell metacharacters can be used to obtain results from `:` that are not otherwise available from the shell. The period metacharacter will match any single character; the asterisk metacharacter will match any number of characters. Therefore, a statement like:

```
expr 'twelve' : '.*'
```

will return the length of the value to the left of the operator, since the expression on the right will match any characters.

The matching operator can also be used to return the right portion of a string of characters, performing a function much like the RIGHT$ function found in most versions of BASIC. Obtaining this type of output requires using metacharacters surrounded by parentheses on the right of the operator; the parentheses must be escaped with the backslash because they have special meaning to the shell. For example, the last word of a string can be retrieved with:

```
a=`expr 'This is a test' : ' \(.*\)'`
```

The expression to the right of the colon begins with a space, followed by metacharacters within parentheses that match any character.

Exporting Values

Shell variables are local to the shell script. In other words, they retain their values only while the script is running. If the value of a variable should be kept after the script completes its execution, the variable must be *exported*.

Assume, for example, that you have changed the default level one prompt to `Have a nice day` and wish to continue to use the changed prompt while you are logged in. To do so, include the following two lines in a shell script:

```
PS1="Have a nice day "
export PS1
```

Most commonly, `export` is used to retain changes in shell variables such as `PS1`, `HOME`, `TERM`, and `PATH`. (See the section Configuring a Working Environment for more details on how these are used.)

Metacharacters for Use in Shell Scripts

In addition to the metacharacters that have been discussed in previous chapters, there are two additional metacharacters that are particularly useful within shell scripts:

1. $: The number of the current process. This value can be assigned to a shell variable with:

   ```
   process.no=$$
   ```

   The first dollar sign instructs the shell to obtain the contents of the second, the current process number.
2. #: The total number of positional parameters passed to the script on the command line. For example, if a user types:

   ```
   list.names jon jan james jake june
   ```

   # will have a value of five and the shell will make the following assignments:

   ```
   1=jon
   2=jan
   3=james
   4=jake
   5=june
   ```

   The # can be used to control looping constructs when the number of parameters is variable. For an example, see the section Using while Loops later in this chapter.

Input and Output

Like other programming languages, the Bourne shell has statements that permit it to collect data from the user and to display data for the user's benefit. The basic output statement is `echo`, which displays a string of text. Data can be collected from the keyboard with the `read` statement.

Writing Text

The `echo` command displays the string of text that follows it to the standard output. For example,

```
echo 'This is a test'
```

displays

```
This is a test
```

on the user's terminal screen.

`Echo` will also display the contents of shell variables. As an example, consider the following:

```
CurrDir=`pwd`
echo 'You are currently working in ' $CurrDir
```

If the user's current directory is `/users/jon`, the two lines above produce:

```
You are working in /users/jon
```

As well as variables, `echo` statements can also contain expressions that are to be evaluated. For example, the two lines above could be written as one in the following manner:

```
echo 'You are currently working in ' `pwd`
```

Remember that the single quotes around `You are currently working in` instruct A/UX to display the characters literally, just as they appear in

the command line. However, the back quotes surrounding `pwd` indicate that the expression is to be evaluated and its value displayed.

By default, `echo` issues a carriage return and newline after displaying text. In other words, it moves the cursor to the far left position on the line below the line on which the text appeared. However, when `echo` is used to display a prompt to which a user should enter data, the cursor should be left on the same line as the text. `Echo` therefore supports a number of *escape* characters that control what happens to the cursor.

The escape sequence `\c` will instruct `echo` to leave the cursor at the right edge of the displayed text. For example,

```
echo 'Enter your name:
```

produces

```
Enter your name:
_
```

while

```
echo 'Enter your name: \c'
```

displays

```
Enter your name: _
```

The `\t` escape sequence will insert a tab into the output. For example:

```
echo 'Name\tPhone #\tBirth Date'
echo '----\t-------\t----------'
echo
echo 'jon\t555-1234\t12-10-62'
echo 'jan\t555-0987\t10-13-50'
```

displays

```
Name     Phone # Birth Date
----     -------- ----------

jon      555-1234 12-10-62
jan      555-0987 10-13-50
```

As you will remember, by default, tab stops are set every eight spaces. The `echo` command on a line by itself without text simply displays a blank line.

Additional escape sequences that you may wish to use with `echo` include:

1. `\b` Backspace.
2. `\f` Form feed (used when the text is being "displayed" on a printer).
3. `\n` Newline (moves the cursor down one line without moving it horizontally).
4. `\r` Carriage return (moves the cursor to the left edge of the line without issuing a line feed).

Although one of the most common uses of `echo` is to display text on the terminal screen, it can also be used to write to a file by redirecting output. For example,

```
echo 'Name\tPhone #\tBirth Date' >user.file
echo '----\t-------\t----------' >>user.file
echo >>user.file
echo 'jon\t555-1234\t12-10-62' >>user.file
echo 'jan\t555-0987\t10-13-50' >>user.file
```

will write five lines to the file `user.file`. Notice that the output in the first `echo` is redirected with >. The > will create a new file if one does not already exist. If the file does exist, it will be overwritten to contain just the first line above. The remainder of the `echo` commands redirect output with >>. The >> appends the remaining lines to the existing file rather than overwriting it each time.

The `echo` command is documented in *A/UX Command Reference (A–L)*. See the section *User Commands (1)*; the commands are in alphabetical order.

Reading Input Data

Data are accepted from the keyboard and stored in a variable by the `read` command. For example,

```
read choice
```

will accept one "word" from the keyboard and store it in the variable named `choice`.

The shell defines a word as a string of characters terminated by a blank or a carriage return. If, for example, a shell script contains:

```
read choice1 choice2
```

and the user types:

```
first second <cr>
```

the characters `first` will be assigned to `choice1`; the characters `second` will be assigned to `choice2`. However, if the user types:

```
first second third
```

the shell will place `first` in `choice1` and `second third` in `choice2`. In other words, the shell places each word of data into the `read` command's variables according to the position of the variables in the command. If there are more words than variables, the last variable contains everything left over. For example, the statements:

```
echo 'Enter your name: \c'
read name
```

```
echo '      Tools Program Main Menu'
echo
echo '1. Check the date and time'
echo '2. Look at a calendar'
echo '3.. See who else is logged in'
echo '4. Read the mail'
echo
echo '9. Quit'
echo
echo 'Enter an option number: \c'
read choice
```

Figure 8.1 A shell script menu.

will prompt the user for his or her name and then store the entire line in the variable name.

Read's input can be redirected to a file, as in:

```
read item, units, on.hand <inventory
```

However, the above command will always read the first line from the file, regardless of how many times the command is executed. For details on how to step through a file, line by line, see the section Repeating Actions later in this chapter.

Creating Menus

The echo and read commands can be used together to create simple menus that will allow users to choose actions. Assume, for example, that you wish to develop a shell script that will simplify the use of some A/UX utilities. The shell script will be called tools; its menu can be found in Figure 8.1.

The program title and the menu items are displayed with echo. The read command then accepts the option number and stores it in choice. This is a very primitive way to create a menu, and may not appeal to users who are used to the Macintosh user interface. However, the shell's language does not have access to Macintosh ToolBox routines. It is, therefore, limited to the type of menu found in Figure 8.1.

File Name Descriptors

In a number of the examples of the command `echo`, output has been redirected to a file. To simplify both input and output redirection, the shell allows single numbers to be associated with file names (*file descriptors*). Three numbers are reserved:

1. 0 (standard input)
2. 1 (standard output)
3. 2 (standard error output)

To associate a file name with a file descriptor other than the three reserved values, use:

```
exec descriptor#<FileName
```

For example, the file descriptor `6` can be associated with `request.file` with:

```
exec 6<request.file
```

When a file descriptor is placed on the right of one of the I/O redirection symbols, the shell cannot distinguish it from a file whose name is a single number. Therefore, when file descriptors are used, they are preceded by an ampersand (`&`). For example, to read from `request.file`, a shell script might contain:

```
more <&6
```

To write to the file, a shell script might contain:

```
echo $Name >&6
```

Choosing Alternatives

The Bourne shell supports two constructs for choosing between alternative actions–`if/then/else` and `case`. `If/then/else` is most convenient when the number of alternatives is limited; `case` can simplify processing when there are more than two or three choices.

Using if/then/else

The general form of the `if/then/else` construct is:

```
if [condition]
then
    statements to execute when condition is true
else
    statements to execute when condition is false
fi
```

or

```
if [condition]
then
    statements to execute when condition is true
elif [condition]
    statements to execute when condition is true
else
    statements to execute when conditions above are false
fi
```

`If` and `elif` can be nested, as needed.

The placement of the components of the construct on separate lines is important; the shell will report an error if the following rules are broken:

1. `if [condition]` must appear on a line by itself, although it may be indented with leading tabs or spaces.

2. `then` must appear on a line by itself, although it may be indented by leading tabs or spaces.
3. `else` or `elif` [*condition*] must be on a line by itself, although either may be indented by leading tabs or spaces.
4. `fi` must appear on a line by itself, although it may be indented by leading tabs or spaces.

The syntax for writing the logical conditions for `if` and `else` is somewhat different from that found in other high-level languages. Conditions can be written:

```
test condition
```

or

```
[condition]
```

Because `test` is a favorite name for temporary and sample files, most people choose to use the bracket notation rather than the `test` command.

When using the bracket notation, place a space after the opening bracket and a space before the closing bracket. Each relational operator (those used to express the relationship being test) must also have a space on either side. The shell will report an error if the spacing rules are not followed.

The operators that can be used to test logical conditions are summarized in Table 9.1. The file operators can be particularly useful. Assume, for example, that you need to determine if a file already exists. If it exists, a new line should be appended to the file; if the file does not exist, it should be created. The shell script code would appear as:

```
filename=New.file
if [ -f "$filename" ]
then
    echo 'Added line' >>$filename
else
    echo 'First line' >$filename
fi
```

Table 9.1
Relational Operators For Bourne Shell Scripts

Operator	**Meaning**
Strings:	
`string1 = string 2`	true if the two strings are identical (must match case)
`string1 != string 2`	true if the two strings are not identical
`string1`	true if the string is not the null string (i.e., has length)
`-z string`	true if the string has length zero
`-n string`	true if the string has length other than zero
`Numbers:`	
`number1 -eq number2`	true if the two quantities are equal additional number comparison operators: `-ne` not equal to `-gt` greater than `-ge` greater than or equal to `-lt` less than `-le` less than or equal to
Files:	
`-r filename`	true if the file exists and can be read
`-w filename`	true if the file exists and can be written to
`-x filename`	true if the file exists and can be executed
`-f filename`	true if the file exists and is a regular file
`-d filename`	true if the file exists and is a directory
`-s filename`	true if the file exists and is greater than zero bytes in size
Modifiers:	
`!`	makes any of the operators above negative
`-a`	links any two conditions with AND
`-o`	links any two conditions with OR

As with any high-level language, any number of executable statements can appear after `then`, `else`, or `elif`.

An `if/then/else` construct to handle the menu choice made by the code in Figure 8.1 appears in Figure 8.2. If you look closely at the code, you will notice that when variable names are used within brackets, they are surrounded by quotes. This will prevent the shell from returning an error message if the variable has no contents. For example, if the user

```
if [ "$choice" -eq 1 ]
then
      date
elif [ "$choice" -eq 2 ]
then
      echo 'What year's calendar? \c'
      read year
      echo 'What month's calendar? \c'
      read month
      if [ -n "$year" -a -n "$month"
      then
            cal $month $year
      elif [ -n "$year" -a -z "$month" ]
      then
            cal $year
      elif [ -z "$year" -a -n "$month" ]
      then
            cal $month
      else
            cal
      fi
elif [ "$choice" -eq 3 ]
then
      who
elif [ "$choice" -eq 4 ]
then
      mail
elif [ "$choice" -eq 5 ]
      exit
else
      echo 'You have entered an invalid choice'
fi
```

Figure 8.2 An `if/then/else` **construct**

wanted to see an entire year's calendar, he or she might simply press the RETURN key when asked to enter the month. In that case, the shell would return an error whenever the contents of `month` were tested. Placing `$month` in double quotes supresses the error trapping and allows execution of the script to proceed.

Figure 8.2 also contains the shell command `exit`. Although shell scripts will automatically terminate when program flow reaches the physical end-of-file, `exit` can be used within a script to terminate execution at some point other than the last line of the script.

Using case

The `case` construct is a shorthand for multiple `if/then/else` constructs. It can be used to simplify the choices between multiple options. The general form of the construct is:

```
case variable_name in
     pattern to match)
          statements to execute ;;
     pattern to match)
          statements to execute ;;
     *)
          action if no preceding patterns are matched
esac
```

Each value of the variable for which statements are to be executed is followed by a right parenthesis. The parenthesis is followed, on the same or following lines, by executable shell commands. All of the commands that apply to a given variable value are terminated by two semicolons. However, semicolons after the last option (i.e., just before the `esac`) are optional.

The values to which the shell matches the contents of the `case` variable can be a constant or any of the shell's metacharacters. For that reason they are called a *pattern*, rather than just *value*. Commonly, the last pattern is `*`, the metacharacter that matches any number of characters. It will trap any values of the variable in the `case` statement that match none of the preceding patterns.

The `if/then/else` construct from Figure 8.2 can be rewritten as a `case` construct. The code can be found in Figure 8.3. There is one pattern for each of the options in the menu. The final option is `*`, which traps anything the user might enter that isn't one of the acceptable options.

It is important to realize that `case` has a major limitation. It can only test for equality between the value of the variable in the `case` statement

```
case $choice in
    1)  date ;;
    2)  echo 'What year's calendar? \c'
        read year
        echo 'What month's calendar? \c'
        read month
        if [ -n "$year" -a -n "$month"
        then
            cal $month $year
        elif [ -n "$year" -a -z "$month" ]
        then
            cal $year
        elif [ -z "$year" -a -n "$month" ]
        then
            cal $month
        else
            cal
        fi ;;
    3)  who ;;
    4)  mail ;;
    9)  exit ;;
    *)  'You've entered an invalid option'
esac
```

Figure 8.3 A `case` construct.

with the patterns in the rest of the construct. It cannot test any other type of relationship. For that reason, the actions following a value of `2` for `choice` in Figure 8.3 must retain the `if/then/else` construct to determine whether `year` and `month` have values.

Repeating Actions

The Bourne shell has three constructs that will perform iteration: `for` loops, `while` loops, and `until` loops. `While` and `until` loops function much like their counterparts in other high-level languages. `For`, however, is somewhat different from other `for` commands.

Using for Loops

The general form of the `for` construct is:

```
for variable_name in list_of_values
do
    commands to be executed
done
```

Unlike the BASIC `for` loop, the shell `for` loop does not increment the value of the variable in the `for` statement. Instead, the variable is given each of the values in the list of values, one at a time. For example, if there are four values in the list, then the loop will execute four times.

A loop that should execute three times might be written:

```
for i in 0 1 2
do
    process these statements
done
```

Because the variable in the `for` statement is not incremented, but instead given the each value in the list, a `for` loop can be used to process a series of unrelated items. For example, assume that a shell script accepts three names as arguments. Each name is processed in the same manner. A loop to perform the processing might be written:

```
for i in $1 $2 $3
do
    echo $i
    process the name that is stored in $i
done
```

The three arguments to the command name are stored in the positional parameters `$1`, `$2`, and `$3`. When the loop begins, the value of `$1` is assigned to `i`. During the second iteration, `i` has the value of `$2`. It will have the value of `$3` during the final iteration.

Using while Loops

A `while` loop has the general format:

```
while executable command or condition
do
     statements to be processed
done
```

A `while` loop executes the statements between `do` and `done` as long as the command following `while` executes successfully.

One common way to write such a loop is to place a logical condition after `while`:

```
counter=1
while [ "$counter" -le $# ]
do
     process some statements
     counter=`expr counter + 1`
done
```

The shell first evaluates the condition following `while`. If the condition is true, it processes all statements between `do` and `done` and then loops back to the `while` statement again. This particular loop will execute once for each positional parameter. Note, however, that it cannot process each of the positional parameters within the body of the loop. Doing so requires a special technique.

Looping Through Positional Parameters

If a script needs to process each of a variable number of positional parameters, the loop is written:

```
while [ -z $1 ]
do
     process parameter 1 in some way
     shift
done
```

The condition in the while statement will be true if $1 has some contents (i.e., its length is greater than zero. Assuming that there is at least one parameter, the body of the loop processes its value in some way. The shift command then deletes the current $1 and renames the remaining parameters. For example, if the shell script was invoked with five parameters, the first shift deletes $1 and renames $2 as $1, $3 as $2, $4 as $3, and $5 as $4. When the last parameter has been deleted (after five iterations of the loop), the test command will be unsuccessful and the loop will stop.

Line-by-line File Processing

As discussed earlier in this chapter, when the input for a read command is redirected to a file, the command will always retrieve the first line of the file. However, a while loop can be used to step through a file.

Assume, for example, that you wish to read each line in an inventory file to determine which items need to be reordered. Shell script statements to perform the analysis might be as follows:

```
exec <inventory
while read item, units, on.hand, reorder.pt
do
    AmtLeft='expr on.hand - reorder.pt'
    if [ "$AmtLeft" -le 0 ]
    then
        echo $item ' ' 4units >>to.order
    fi
done
exec </dev/tty
```

The first line of the code redirects input to the file inventory. The while statement processes the read. Each execution of the while reads a successive line from inventory. When the end of the file is reached, the read will be unsuccessful and the loop will stop. The final step is to redirect input back to the terminal keyboard.

Using until Loops

The general format of the `until` loop is very similar to the `while` loop:

```
until command or condition
do
     statements to be processed
done
```

The loop will continue as long as the command following `until` is unsuccessful or the condition is not met.

An `until` loop might be used to repeat the actions of an entire shell script until the user decides to quit:

```
stop=n
until [ "$stop" = y ]
do
     perform the script's work
     echo 'Do it again? \c'
     read stop
done
```

Loop Control

All of the three looping constructs will loop whenever the bottom of the loop is reached and end when controlling criteria are met. However, there are circumstances where you may wish to exit a loop prematurely or cause a loop to iterate before it reaches the bottom.

The `break` command will exit a loop. If the loop containing the `break` is nested within another loop, `break` will exit only the innermost loop. For example, in the loop in Figure 8.4, the `break` causes execution to resume below the `done` statement of the `for` loop.

The `continue` command will force a loop to iterate (i.e., switch the flow of control from the current statement to the top of the loop). It can be useful in situations where looping is controlled by a variety of conditions, as in Figure 8.5. In the example above, if the condition following `if` is met, the script will execute some statements and then return to the top of the

```
while [ "$cont" = y ]
do
    for i in 0 1 2 3 4
        echo 'Keep going? \c'
        read go
        if [ "$go" = n]
        then
            break
        fi
    done
    echo 'Do it again? \c'
    read cont
done
```

Figure 8.4 Using `break` **to exit a loop.**

```
while [ 2 -gt 1 ]
do
    if [ condition ]
    then
        execute statements
        continue
    elif [ condition ]
    then
        break
    else
        continue
    fi
done
```

Figure 8.5 Using `continue` **to force a loop to iterate.**

loop. If the condition following `elif` is met, processing will exit the loop and continue with whatever statement follows `done`. (The `break` is essential because the condition in the `while` statement will always be true,

creating an infinite loop.) If neither condition is met, no processing is performed; the loop simply iterates.

Configuring a Working Environment

Early in this chapter, you were introduced to a number of environmental variables that are maintained by the shell for each user. Although these variables can be assigned values at the shell's prompt, it can be tedious to do so every time you log in. For that reason, most UNIX users place a file named `.profile` in their login directory. The `.profile` is a shell script that is executed automatically by the shell whenever a user logs in.

By default, an A/UX user account has no `.profile`. However, the following enviornmental variables are set:

```
HOME=path name of login directory
MAILCHECK=60
SHELL=/bin/sh
PATH=:/bin:/usr/bin:/usr/ucb
TZ=current time zone
```

To see the values for all environmental variables that have been set, type either `env` or `printenv` at the shell's prompt. The output is similar to the listing above.

In most cases, you will want to create a `.profile` that does the following:

1. Adds the `/etc` and `/usr/toolboxbin` directories to `PATH`. This will make it easier to run commands in those directories.
2. Assigns a value to `TERM` describing the type of terminal that you most commonly use to log in to A/UX

A typical .profile is therefore:

```
PATH=$PATH:/etc:/usr/toolboxbin
export PATH
TERM=mac2
export TERM
```

Keep in mind that variables are local to the shell script in which their values are assigned. If PATH and TERM are to retain their values after the .profile finishes executing, they must be exported with the export command. Notice also that the directory path names in PATH are separated by colons. The first statement in the above .profile takes the existing contents of PATH and adds two new directories.

Some Sample Scripts

The following Bourne shell scripts are illustrative of the way in which a user can use scripts to customize his or her A/UX environment. The first three are useful utilities; the last is just for fun.

Checking the Time

As you will remember, the date command displays both the date and time. A simple shell script, saved with the file name time, will extract just the time portion. The time script has only two lines:

```
t=`date |cut -c12-19`
echo "The current time is: $t"
```

The script first issues the date command and pipes its result to cut. Because columns 12 through 19 of the date contain the time, the shell variable t will contain just the time. The second line displays the string The current time is and the contents of t.

Safe Deletes

When an A/UX file is deleted with `rm`, there is no practical way to recover the file. A shell script named `del` will give you a chance to change your mind before an `rm` is actually performed.

The script contains ten lines. They are numbered for ease of discussion; the numbers are not part of the script.

```
1    echo "Name of file or directory to Delete: \c"
2    read dname;
3    echo "Are You Sure? y/n \c"
4    read x
5    if [ "$x" = y ]
6    then
7        rm $dname
8    else
9        echo "Nothing deleted"
10   fi
```

Lines 1 and 2 store the name of the file or directory to be deleted in the variable `dname`. Lines 3 and 4 then ask for confirmation of the delete command. If the delete is confirmed (i.e., the condition in line 5 returns a value of true), line 7 deletes the file. Otherwise, line 9 displays a message on the standard output indicating that the delete has not been performed.

Bulk Mail

The bulk mail shell script makes it easy to send the same message to more than one recipient. You can either create the message with a text editor or enter it from within the script. As before, the line numbers have been added for discussion only; they are not part of the script.

```
echo "Name of user (or list of users) to send mail to: \c"
read mailnames
echo "Name of file to be sent to user(s): \c"
echo "Press RETURN if no file to send and then type message."
read filename
```

```
6    if [ -z "$filename" ]
7         tput clear
8         echo "Type CTRL-D when finished."
9         mail $mailnames
10   elif [ -f "$filename" ]
11   then
12        mail $mailnames <$filename
13   elif [ -z "$mailnames" ]
14   then
15        tput clear; echo "You must supply a user name to send mail to."
16   fi
```

The first five lines of the script collect the names of the users who are to receive the message and the file in which the message is stored. Line 6 checks the length of the variable `filename`. If it is zero (i.e., `[ -z "$filename" ]` is true), the script then invokes `mail` to allow you to enter the message.

Line 7 issues the command `tput clear`. The `tput` command reads information from a terminal information file. When followed by the argument `clear`, it issues whatever commands are needed to clear the terminal screen.

> **The `tput` command is documented in *A/UX Command Reference (M–Z and Games)*; see the section *User Commands (1)*; the commands are in alphabetical order. The terminal characteristics that `tput` will display can be found in *A/UX Programmer's Reference*. See the `terminfo` entry in the section *File Formats (4)*; the file formats are in alphabetical order.**

If the file name stored in `filename` is a regular file (i.e., `[-f "$filename" ]` in line 10 is true), the script redirects input to `filename` and sends the mail without further intervention (line 9). The final section of the script, lines 14 through 16, alert the user that mail cannot be sent without the name of at least one user to whom mail should be sent.

Fortunes in a .profile

Although configuring a working environment is generally a serious business, many people also place shell commands in their `.profile` that have

no purpose other than to be entertaining. One such set of statements are those that randomly select and display a quotation from a file of favorite quotes.

The code that selects and displays the quotation is actually quite short:

```
number=`expr $$ % 20`
expr "    $number" : '.*\(...\)'   | \
join -t% -o 2.2 - quotes
```

The Bourne shell has no way to generate a random number. Therefore, the first statement divides the current process number ($$) by the total number of quotations in the file and returns the remainder. For the purposes of this example, the number of quotations has been limited to 20. However, in practice, you may wish to create a quote file with several hundred quotations.

To understand the remainder of these statements, look first at the contents of the file named `quotes` (these quotations are all taken from Arthur Conan Doyle's Sherlock Holmes stories):

```
0%"Dr. Watson, Mr. Sherlock Holmes," said Stamford, introducing us.
0%     "A Study in Scarlet"
1%"Read it up - you really should. There is nothing new under the sun. It has
1% all been done before."
1%     Sherlock Holmes. "A Study in Scarlet"
2%"Which is it today," I asked, "morphine or cocaine?"
2%He raised his eyes languidly from the old black-letter volume which he had opened.
2%"It is cocaine," he said, "a seven-per-cent solution. Would you care to try it?"
2%     The Sign of Four
3%And that what how a great scandal threatened to affect the kingdom of Bohemia,
3%and how the best plans of Mr. Sherlock Holmes were beaten by a woman's wit. He
3%used to make merry over the cleverness of women, but I have not heard him do it
3%of late. And when he speaks of Irene Adler, or when he refers to her photograph,
3%it is always under the honourable title of _the_ woman.
3%     A Scandal in Bohemia
4%"You see, Watson," he explained in the early hours of the morning as we sat over
4%a glass of whisky and soda in Baker Street, "it was perfectly obvious from the
4%first..."
4%     The Red Headed League
5%"My dear fellow," said Sherlock Holmes as we sat on either side of the fire in his
5%lodgings at Baker Street, "life is infinitely stranger than anything which the
```

```
 5%mind of man could invent."
 5%    A Case of Identity
 6%"You have a grand gift of silence, Watson," said he. "It makes you quite invaluable
 6%as a companion."
 6%    The Man With the Twisted Lip
 7%"The band! The speckled band!" whispered Holmes.
 7%    The Speckled Band
 8%"To the man who loves art for its own sake," remarked Sherlock Holmes, tossing
 8%aside the advertisement sheet of the _Daily Telegraph_, "it is frequently in its
 8%least important and lowliest manifestations that the keenest pleasure is to be
 8%derived."
 8%    The Adventure of the Copper Beeches
 9%Sherlock Holmes was a man who seldom took exercise for exercise's sake. Few men
 9%were capable of greater muscular effort, and he was undoubtedly one of the finest
 9%boxers of his weight that I have ever seen; but he looked upon aimless bodily
 9%exertion as a waste of energy...
 9%    The Yellow Face
10%An anomaly which often struck me in the character of my friend Sherlock Holmes was
10%that, although in his methods of thought he was the neatest and most metholodical
10%of mankind, and although also he affect a certain quiet primness of dress, he was
10%none the less in his personal habits one of the most untidy men that ever drove
10%a fellow-lodger to distraction.
10%    The Musgrave Ritual
11%"Holmes," said I as I stood one morning in our bow-window looking down the street,
11%"here is a madman coming along. It seems rather sad that his relatives should
11%allow him to come out alone."
11%    The Adventure of the Beryl Coronet
12%"My dear Watson," said he, "I cannot agree with those who rank modesty among the
12%virtues."
12%    The Greek Interpreter
13%It is with a heavy heart that I take up my pen to write these the last words in
13%which I shall ever record the singular gifts by which my friend Mr. Sherlock
13%Holmes was distinguished.
13%    The Final Problem
14%"He is the Napoleon of crime, Watson. He is the organizer of half that is evil
14%and of nearly all that is undetected in this great city. He is a genius, a
14%philosopher, an abstract thinker."
14%    The Final Problem
15%I moved my head to look at the cabinet behind me. When I turned again, Sherlock
15%Holmes was standing smiling at me across the study table. I rose to my feet,
15%stared at him for some second in utter amazement, and then it appears that I
15%must have fainted for the first and last time in my life.
15%    The Adventure of the Empty House
16%"Come, Watson, come!" he cried. "The game is afoot. Not a word! Into your clothes
16%and come!"
```

```
16%     The Adventures of the Abbey Grange
17%"Mr. Holmes, they were the footprints of a gigantic hound."
17%     Dr. Mortimer. The Hound of the Baskervilles
18%One of Shelock Holmes's defects - if, indeed, one may call it a defect - was that
18%he was exceedingly loath to communicate his full plans to any other person
18%until the instant of their fulfilment.
18%     The Hound of the Baskervilles
19%A hound it was, an enormous coal-black hound, but not such a hound as mortal eyes
19%have every seen. Fire burst from its open mouth, its eyes glowed with a smoulderng
19%glare, its muzzle and hackles and dewlap were outlined in flickering flame.
19%     The Hound of the Baskervilles
20%Holmes had the impersonal joy of the true artistry in his better work, even as he
20%mourned darkly when it fell below the high level to which he aspired.
20%     The Valley of Fear
```

The first three characters of the file are reserved for the quote number. If the number is between 10 and 99, the first character is a blank; if the number is less than 10, the first two characters are blank. The second field of the file contains a portion of a quote; the two fields are separated by a percent sign.

If the `join` is to work properly, the quote number generated by the first statement must be of the same length as the quote number in the `quotes` file. However, numbers less than 100 will be shorter than the three characters allocated for the number in the file. The solution is to use `expr`'s matching operator. The left side of the operator contains three blanks and the contents of the `number` variable (`"   $number"`). The right side of the operator contains an expression that will match exactly three characters (`.*\(...\)`). As discussed earlier in this chapter, this particular form of the matching operator returns characters from the right of the value on the left.

The result of `expr` is piped into the `join` command. Since the result corresponds to the first file being joined, a hyphen appears in the `join` command in place of the first file name.

To display your own quotation each time you log in, first place the three lines of shell script code in your `.profile`. Then create a file of your favorite quotes. Pay special attention to the spacing of the quotation numbers. Quotes that are longer than one line should be entered on multiple lines, each preceded with the same quotation number.

Chapter 9

A/UX's Korn Shell

Although the Bourne shell is A/UX's default shell, many users choose to use an alternate shell. The Korn shell (`ksh`) is similar to the Bourne shell, but has some additional features (e.g., the ability to use a text editor to edit a command line) that make it extremely useful. This chapter looks at A/UX's implementation of the Korn shell. In particular, it focuses on those aspects of the Korn shell that are different from the Bourne shell.

Keep in mind that because a shell is a command interpreter, the A/UX commands about which you have been reading are issued in the same way to all three of A/UX's shells. The differences between the shells are found in shell commands only. This also means that there are differences in shell programming.

An introduction to the Korn shell can be found in Chapter 3 of *A/UX User Interface*. Complete documentation of all shell commands and features appears in *A/UX Command Reference (A–L)*. See the `ksh` entry in *User Commands (1)*; the commands are in alphabetical order.

Invoking the Korn Shell

The login shell for a new A/UX account is set in the `/etc/passwd` file when the account is created by the system administrator. In most cases, this will be the Bourne shell (`/bin/sh`). However, there are several ways in which you can invoke the Korn shell so that you can work with it temporarily or make it your permanent login shell.

Spawning the Korn Shell as a Child Process

Regardless of which shell is your default shell, you can work temporarily with the Korn shell by typing:

```
ksh
```

at the default shell's prompt. Because the Korn shell uses the same prompts as the Bourne shell, there will be no outward sign that the shell has changed.

To return to the default shell, type either:

```
exit
```

or CTRL-D.

Temporarily Changing the Default Shell

The command:

```
exec ksh
```

will kill the current default shell and replace it with the Korn shell. To return to the original shell (e.g., the Bourne shell), reissue the command:

```
exec sh
```

Permanently Changing the Login Shell

To make the Korn shell the login shell, use the chsh command. The command has general format:

```
chsh <user name> <new login shell>
```

If jon wants to make the Korn shell his login shell, the command is typed:

```
chsh jon /bin/ksh
```

Note that chsh requires the full path name of the shell.

Because chsh modifies /etc/passwd, you will be able to change the login shell only for the use name under which you are logged in. The exception to this restriction is the superuser; the superuser can change any user's login shell.

The chsh command is documented in *A/UX Command Reference (A–L)*. See the section *User Commands (1)*; the commands are in alphabetical order.

Command Editing

The Bourne shell provides very limited facilities for editing command lines before a command is executed (i.e., all you can do is erase characters with the backspace key or kill the entire line). The Korn shell, however, will allow you to invoke a text editor to modify command lines.

To edit a command line with a text editor, press ESC any time before pressing ENTER or RETURN. Edit the command line using any of the text editor's commands that apply to a single line.[1] Press CTRL-D to return to the shell. Then press ENTER or RETURN to execute the command.

The default editor for command line editing is ed. It can be changed to any other text editor (e.g., vi) in two ways. To change the editor for the current session to vi, type:

```
set -o vi
```

at the Korn shell prompt.

The editor can be set each time you log in by placing the set command above in your .profile. Alternatively, the .profile can assign vi to two environment variables:

```
typeset -x EDITOR=vi
typeset -x VISUAL=vi
```

Command History

The Korn shell retains a log of commands that have been entered. Commands in that file can be edited and reexecuted. By default, the last 128 commands are stored in a file named sh_history. The file, editor, and number of commands stored can be changed by setting three environment variables:

FCEDIT=vi   make vi the editor for modifying the history file

1. Even if you are using a full screen editor such as vi, Korn shell command line editing will allow you to edit only a single line.

`HISTFILE=history`	store commands in a file named `history`
`HISTSIZE=20`	retain only the last 20 commands

Place these in a `.profile` to set them every time you log in.

Editing and Executing Previous Commands

To edit and execute commands from the history file, use the `fc` command. `Fc` locates commands within the history file two ways. You may specify the command's number, as in:

```
fc 15
```

This command will invoke the editor specified by `FCEDIT` and present the 15th command for editing. The command will be executed when you leave the editor. To edit and execute a series of commands, give `fc` a range of command numbers. For example, the command:

```
fc 20 25
```

will place commands 20 through 25 in an editor window. When more than one command appears, any editing commands can be used to modify what appears on the screen. The commands will be executed in order when you leave the editor.

Alternatively, `fc` can be given a string to match. It will retrieve the most recent command (i.e., the command with the highest number) that matches the string. For example, to edit and execute the last `cu` command, type:

```
fc cu
```

Executing Commands Without Editing

Commands stored in the history file can be executed without editing. To do so, type the command as:

```
fc -e - <command number or range>
```

or:

```
fc -e - <string to match>
```

For example, the 35th command will be executed without editing with:

```
fc -e - 35
```

The first `cu` command in the history file will be executed with:

```
fc -e - cu
```

The `-e -` option of the `fc` command supports string substitution within the command line. Assume, for example, that the first `cu` command in the history file calls a system named `chimera`. You would like to place another `cu` command, using the same dialing parameters, but to a system named `dragon`. The `fc` command might be issued as:

```
fc -e - chimera=dragon cu
```

`Fc` will find the most recent command in the history file that contains `cu`. It will then search the command line for the string on the left of the equals sign (`chimera`) and substitute the string on the right (`dragon`) before executing the command.

Because `fc -e -` can be tedious to type repeatedly, the Korn shell uses `r` as an alias. The above command can, therefore, be typed as:

```
r chimera=dragon cu
```

The `r` can be used anywhere `fc -e -` is used.

Viewing the Contents of the History File

To see the commands currently stored in the history file, use the `fc` command's `-l` option with the general format:

```
fc -l <first number to view> <last number to view>
```

For example, the 12th through 25th commands will be displayed on the standard output with:

```
fc -l 12 25
```

If the highest number exceeds the number of commands in the history file, or if the lowest number references a command that has been purged from the file to make room for more recent commands, the shell will display:

```
Bad number
```

The `-l` option will also search for all commands that match a given string. For example, to see all `cu` commands in the history file, type:

```
fc -l cu
```

Configuring a Working Environment

When invoked, the Korn shell will read and execute the commands stored in a `.profile` in the account's login directory. The `.profile` can contain any Bourne shell commands, including Bourne shell environment variables. In addition, it can contain syntax specific to the Korn shell.

For example, the Bourne shell requires that environment variables be exported from the `.profile`, as in:

```
FCEDIT=vi
HISTFILE=history
```

```
HISTSIZE=20
export FCEDIT HISTFILE HISTSIZE
```

However, the Korn shell supports the `typeset` command. Using `typeset`'s `-x` option, variables will be automatically exported. The above commands can, therefore, be written:

```
typeset -x FCEDIT=vi
typeset -x HISTFILE=history
typeset -x HISTSIZE=20
```

Keep in mind that if a `.profile` contains Korn shell syntax, it cannot be executed successfully by the Bourne shell. Therefore, if you plan to switch between the two shells, use only Bourne shell commands.

The problem with a `.profile` is that the variables set within it affect only the login shell. Any child shells spawned do not get the values assigned to the environment variables. However, if environment variables are set in a file named `.kshrc`, then they will be in effect for all instances of the Korn shell. While `.profile` is read only when you log in, `.kshrc` is read each time a new shell is spawned.

Command Aliases

An alias is a single string to which a command is assigned. For example, the command:

```
alias cufast='cu -l tty0 -s2400'
```

creates a new command, `cufast`, that sends the entire command line within single quotes to the Korn shell. Using aliases is similar to placing a command within a shell file, making the file executable, and executing the shell script. However, commands assigned to aliases with the `alias` command cannot take parameters like shell scripts, but must consist of a single, constant string.

Aliases can be set from the command line. Alternatively, you can place `alias` commands in the `.kshrc` file.

The Korn shell automatically sets a number of aliases when it is invoked:

1. `false='let 0'`
2. `history='fc -l'`
3. `integer='typeset -i'`
4. `r='fc -e -'`
5. `true='let 1'`
6. `hash='alias -t'`
7. `functions='typeset -f'`

A number of the commands above are part of the Korn shell's programming language and will be discussed in the last section of this chapter.

Controlling Jobs

The Korn shell provides control for processes, or *jobs*, that you are running. Whenever you issue a command, it is given a job number. This job number applies to commands issued by you from the time you logged in; it is unrelated to the job's process ID.

When a process is placed in the background, its job number is displayed on the standard output along with its process ID. For example, when the command:

```
cp long.file1 long.file2 &
```

is issued, the Korn shell responds with:

```
[12] 20456
```

The number within brackets is the job number; it is followed by the process ID.

Checking Job Status

A job can be *running* or *stopped*. At any given time, one job can be running in the foreground; any number of jobs can be running in the background.

In addition, any number of jobs can be stopped. When a job is stopped, its execution is suspended until its status is changed in some way.

To see the status of all jobs, type:

```
jobs
```

The jobs are listed in descending numerical order, as in:

```
[6] + Running nroff -man month.1 >month.doc &
[5] - Running pr log.file >log.out &
[4]   Stopped vi memo
[3]   Stopped vi letter
```

The + indicates the job that was run most recently (the *current job*); the - marks the previous job. The output above indicates that the user began editing a file named `letter`, suspended the job, edited a file named `memo`, suspended the job, sent a `pr` command to the background, and finally sent an `nroff` command to the background.

Stopping Jobs

If it is to be stopped, a job must be running in the foreground. To stop the current foreground process, press CTRL-Z.[2] A/UX will discard any input or output requests that have not been completed and save information about the state of the process.

Assume, for example, that the file `memo` is being edited with `vi`. The job is suspended by pressing CTRL-Z. A/UX responds with:

```
[4] + Stopped vi memo
```

---

2. CTRL-Z is the default suspend character. If it doesn't work, the suspend character may have been redefined. To set it back to CTRL-Z, type:

```
stty susp ^z
```

Managing Stopped Jobs

Once a job has been stopped, it may be:

1. left suspended
2. restarted in the background
3. restarted in the foreground
4. killed

Jobs that are left suspended remain in their frozen state until you log out. For details, see Jobs and Logging Out below.

Restarting Jobs in the Background

To restart a suspended job in the background, use the `bg` command. The job that is affected by the command can be specified in one of five ways:

1. `bg` (restarts the current job in the background)
2. `bg %+` (restarts the current job in the background)
3. `bg %-` (restarts the previous job in the background)
4. `bg %`*`n`* (restarts job number *n* in the background)
5. `bg %`*`string`* (restarts the most recent job matching *string*, as in:

   ```
   bg %cp
   ```

   which restarts the most recent `cp` command in the background)

Placing Jobs in the Foreground

Jobs are placed in the foreground with the `fg` command. The job can be identified in any of the five ways used with `bg`. For example:

```
fg %3
```

will place job number 3 in the foreground. If the job has been suspended, the command will resume execution in the foreground. If the job is running in the background, the command will bring it to the foreground.

Because jobs can only be suspended when they are in the foreground, the `fg` command is handy for temporarily bringing background jobs to the foreground for that purpose. For example, consider the following sequence of commands:

```
cp long.file1 long.file2 &
vi memo
CTRL-Z
fg %1
CTRL-Z
fg %2
```

The first command places the `cp` job in the background as job number 1. The user then begins editing a memo (job number 2). The editing is suspended with CTRL-Z. The `cp` job is then returned to the foreground where it can be suspended. The user can then resume editing the memo.

Killing Jobs

Although processes can be killed by using the `kill` command followed by the process ID, the Korn shell allows `kill` to also recognize the percent sign notation for referencing jobs. For example:

```
kill %+
```

will kill the current job and:

```
kill %cp
```

will kill the most recent `cp` job.

Jobs and Logging Out

If jobs are suspended when you attempt to log out, A/UX will warn you with:

```
You have stopped jobs.
```

The logout attempt will be aborted. At this point, you can deal with the suspended jobs if you so choose. However, if you type `exit` or CTRL-D again, the logout will be permitted and all suspended jobs killed.

If background jobs are running when you attempt to log out, the shell will abort the logout attempt and display:

```
You have running jobs.
```

You may deal with the background jobs or repeat the logout command. If you do the latter, background jobs will be killed.

The shell can be instructed to continue running background jobs even after you log out with the `nohup` (no hangup) command. To run a background job in that manner, precede the command with `nohup`, as in:

```
nohup cp long.file1 long.file2 &
```

The `nohup` command is documented in *A/UX Command Reference (M–Z and Games)*. See the section *User Commands (1)*; the commands are in alphabetical order.

Korn Shell Programming

With the exceptions discussed in the remainder of this chapter, Korn shell programming is the same as Bourne shell programming. Because it supports array variables and better arithmetic operations, many users prefer to write scripts using the Korn shell.

Array Variables

The Korn shell's programming language supports one-dimensional arrays. The syntax is similar to Pascal in that subscripts are surrounded by brackets. However, arrays do not need to be declared before they are used. Any reference to an array element within the subscript range—0 through 511--will create the element if needed.

For example, the following shell program statements will assign values to the first five elements of an array:

```
number[1]=one
number[2]=two
number[3]=three
number[4]=four
number[5]=five
```

Array variables can be used anywhere simple variables are used. However, while a simple variable's value is represented by:

```
$VariableName
```

an array variable and its subscript must be surrounded by braces, as in:

```
${Array[2]}
```

The special subscript `[*]` represents all the elements in an array. It can be used, for example, to display the entire contents of an array. The output of the statements:

```
array[1]=one
array[2]=two
array[3]=three
array[4]=four
echo $array[*]
```

will be:

```
one two three four
```

To find out the total number of elements currently stored in an array, use a statement like:

```
TotalElements=${#Array[*]}
```

Declaring Variable Types: typeset

The Korn shell accepts the direct assignment of values to variables across an equals sign, just as does the Bourne shell. The data type of a variable given a value in this way is determined by the data assigned to it. However, the Korn shell also supports the `typeset` command to provide explicit data typing as well as some formatting of values when they are stored in variables.

`Typeset` has two general formats:

```
typeset <flag option(s)> <variable name>
```

or

```
typeset <flag option(s)> <variable name>=<variable or constant>
```

For example, earlier in this chapter you were introduced to the `-x` flag option that indicates that the value of a variable should be automatically exported to the shell when the script terminates. This option is particularly useful for `.profile` and `.kshrc` files.

Other `typeset` options that you may find useful include:

1. `-L` (remove leading blanks and left justify). The statement:

   ```
   typeset -L name=Jones
   ```

   will create the variable `name` as a five-character string variable. Using the alternate format, the syntax:

   ```
   typeset -L5 name
   ```

   will define the same five-character string variable without assigning it a value. The statement:

   ```
   name=Hathaway
   ```

will then assign the characters `Hatha` to `name` (any characters after the fifth will be truncated).

2. `-R` (remove trailing blanks and right justify). The statement:

```
typeset -R quantity=1544
```

will create a four-character string variable. Using the alternate format, the syntax:

```
typeset -R4 quantity
```

will create the same four-character string variable without assigning it a value. As with left justified variables, any values assigned that are longer than the length of the variable will be truncated. For example:

```
quantity=25349
```

will place `5349` in the variable.

3. `-Z` (pad a right-justified variable with leading zeros; remove any leading zeros from a left-justified variable). The statements:

```
typeset -R6 quantity
typeset -Z quantity=123
```

will store `00123` in `quantity`. The statements:

```
typeset -L6 quantity
typeset -Z quantity=00123
```

will store `123` in `quantity`.

4. `-i` (define an integer variable). The statement:

```
typeset -i value=123.45
```

will store `123` in `value`. Remember that the alias `integer` has been defined as `typeset -i`. The expression:

```
integer value=123.45
```

is, therefore, equivalent to the `typeset` command above.

5. `-l` (convert all characters to lowercase). The statement:

```
typeset -Ll string=HandHold
```

will create an eight-character, left-justified variable with the contents `handhold`.

6. `-r` (make the variable read-only). The statement:

```
typeset -r one=1
```

assigns the value `1` to `one` and prevents the value from being changed by a subsequent assignment statement.

7. `-u` (convert all characters to uppercase). The statement:

```
typeset -Lu string=HandHold
```

will create an eight-character, left-justified variable with the contents `HANDHOLD`.

The effect of `typeset` is removed with the `unset` command. For example, the command:

```
unset array, string
```

removes all variable attributes set with `typeset` and erases variable contents. The only variables that cannot be `unset` are those `typeset` with the `-r` (read-only) flag option.

Shell Arithmetic: let

Arithmetic operations are performed with the `let` statement. The operators that can be used, in order of their default precedence, include:

1. − (negation and subtraction)
2. ! (not)
3. * (multiplication)
4. / (division)
5. % (modulo–remainder of an integer division)
6. + (addition)
7. <=, >=, <, and > (logical comparisons)
8. ==, != (logical equal to, logical not equal to)

Parentheses can be used as needed for grouping and to override precedence.

The average of a series of numbers can be computed with:

```
integer number sum count
count=0
sum=0
echo "Enter a number: \c"
read number
while number != 0
do
    let sum=sum+number
    let count=count+1
    echo "Enter a number: \c"
    read number
done
average=sum/count
echo "The average is $average"
```

Notice that there are no spaces within the arithmetic expressions above. If an expression contains spaces or if it contains an asterisk for multiplication, then it must be surrounded by quotes. The expressions below are legal:

```
count=count+1
"count = count + 1"
"cost=price*quantity"
```

However, the expressions:

```
count = count + 1
cost=price*quantity
```

are not.

Chapter 10

A/UX's C Shell

A/UX's C shell provides many of the same features as the Korn shell. However, the syntax differs a great deal from both the Korn and Bourne shells. This chapter, therefore, looks at the features of the C shell that are different from the Bourne shell. It also discusses the C shell's programming language, which shares many characteristics with C.

An introduction to the C shell can be found in Chapter 4 of *A/UX User Interface*. Complete documentation of the shell commands and features appears in *A/UX Command Reference (A–L)*. See the `csh` entry in *User Commands (1)*; the commands are in alphabetical order.

Invoking the C Shell

As you will remember, a new A/UX account uses the Bourne shell as its login shell. However, the C shell can be:

1. Run as a child process of the default shell.
2. Made the default shell temporarily.
3. Installed as the permanent login shell.

The C shell uses a percent sign (`%`) as its default prompt. If the C shell is invoked from either the Korn or Bourne shells, the dollar sign prompt will be replaced with the percent sign.

Spawning the C Shell as a Child Process

To work with the C shell as a child process of the current default shell, type:

```
csh
```

To return to the default shell, type either:

```
exit
```

or CTRL-D.

Temporarily Changing the Default Shell

The command:

```
exec csh
```

will kill the current default shell and replace it with the C shell. To switch to either the Korn or Bourne shell type:

```
exec ksh
```

for the Korn shell or:

```
exec sh
```

for the Bourne shell.

Permanently Changing the Login Shell

To make the C shell the login shell, use the `chsh` command. The command has the general format:

```
chsh <user name> <new login shell>
```

If `jon` want to make the C shell his login shell, the command is typed:

```
chsh jon /bin/csh
```

Note that `chsh` requires the full path name of the shell.

Because `chsh` modifies `/etc/passwd`, you will be able to change the login shell only for the user name under which you are logged in. The exception to this restriction is the superuser; the superuser can change any user's login shell.

The `chsh` command is documented in *A/UX Command Reference (A–L)*. See the section *User Commands (1)*; the commands are in alphabetical order.

Command History

Like the Bourne shell, the C shell permits only the use of the BACKSPACE key for editing a command before the RETURN or ENTER key is pressed. However, like the Korn shell, the C shell does retain a log of previous commands. Commands in the history file can be edited and reused.

The C shell retains its history list in main memory. By default, the last 200 commands are stored. To change the number of commands, assign a new value to the `history` environment variable with:

```
set history=n
```

where *n* is the number of command that should be retained. (This command can be placed in a `.login` or `.cshrc` file so that it is invoked automatically with the C shell. For details, see the section **Configuring a Working Environment** later in this chapter.) Keep in mind that the more commands stored, the more main memory that is used to retain them; a large number of commands will slow down overall system performance.

Viewing Command History

To see the most recent 50 commands, type:

```
history
```

To change the number of commands displayed, place a number after `history`, as in:

```
history 10
```

Each command in the output is preceded by its number in the log. The ten most recent commands (displayed by `history 10` above) might appear as:

```
95   vi memo
96   vi letter
97   cu -l tty0 -s2400
```

```
98   cp long.file1 long.file2 &
99   nroff -man big.manual >big.pages &
100  vi memo2
101  vi small.manual
102  nroff -man small.manual >small.pages &
103  lp memo &
104  lp memo2 &
```

The command numbers can be used to reference the commands for editing and/or re-execution.

Working with the Most Recent Command

To repeat the most recent command without any changes, type:

```
!!
```

The first exclamation point alerts the C shell that what follows is a reference to a historical command. The second references the most recent command.

To edit the most recent command before re-executing it, use the syntax:

^*old_string*^*new_string*^

The C shell will search the most recent command for *old_string* and replace it with *new_string*. For example, assume that the command:

```
lp snall.pages
```

returns the error message:

```
lp: cannot open /users/jon/snall.pages
```

To correct the command, type:

```
^snall^small^
```

Typing `!!` immediately after editing the command line will re–execute the corrected command.

Re–executing Other Commands Without Editing

The exclamation point notation can be used to re–execute commands other than the most recent:

1. `!`*n* (Re–execute command number *n*, where *n* is the number of a historical command.)
2. `!-`*n* (Re–execute the command *n* commands prior to the current command.)
3. `!`*string* (Execute the most recent command that *begins* with the characters in *string*.)
4. `!?`*string*`!` (Execute the most recent command the *contains* the characters in *string*.)

The most `cp` command (number 98 in the listing above) can be re–executed with any of the following:

```
!98
!-6
!cp
!?long.file1?
```

Editing and Re–executing Other Commands

The C shell provides syntax for editing and re–executing previous commands. In its simplest form, the syntax appends a string to a command and then re–executes it. The general format of the shell command is:

`!{`*identifier*`}` *string*

The *identifier* is either a command number or a string with which a previous command begins. The contents of *string* are appended to the previous command without any spaces. For example, if the `history` command displays:

```
25   lp part1
```

then the command:

```
!{25}a
```

will execute the command:

```
lp part1a
```

More sophisticated editing is possible using the general format:

```
!identifier:s/old_string/new_string/
```

The command identifier can be either a command number or a string with which the command begins. The `:s` is what is known as a *modifier*, since it modifies the action of the exclamation point command. The C shell searches the command for the first occurrence of *old_string* and replaces it with *new_string*. Even if *old_string* appears more than once in the command, only the first occurrence will be replaced.

Assume, for example, that you wish to format and print a series of files. The first command is issued at the percent sign prompt as:

```
nroff -man part1 | lp &
```

Assuming that the command is number 110, it can be edited and re–executed on the file named `part2` with:

```
!110:s/1/2
```

or:

```
!nroff:s/1/2
```

The :gs modifier will replace *all* occurrence of *old_string* within a previous command. For example, assume that you wish to change the names of a sequence of files. The first command is issued as:

```
mv part1 man.page1
```

The remaining files (part2, part3, and part4) can be moved with:

```
!mv:gs/1/2
!mv:gs/2/3
!mv:gs/3/4
```

The result will be the files man.page2, man.page3, and man.page4.

A number of other modifiers can be used to edit historical command lines. These include:

1. :h (Remove the last file or directory name in a path name.) Assume, for example, that you have issued the command:

   ```
   ls -l /users/jon/open.memo
   ```

   This becomes command number 25. Unfortunately, open.memo is not the file in which you are interested (the modification date is wrong). The entire contents of jon's directory can be displayed with:

   ```
   ls -al !25:h
   ```

2. :t (Remove everything but the last file or directory name in a path name.) Assume that the ls -al command above revealed that the correct file was named public.memo. One way to edit the file would be to issue the following commands:

   ```
   cd !ls:h
   vi !!:t
   ```

The `cd` statement uses the path name from the previous `ls` command. The `vi` command edits the file name from the previous command (the `!!`).

3. `:p` (Display a command but do not execute it.) This modifier can be combined with any of the others. For example, to see the effect of the substitution:

```
!150:s/1/2
```

the command is typed:

```
!150:s/1/2 :p
```

If command number 150 was:

```
nroff -man man.pages1
```

then the `:p` command line will display:

```
nroff -man man.pages2
```

Configuring a Working Environment

When invoked as a login shell, the C shell executes a file named `.login`. In addition, each instance of the shell that is spawned also executes a `.cshrc` file. In most cases, commands that set environment variables are placed in `.cshrc` so that they will be enforced when subshells of the default shell are spawned.[1]

In addition to the environment variables such as `TERM` and `PATH` that are used by all three shells, the C shell supports its own environment

1. The `.login` file is similar to the Korn shell's use of a `.profile`; the `.cshrc` file is similar to the Korn shell's `.kshrc`.

variables. The general syntax for giving the C shell variables values is:

```
set <variable name>=<value>
```

To ensure that the variables are enforced for every C shell that is spawned, the `set` commands are generally placed in the `.cshrc` command.

The C shell variables include:

1. `echo`: Displays every command on the screen before it is executed. If metacharacters appear in the command, each individual command generated when the metacharacters are expanded will be displayed.
2. `histchars`: Changes the characters used for invoking command history substitution. The command is issued as:

   ```
   set histchars char1 char2
   ```

   where *char1* is the character that should replace `!` and *char2* is the character that should replace `^`.
3. `history`: Sets the number of historical commands that are to be retained in main memory.
4. `prompt`: Changes the prompt from `%` to any other string of characters.
5. `savehist`: Indicates the number of historical commands that should be saved in a file when you log out. The history file, named `.history`, is placed in the login directory. Its contents are read into main memory at the next login.

Command Aliases

An alias is a single string to which a command is assigned. For example, the command:

```
alias cufast='su -l tty0 -s2400'
```

creates a new command, `cufast`, that sends the entire command line

within single quotes to the C shell. Aliases can be set from the command line. Alternatively, you can place `alias` commands in the `.cshrc` file.

C shell aliases will accept arguments on the command line. Assume, for example, that you mail a file named `daily.memo` to four different users each day. An alias that will permit the inclusion of the user name on the command line is written:

```
alias daily='mail \!^ <daily.memo'
```

The `\!^` indicates that an argument is required; the error message:

```
bad ! arg selector
```

will appear if no argument is used. To send a copy of the memo, the command is typed:

```
daily jon
```

Optional arguments are specified with `\!*` rather than `\!^`.

Controlling Jobs

The C shell provides job control identical to that available with the Korn shell. If you are familiar with the Korn shell's job control, then you may skip this section.

Whenever you issue a command, the C shell gives it a job number. This job number applies to commands issued by you from the time you logged in; it is unrelated to the job's process ID.

When a process is placed in the background, its job number is displayed on the standard output along with its process ID. For example, when the command:

```
cp long.file1 long.file2 &
```

is issued, the C shell responds with:

```
[12] 20456
```

The number within brackets is the job number; it is followed by the process ID.

Checking Job Status

A job can be *running* or *stopped*. At any given time, one job can be running in the foreground; any number of jobs can be running in the background. In addition, any number of jobs can be stopped. When a job is stopped, its execution is suspended until its status is changed in some way.

To see the status of all jobs, type:

```
jobs
```

The jobs are listed in descending numerical order, as in:

```
[6] + Running nroff -man month.1 >month.doc &
[5] - Running pr log.file >log.out &
[4]   Stopped vi memo
[3]   Stopped vi letter
```

The + indicates the job that was run most recently (the *current job*); the - marks the previous job. The output above indicates that the user began editing a file named `letter`, suspended the job, edited a file named `memo`, suspended the job, sent a `pr` command to the background, and finally sent an `nroff` command to the background.

Stopping Jobs

If it is to be stopped, a job must be running in the foreground. To stop the

current foreground process, press CTRL-Z.[2] A/UX will discard any input or output requests that have not been completed and save information about the state of the process.

Assume, for example, that the file `memo` is being edited with `vi`. The job is suspended by pressing CTRL-Z. A/UX responds with:

```
[4] + Stopped vi memo
```

Managing Stopped Jobs

Once a job has been stopped, it may be:

1. left suspended
2. restarted in the background
3. restarted in the foreground
4. killed

Jobs that are left suspended remain in their frozen state until you log out. For details, see Jobs and Logging Out, below.

Restarting Jobs in the Background

To restart a suspended job in the background, use the `bg` command. The job that is affected by the command can be specified in one of five ways:

1. `bg` (Restarts the current job in the background.)
2. `bg %+` (Restarts the current job in the background.)
3. `bg %-` (Restarts the previous job in the background.)
4. `bg %`*`n`* (Restarts job number *n* in the background.)
5. `bg %`*`string`* (Restarts the most recent job matching *`string`*, as in:

```
bg %cp
```

---

2. CTRL-Z is the default suspend character. If it doesn't work, the suspend character may have been redefined. To set it back to CTRL-Z, type:

```
stty susp ^z
```

which restarts the most recent cp command in the background.)

Placing Jobs in the Foreground

Jobs are placed in the foreground with the fg command. The job can be identified in any of the five ways used with bg. For example:

```
fg %3
```

will place job number 3 in the foreground. If the job has been suspended, the command will resume execution in the foreground. If the job is running in the background, the command will bring it to the foreground.

Because jobs can only be suspended when they are in the foreground, the fg command is handy for temporarily bringing background jobs to the foreground for that purpose. For example, consider the following sequence of commands:

```
cp long.file1 long.file2 &
vi memo
CTRL-Z
fg %1
CTRL-Z
fg %2
```

The first command places the cp job in the background as job number 1. The user then begins editing a memo (job number 2). The editing is suspended with CTRL-Z. The cp job is then returned to the foreground where it can be suspended. The user can then resume editing the memo.

Killing Jobs

Although processes can be killed by using the kill command followed by the process ID, the C shell allows kill to also recognize the percent sign notation for referencing jobs. For example:

```
kill %+
```

will kill the current job and:

```
kill %cp
```

will kill the most recent `cp` job.

Jobs and Logging Out

If jobs are suspended when you attempt to log out, A/UX will warn you with:

```
You have stopped jobs.
```

The logout attempt will be aborted. At this point, you can deal with the suspended jobs if you so choose. However, if you type `exit` or CTRL-D again, the logout will be permitted and all suspended jobs killed.

If background jobs are running when you attempt to log out, the shell will abort the logout attempt and display:

```
You have running jobs.
```

You may deal with the background jobs or repeat the logout command. If you do the latter, background jobs will be killed.

The shell can be instructed to continue running background jobs even after you log out with the `nohup` (no hangup) command. To run a background job in that manner, precede the command with `nohup`, as in:

```
nohup cp long.file1 long.file2 &
```

The `nohup` command is documented in *A/UX Command Reference (M–Z and Games)*. See the section *User Commands (1)*; the commands are in alphabetical order.

C Shell Programming

With the exceptions discussed in the remainder of this chapter, C shell programming is the same as Bourne shell programming. Because it provides bit-level arithmetic operations (e.g., shifts) not available with either the Bourne or Korn shells, some users prefer programming under the C shell.

Variables and Assignment Statements

The C shell supports simple and one-dimensional array variables. Unlike the Korn shell, there are no numeric variables; all variables are strings. Array subscripts begin with 1 and are surrounded by brackets. For example:

```
array[6]
```

references the sixth element in an array. The special subscript * represents all subscripts.

Values are assigned to variables with the `set` command, as in:

```
set WorkingPath=/usr/bin
set value[1]=yes
set value[2]=no
set value[3]=maybe
```

If a string contains blanks, it must be surrounded by quotes:

```
set prompt2="Hit any key to continue: "
```

C shell variables cannot be used in any statement until they are initialized by a `set` statement.

Variables can be assigned the null string with the `unset` command. The statement:

```
unset value[*]
```

will assign the null string to every element in the array `value`.

Flow-of-control Statements

There are minor differences between the C and Bourne shells in the syntax of flow-of-control statements. These include the `switch` (i.e., `case`), `if/then/else`, `for`, and `while` constructs.

The C Shell's Switch and If/Then/Else Constructs

The C shell's `switch` statement is similar to the `case` statement supported by the Bourne and Korn shells. It has the general format:

```
switch variable_name
     case pattern_to_match:
          statements to execute
     breaksw
     default:
          statements to execute
     breaksw
endsw
```

Each value of the variable for which statements are to be executed is followed by a colon. The colon is followed, on the same or following lines, by executable shell commands. All of the commands that apply to a given variable value are terminated by a `breaksw` statement.

The values to which the shell matches the contents of the `switch` variable can be a constant or any of the shell's metacharacters. For that reason, they are called a *pattern*, rather than a *value*. Commonly, the last pattern to match is `default`. Any values of the `switch` value that are not matched by preceding patterns will be trapped by `default` and the statements following it executed.

A sample `switch` construct, representing the same code as that in Figure 8.3, can be found in Figure 10.1. This code also illustrates the C shell's `if/then/else` construct. It has the general format:

```
if logical_expression then
     statements to execute
else if logical_expression then
     statements to execute
else
     statements to execute
end if
```

```
switch ($choice)
     case 1:
          date
     breaksw
     case 2:
          echo "What year's calendar? \c"
          read year
          echo "What month's calendar? \c"
          read month
          if [ -n "$year" -a -n "$month" ] then
               cal $month $year
          else if [ -n "$year" -a -z "$month" ] then
               cal $year
          else if [ -z "$year" -a -n "$month" ] then
               cal $month
          else
               cal
          end if
     breaksw
     case 3:
          who
     breaksw
     case 4:
          mail
     breaksw
     case 9:
          exit
     breaksw
     default:
          "You've entered an invalid option"
     breaksw
endsw
```

Figure 10.1 A C shell `switch` **construct.**

The C Shell's For Construct

The C shell's `for` construct has the general format:

```
foreach variable name (value list)
     statements to execute
end
```

Unlike the BASIC for loop, the C shell's for loop does not increment the value of the variable in the for statement. Instead, the variable is given each of the values in the value list, one at a time. A loop that is to be executed three times might, therefore, be written:

```
foreach i (0 1 2)
     process these statements
end
```

The C Shell's While Construct

The C shell's while construct has the general format:

```
while logical_expression
     statements to be processed
end
```

The loop will continue to execute as long as the logical expression following while evaluates a true. When the expression evaluates as false, execution of the loop stops and the shell script continues with the statement below end.

A while loop that processes all of the positional parameters passed to the shell script on the command line might be written:

```
set counter=1
while [ "$counter" -le $# ]
     process some statements
     @ counter = counter + 1
end
```

When looking at this loop, remember that # represents the total number of positional parameters passed to the script.

Shell Arithmetic

The C shell performs only integer arithmetic. Arithmetic statements have the general format:

```
@ <variable name> = <arithmetic expression>
```

For example, the Korn shell script that appears in Chapter 9 to compute the average of a series of numbers is written for the C shell in the following manner:

```
set count=0
set sum=0
set number=0
echo "Enter a number: \c"
read number
while number !=0
    @ sum = sum + number
    @ count = count + 1
    echo "Enter a number: \c"
    read number
end
@ average = sum / count
echo "The average is $average"
```

Note that the spaces surrounding the assignment operator (the equals sign) and the variables, numbers, and constants in the arithmetic expression are required.

C shell arithmetic statements can use the following operations (listing in order of decreasing precedence):

1. `-` (negation)
2. `!` (logical NOT)
3. `*`, `/`, and `%` (multiplication, division, and remainder [modulus])
4. `+`, `-` (addition and subtraction)
5. `<<`, `>>` (left shift, right shift)

6. `<=, >=, <, >` (less than or equal to, greater than or equal to, less than, greater than)
7. `==, !=, =~, !~` (equal to, not equal to, equal to, not equal to)
8. `&` (binary AND)
9. `^` (binary exclusive OR)
10. `|` (binary OR)
11. `&&` (logical [bit-wise] AND)
12. `||` (logical [bit-wise] OR)

Parentheses can be used as needed for clarity and to override the default precedence. Expressions that conta,in characters that have special meaning to the shell (e.g., `&`, `&&`, `|`, `||`, `<`, `>`, `(`, `)`, and `*`) should be surrounded by quotes.

Part III

Administering A/UX

Chapter 11

Starting Up and Shutting Down

Although it's relatively easy to follow the step-by-step instructions in the *A/UX Installation Guide* to get A/UX up and running, there's little in that manual to help you understand why the procedures are performed in the way they are. This chapter, therefore, looks at a variety of issues surrounding the start–up and shutdown of an A/UX system, including the stand-alone shell (`sash`) and the system files that A/UX processes when it starts up.

The Superuser

The superuser is a highly privileged user account with the login name of `root`. Any individual logged in as the superuser has access to every file on the system and can perform any actions he or she desires. For that reason, the superuser password must be managed very carefully.[1]

There are two ways to become the superuser. The first is to log in directly to `root`. However, under most circumstances, you should avoid doing so, primarily for security reasons. Any user using the `who` command will be aware that a superuser is currently working on the system, providing a potential system cracker with information that he or she should not have.

The preferred alternative is to log in to a regular account (often called `sysop`) and then become the superuser as needed to perform maintenance tasks. To become the superuser, type:

```
su
```

at the shell's prompt. A/UX will then prompt you for the `root` account's password. Type the password and press enter. If you have entered the correct password, the prompt will change to a pound sign (#). To leave superuser status and return to the regular shell, enter `CTRL-D`.

---

1. For details on password management, see Chapter 13, System Security.

```
 File  Edit  Execute  Preferences
Standalone Shell Window (1.1)
-rwx------     1 root     root      75252 Jan 23 11:07 ypserv
drwxr-xr-x     7 sys      sys         912 Apr 11 07:02 zoneinfo
sash# ls -al (1,0,0)/
total 2043
drwxr-xr-x    11 root     root        336 Jun  3 07:01 .
drwxr-xr-x    11 root     root        336 Jun  3 07:01 ..
-rw-r--r--     1 root     root          0 May  7 06:42 .clipboard
-rw-r--r--     1 root     root        160 Aug 24  1987 .cshrc
-rw-r--r--     1 root     root        482 Apr  7  1988 .login
-rw-r--r--     1 root     root        387 Apr  7  1988 .profile
-r--r--r--     2 root     root     292686 Feb 10 16:48 FILES
drwxr-xr-x     2 bin      bin        2288 Jan 23 10:10 bin
drwxr-xr-x     5 bin      sys        1488 Jun  5 12:06 dev
drwxrwxr-x    14 bin      sys        2208 Jun  5 12:06 etc
-rw-rw-r--     1 root     root       1240 Apr 24 14:52 install.files
drwxr-xr-x     4 bin      bin         400 Jan 23 11:00 lib
-rw-r--r--     1 root     root        502 Apr 16 12:10 long.list
drwxrwxrwx     2 root     root       4128 Jan 23 11:01 lost+found
drwxrwxrwx     2 root     root         32 May 12  1987 mnt
-rw-r--r--     1 sys      sys      354661 Feb 10 16:21 newunix
-rw-r--r--     1 root     root          6 Jan 22 09:56 nextunix
drwxrwxrwx     2 bin      bin         208 Jun  5 09:04 tmp
-rw-r--r--     1 sys      sys      368776 Jan 22 09:56 unix
drwxr-xr-x     5 root     root         80 Apr 11 07:06 users
```

Figure 11.1 The stand-alone shell screen.

The Stand-alone Shell

When you want to boot A/UX, you first run an application known as the stand–alone shell, or `sash`, from the Macintosh OS desktop. The stand-alone shell screen (Figure 11.1) contains a window with the prompt `sash#`. Most of the time, you simply press Command-b at that prompt to boot A/UX. However, `sash` is a UNIX shell, similar to the Bourne, Korn, and C shells. It provides access to A/UX hard disk partitions and can be invaluable for repairing damage or modifying files that are used during system startup.

Although the stand-alone shell is key to some A/UX management activities, it can also present a significant security risk. If an unauthorized user gains access to the stand-alone shell, he or she could, for example,

Table 11.1
Stand-alone Shell Commands

cat	kconfig
chgrp	launch
chmod	ln
chown	ls
cp	mkdir
date	mkfs
dd	mknod
dp	mv
ed	od
esch	pname
fsck	rm
fsdb	stty

change the password on the the `root` account. Doing so would make the unauthorized user the only one who could become the superuser. What this means is that the physical security of the A/UX Macintosh is just as important as any other type of security that is applied to the system.

The `sash` is documented in *A/UX System Administrator's Reference*. See the section *Stand-Alone Commands (8)*; the commands are in alphabetical order.

The `sash` supports a subset of the commands available with the standard A/UX shells (see Table 11.1). Any of its commands can be entered in the `sash` window. This window acts like a `term` window that always records lines as they scroll off the top.

The problem with the `sash` is that it doesn't provide the `mount` command, the command that makes file systems available to A/UX. (The `mount` command is discussed in detail in Chapter 12.) However, there is a way to access files on A/UX disk partitions.

As you will remember, each A/UX device is represented as a file in `/dev`. For example, if the A/UX root file system resides on an internal hard disk (SCSI address 0), its file name will be `/dev/c0d0s0`; if the root file system is stored on an external drive at SCSI address 1, the file name is `/dev/c1d0s0`. To access a drive from the `sash`, you must know the three

numbers in the file name. The first represents the SCSI address of the disk drive, the second the disk, and the third the disk partition.

To use the numbers, place them in parentheses separated by commas, preceding the path name of the file you wish to access. For example, to see the contents of /etc on an internal A/UX drive, the command is issued as:

```
ls -al (0,0,0)/etc
```

Any file on any A/UX formatted hard disk can be reached in this way.

The sash window does not support full-screen operations. Therefore, the only text editor available is ed. In most cases, it is adequate for modifying system files and making minor repairs.

As mentioned earlier, the sash can be a significant security risk. It runs only as the superuser; it cannot be passworded. Because it has access to every file on every A/UX disk partition, access to it should be guarded very carefully. The only place that sash will run is from the system console (the monitor attached to the A/UX Macintosh). Therefore, the best form of security is to physically restrict access to that machine.

Start–up Notes

The A/UX documentation assumes that the hard disk on which the sash and the A/UX root file system reside will be the disk from which the Macintosh boots. However, that need not be the case. In fact, if your Macintosh is used part of the time for the Macintosh OS and part of the time for A/UX, it may be more convenient to boot from an alternative drive.[1]

---

1. Some people may suggest that you copy all of your Macintosh OS applications to A/UX and run them with launch. In that way, you would never have to use the Macintosh OS except to boot A/UX. However, there are two reasons this isn't particularly practical at this time. Although the compatibility of Macintosh OS applications with A/UX has increased greatly with the release of A/UX 1.1, there are still many that will not run. In addition, unless the A/UX has an AppleTalk communications board, it is not possible to print from Macintosh OS applications that are running under A/UX.

To boot from another drive (presumably a hard drive), open the desk accessory Control Panel (in the menu) and scroll the icons on the left until you can see Startup Device. Click on that icon. The right portion of the window will contain icon for each hard disk partition known to the Macintosh OS. Click on the partition from which you would like to boot and then close the desk accessory.

When booting from a partition other than `sash`, start A/UX by first double-clicking on the `sash` icon. When the `sash` screen appears, boot A/UX as usual (pressing Command-b is the easiest way).

Start–up Processes: inittab

When A/UX is booted, it places the system in single-user mode. Although some maintenance activities should only be performed with the system in that state, most of the time the system should be in multiuser mode. The command that places the system in multiuser mode is:

```
init 2
```

`Init` is a command that creates, or *spawns*, processes based on the contents of the file `/etc/inittab`. The `2` argument represents a *run level.*

An A/UX system may be at any of run levels 0 through 6 or in single-user mode (run levels `s` or `S`). By convention, run level 2 is multiuser mode. The processes that `init` creates for any given run level are indicated in `/etc/inittab` by that run level number.

In Figure 11.2, you will see the contents of A/UX's default `/etc/inittab`. The file has four fields:

1. ID: One to four characters that uniquely identify each entry.
2. Run level: A number indicating that run level at which the entry is to be used.
3. Action: A word that tells what A/UX is to do with the process. Common actions include:
   a. `boot`: Process the entry only on system boot and place the process in the background.

```
sy::sysinit:/etc/sysinitrc </dev/syscon >/dev/syscon 2>&1          #System Init
is:s:initdefault:                                           #First Init State
bl::bootwait:/etc/bcheckrc </dev/syscon >/dev/syscon 2>&1          #Bootlog
bc::bootwait:/etc/brc </dev/syscon >/dev/syscon 2>&1               #Bootrun
command
rc::wait:/etc/rc 1>/dev/syscon 2>&1          #System initialization - runcom
sl::wait:(rm -f /dev/syscon;ln /dev/systty /dev/syscon;) 1>/dev/systty 2>&1
pf::powerfail:/etc/powerfail 1>/dev/syscon 2>&1 #Power fail routines
co::respawn:/etc/getty console co_9600                      # Console Port
er:2:wait:/usr/lib/errdemon
cr:2:wait:/etc/cron </dev/syscon >/dev/syscon 2>&1
lp:2:wait:/usr/lib/lpsched >/dev/syscon 2>&1 # Set to "wait" for lp
tb0:2:once:/etc/toolboxdaemon >/dev/syscon 2>&1 # Set to "once" for toolbox
at0:2:off:/etc/at_nbpd >/dev/syscon 2>&1 # Set to "once" for AppleTalk
nfs0:2:off:/etc/portmap                       # set to "wait" for networking
nfs1:2:off:/etc/ypserv          # set to "wait" for yellow page server
nfs2:2:off:/etc/ypbind          # set to "wait" for yellow page client
nfs3:2:off:/etc/nfsd 4          # set to "wait" for NFS server
nfs4:2:off:/etc/biod 4          # set to "wait" for NFS client
nfs8:2:off:/etc/mount -at nfs > /dev/syscon 2>&1 # set to "once" for NFS
net4:2:off:/etc/in.routed       # set to "wait" for routing
net5:2:off:/usr/etc/in.rwhod    # set to "once" for rwho
net8:2:off:/usr/lib/sendmail -bd -q30m      # set to "once" for mail
net9:2:off:/etc/inetd           # set to "respawn" for networking
net0:2:off:/etc/named /etc/named.boot       # set to "wait" to be a nameserver
net6:2:off:/etc/syslogd                     # set to "wait" to run a syslog daemon
00:2:off:/etc/getty tty0 at_9600  #Port tty0 (modem); set to "respawn"
01:2:off:/etc/getty tty1 at_9600  #Port tty1 (print); set to "respawn"
```

Figure 11.2 A/UX's default `/etc/inittab`.

b. `bootwait`: Process the entry when the system is booted, but do not place it in the background (i.e., wait until the process finishes before proceeding).

b. `once`: Start the process once; if it dies, do not restart it; if it is running when the run level is changed, do not restart it (these processes are placed in the background).

c. `wait`: Run this process upon entering the associated run level; wait for the process to end before proceeding (i.e., do not place the process in the background).

d. `respawn`: If the process does not exist, start it; if the process dies, restart it (these processes are placed in the background).

   e. `off`: If the process is running, kill it; if the process is not running, do not start it.
   f. `sysinit`: Execute this process before trying to access the system console; wait for the process to finish before proceeding (do not place it in the background).
   g `powerfail`: Execute this process on a power failure.
   h. `initdefault`: Process this entry only the first time the system looks at `/etc/inittab` (this entry is used to determine the initial run level).
4. Process: The path name of an executable program that is to be run.

As you can see from Figure 11.2, the first eight entries are processed before the system is brought into multiuser mode. Those in which the run level field is blank are processed at boot time; the entry named `is` is used to bring the system into single-user mode (the initial run level). The remainder of the entries are all assigned to run level 2.

When the system is brought to run level 2, the following processes are started:

1. The error daemon (the daemon that traps system errors and displays error messages).
2. `Cron` (the daemon that handles timed command execution; `cron` is discussed later in this chapter).
3. The printer scheduler (the daemon that handles the print queues).
4. The ToolBox daemon (the daemon that acts as an interface between A/UX and the Macintosh ToolBox).

The remainder of the entries have an action of `off` and will, therefore, not be started. Their action is changed by the system administrator as needed to configure the system. (`/etc/inittab` can be edited with `vi` or another text editor by the superuser.)

As capabilities are added to an A/UX system, `/etc/inittab` entries are modified. For example, if A/UX is to check the modem port for incoming calls, the second to the last line must have its action changed to `respawn` so that there will be a `getty` process for that port. Specific

instructions on making changes to /etc/inittab will be discussed throughout the remainder of this book as needed.

The init command is documented in *A/UX System Administrator's Reference.* See the section *Maintenance Commands (1M)*; the commands are in alphabetical order. The format of the inittab file is documented in *A/UX Programmer's Reference.* See the section *File Formats (4)*; the file names are in alphabetical order.

Configuring the System

This section discusses some of things you may need to do to configure an A/UX system, including manage the system's name and the current date and time.

Setting a System Name

When you installed A/UX, you gave your system a name. That name is stored in /etc/HOSTNAME. The file contains only one line with two fields separated by tabs; the first field contains the local system name. System names are essential for networking. In fact, the entire uucp network relies on each system having a unique name. If you discover that the name you originally gave your system is not unique, then you should probably choose another name. To do so, become the superuser and edit /etc/HOSTNAME, replacing the first field only. The change will take effect the next time you boot A/UX.

System Date and Time

UNIX systems make a great deal of use of dates and times. Each file is stamped with the date and time of last modification; the date and time of each login and logout are also recorded. The system accounting routines also make heavy use of dates and times. In addition, the cron facility (discussed in the next section of this chapter) needs a clock to determine when to perform given tasks. For that reason, the A/UX system date and time should be as accurate as possible.

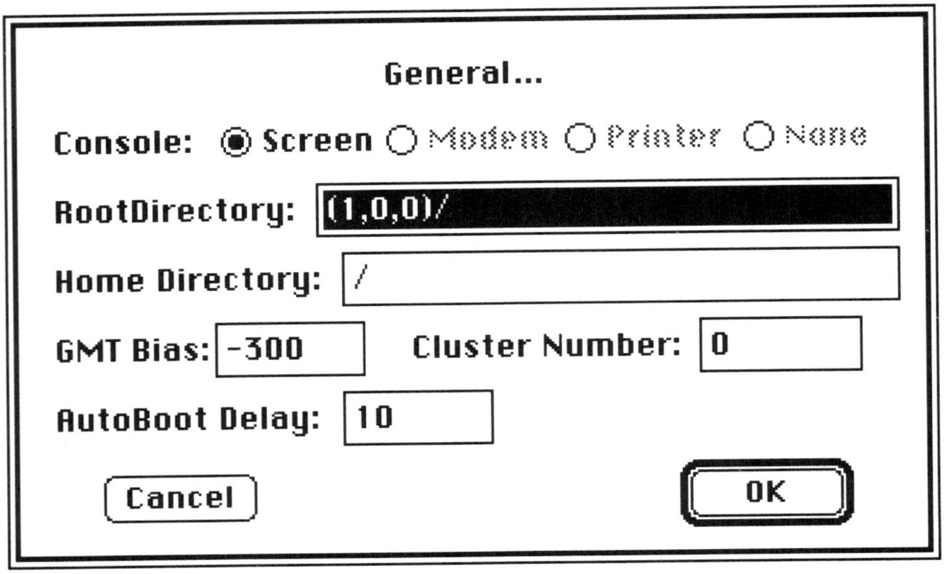

General...

Console: Screen Modem Printer None

RootDirectory: (1,0,0)/

Home Directory: /

GMT Bias: -300 Cluster Number: 0

AutoBoot Delay: 10

Cancel OK

Figure 11.3 The General dialog box.

By default, A/UX will use the time and date set in the Macintosh OS Control Panel. However, A/UX is much smarter than the Macintosh OS when it comes to daylight savings time; it will automatically adjust its clock while the Macintosh OS will not. To do so, it needs to know how far the system is from Greenwhich Mean Time (GMT), the GMT bias.

To set the GMT bias, boot the stand-alone shell (`sash`) and then choose General from the Preferences menu. Use the General dialog box (Figure 11.3) to enter the appropriate bias. The -300 that you see in Figure 11.3 represents Eastern Standard Time.

A/UX also needs to your system's time zone. Time zone files are stored in the directory `/etc/zoneinfo`. The names of the files correspond to the time zone they represent. For example, Eastern time is `EST5EDT`. Perform an `ls` on the directory and select your time zone (the zone files for countries other than the United States are gathered into subdirectories by country name). You will then link the file to a file called `localtime`.

First, delete the existing link with:

```
/etc/zoneinfo/localtime
```

Create the new link with:

```
ln <path name of time zone file> /etc/zoneinfo/localtime
```

For example, Eastern time is linked with:

```
ln /etc/zoneinfo/EST5EDT /etc/zoneinfo/localtime
```

Once the GMT bias and time zone have been set, the date and time can be set with the `date` command:

date *mmddhhmmyy*

The date will be set to October 13, 1950, 6:12 a.m. with:

```
date 1013061250
```

The last two digits of the year are optional. If they are left off, A/UX assumes you mean the current year (whatever is set in the Macintosh OS's control panel). Be sure to set the date only when A/UX is in single–user mode.

The `date` command is documented in *A/UX Command Reference (A–L)*. See the section *User Commands (1)*; the commands are in alphabetical order.

Dealing with Daylight Savings Time

Daylight savings time presents a bit of a dilemma. Although A/UX automatically adjusts for the change, the Macintosh operating system does not. That leaves the system administrator with two options. The first is to leave the Macintosh OS clock on standard time throughout the year; the A/UX time will adjust for daylight savings time and be correct.

The second option is to change the Macintosh OS clock and also A/UX's GMT bias. For example, if the Macintosh OS clock is set one hour ahead, the -300 GMT bias for Eastern Standard Time must be changed to -240 for Eastern Daylight Time.

Message of the Day

Every UNIX system contains a file called `/etc/motd`. This text file, the "message of the day," contains a message that is to be displayed whenever a user logs in. In most UNIX systems, `/etc/motd` is displayed automatically. However, A/UX does not do so. If you wish users to see a login message, place a command like:

```
more /etc/motd
```

in each default `.profile`.

Desk Accessories

Users working with `term` have access to the desk accessories (DAs) installed in the System file in the `sash` partition. This is true even if the Macintosh is booted from another disk (i.e., the start–up disk is something other than the disk on which `sash` and A/UX reside). As shipped, the `sash` System file has a minimal set of DAs installed. To add more, use the Macintosh OS's Font/DA Mover application, just as you would if you were adding DAs for use under the Macintosh OS. Although the Font/DA Mover can be copied to A/UX and run with `launch`, it's probably easier to install the DAs from the Macintosh OS before booting A/UX.

Automating System Activities: cron

The UNIX `cron` utility provides a mechanism through which the system will execute programs at prespecified intervals. If you look back at Figure 11.2, you will see that `cron`, the clock daemon, is started when the system is brought to run level 2. At that time it reads files known as `cron` tables to discover when programs should be run. In addition, it will read a `cron` table whenever the `crontab` command is run against it.

The `cron` command is documented in *A/UX System Administrator's Reference*. See the section *Maintenance Commands (1M)*; the commands are in alphabetical order.

Cron Tables

`Cron` tables are stored in the directory `/usr/spool/cron/crontabs`. Although it is possible to administer a system with only one `cron` table, most UNIX systems keep several, organizing the programs by general function. A `crontab` is a text file with six fields per line:

```
mi ho da mo dw <program to execute>
```

The first field indicates the minute(s) after the hour that the command should be executed; the hour(s) that the command should be executed appear in the second field. The third field contains the day of the month, the fourth field the month, and the fifth the day of the week. If any of the fields should be ignored, they are replaced with asterisks.

For example, the file `/usr/spool/cron/crontabs/adm` contains the line:

```
5 * * * * /usr/lib/acct/ckpacct
```

The program `/usr/lib/acct/ckpacct` will therefore be run at five minutes after every hour of every day. The line:

```
0 18-7 * * 1-5 /usr/lib/sa/sal
```

will run the program `/usr/lib/sa/sal` on the hour from 18:00 to 07:00 on the first five days of the week (days of the week are numbered from 0 to 6, beginning with Sunday). In other words, this command is set up to run during the work week, but during nonworking hours (hours are specified using a 24–hour clock, with 0 as midnight). Note that ranges of days or times are separated by a hyphen. To get a discontinuous set of days or times, separate them by commas. Be certain that there are no spaces within each field and that each field is separated by a space or a tab.

To make a change to an existing `cron` table, use a text editor such as `vi`. If you want the change to be recognized by the system immediately, run the `crontab` command as described in the next section.

Throughout the other chapters of Part III of this book, you find suggestions of additions and changes you should make to the `cron` tables. In particular, these relate to automating system accounting and communications clean up. However, there is no reason that you cannot add any command that you feel is necessary.

The Crontab Command

Because A/UX only reads `cron` tables when the system is brought to run level 2, any changes made to the `cron` tables while in multiuser mode will not take effect. However, there is no need to bring the system down to single user mode and reissue the `init 2` command.

The `crontab` command takes a file and copies it into a file in `/usr/spool/cron/crontabs`. The file has the name of the user issuing the command. For example, if `jon` issues:

```
crontab my.programs
```

a file named `/usr/spool/cron/crontabs/jon` will be created. `Cron` will read the file at that time.

If `crontab` is issued on an existing `cron` table, then the table will not be copied into the `cron` directory, but merely read by `cron`. For example, if you have just made a change to `/usr/spool/uucp/crontabs/adm`, the command:

```
crontab /usr/spool/uucp/crontabs/adm
```

will force `cron` to read the file and, therefore, recognize any new entries that have been made since the system was brought to multiuser mode.

Not every user can issue the `crontab` command. By default, only the superuser (the `root`) can do so. However, there are two ways to give other users that freedom. Any user whose name appears in `/usr/lib/cron/cron.allow` will be permitted to use the command; all other users except the superuser will not be able to execute it. Alternatively, the names of users who should *not* be allowed to issue to command can be stored in `/usr/spool/cron/cron.deny`; all other users will be permitted to do so. Both the `cron.allow` and `cron.deny` files are text files with one user name per line.

The `crontab` command is documented in *A/UX Command Reference (A–L)*. See the section *User Commands (1)*; the commands are in alphabetical order.

System Shutdown Issues

One of the nastiest things you can do to your A/UX system is shut it down by just turning off the power switch on the back of the Macintosh. Doing so is guaranteed to corrupt the file system in some way. (For that reason, power failures are similarly dreadful.) Instead, you should shut the system down gracefully.

A graceful shutdown requires three steps:

1. Shutting the system down to single user mode (the `shutdown` command).
2. Forcing the contents of the I/O buffers to the disk (the `sync`) command.
3. Powering down the machine (the `powerdown` command).

In essence, the `shutdown` command reverses everything that happened when the system was brought to multiuser mode. It unmounts all file systems except the root file system (it is permanently mounted). It also kills all running processes that were spawned after `init 2` was issued.

If you wish to reboot the Macintosh rather than powering it down, you may use the `reboot` command rather than `powerdown`. Do so only after shutting down to single user mode so that all file systems will be unmounted and processes killed gracefully.

Going to Single User Mode

A/UX is brought from multiuser mode to single user mode with the `shutdown` command, Shutdown may be immediate or delayed for a few minutes. The purpose of a delay is to give users a chance to save their work and log off gracefully. Because shutdown kills all processes that were started from the time the system went to run level 2, users will lose any work in progress when `shutdown` is executed.

Shutdown first prompts for the delay before the process begins:

```
SHUTDOWN PROGRAM
Wed Jun  7 14:55:50 1989

Do you wish to enter your own delay to shutdown
Default is 1 minute, (y or n):Enter your delay in minutes (0-60)
(No warning messages will be sent if input is 0):/dev/dsk/c1d0s0 on / type
5.2 (rw,noquota)
```

Unless the delay is zero (shutdown immediately), shutdown will broadcast messages to all users, stating that the system will be coming down after the specified delay.

The shutdown command is documented in *A/UX System Administrator's Reference*. See the section *Maintenance Commands (1M)*; the commands are in alphabetical order.

Securing the Root File System

Before the system can be powered down, one additional step must be performed to ensure the integrity of the root file system. To do so, issue the sync command at least once. Sync forces whatever is stored in disk I/O buffers to be written to disk and then updates the *superblock*, a disk block that stores information about the file system. If A/UX is powered down without syncing the boot drive, it is highly likely that the root file system will be corrupted in some way. Although most of the damage can be repaired by fsck (discussed in Chapter 12), the possibility exists for the introduction of serious file system problems that cannot be easily repaired.

The sync command is documented in *A/UX Command Reference (M–Z and Games)*. See the section *User Commands (1)*; the commands are in alphabetical order.

Turning It Off

Rather than reaching around to the back of the A/UX Macintosh and using the master power switch, turn the machine off with the powerdown command. Powerdown turns off the Macintosh in such a way that it can be restarted by the power key on the keyboard.

The `powerdown` command is documented in *A/UX System Administrator's Reference*. See the section *Maintenance Commands (1M)*; the commands are in alphabetical order.

If you wish to reboot the Macintosh (i.e., to work with the Macintosh OS), use the `reboot` command instead. `Reboot` performs a warm boot just like the Macintosh OS Restart menu option.

The `reboot` command is documented in *A/UX System Administrator's Reference*. See the section *Maintenance Commands (1M)*; the commands are in alphabetical order.

Chapter 12

Routine Maintenance

This chapter examines routine maintenance tasks, including handling groups and user accounts, automating system activities, and handling printers. All of the procedures discussed must be performed by the super-user.

Managing Groups

Each A/UX user belongs to one or more groups. The groups on any given A/UX machine are defined in the file `/etc/group`. A sample of an `/etc/group` file appears in Figure 12.1. The bottom two lines were added by the system administrator; the remainder are shipped with A/UX.

The `/etc/group` file has four fields, delimited by colons. The fields are:

1. Group name: A unique name given to each group.
2. Encrypted group password.
3. Group ID: A unique number identifying the group.
4. Group members: Names of user accounts that are a member of the group.

In Figure 12.1, the password fields have been filled with asterisks. This prevents A/UX from asking for a password when a user enters the `newgrp` command. This is not as much of a security hole as might be

```
root:****:0:
daemon:**:1:
bin:*****:2:
sys:*****:3:
adm:*****:4:
uucp:****:5;
lp:******:7:
mail:****:8:
project:*:100:
users:***:200:jon,jan,sysop
stndts:**:300:mark,millie,sysop
```

Figure 12.1 A sample `/etc/group` file.

expected. Although any user can attempt to change to any group, only those users whose login names actually appear in /etc/group with the group name will be permitted to make the change. A password on a group, therefore, serves very little purpose.

To create a new group, become the superuser and use a text editor such as vi to edit /etc/group. Add users to a group in the same way. The system whose /etc/group file appears in Figure 12.1 has two custom groups. The users group is the default group for all users who have full system access. The stndts group is for student users whose access to the system must be restricted.

The /etc/group file is documented in *A/UX Local System Administration* (see pages 3-5 to 3-8) and *A/UX Programmer's Reference* (see the section *File Formats (4)*; the file names are in alphabetical order.).

User Accounts

Creating an account for a new user requires four steps:

1. Add an entry for the account to the file /etc/passwd.
2.. Create a home directory for the account and install a default .profile.
3. Make the new account the owner of its home directory and default .profile.
4. Give the user an initial password.

An A/UX /etc/passwd file can be seen in Figure 12.2. The two bottom lines are user accounts (jon and sysop). The remainder are accounts that are shipped with A/UX. Each line in the file has six fields, delimited by colons. From left to right the fields are:

1. Account name: The account's login name.
2. Encrypted password: The encrypted version of the password.
3. User ID: A unique number identifying the user.
4. Group ID: A number identifying the user's default group.
5. User's real name: Text that identifies the account holder.

```
root:Zw983NAakkd81:0:0::/:/bin/sh
rootcsh:D1089Zd9gj39bi:0:0::/:/bin/csh
rootksh:ZW03j8Gge902kjc:0:0::/:/bin/ksh
daemon:xxxxxxxxxxxxx:1:1::/:
bin:xxxxxxxxxxxxx:2:2::/bin:
sys:xxxxxxxxxxxxx:3:3::/bin:
adm:xxxxxxxxxxxxx:4:4::/usr/adm:
uucp::5:5:UUCP admin:/usr/spool/uucppublic:/usr/lib/uucp/uushell
lp:xxxxxxxxxxxxx:7:7:lp:/usr/spool/lp:
ftp:xxxxxxxxxxxxx:8:2:ftp:/usr/spool/ftp:
who::22:0:who command:/bin:/bin/who
nobody:xxxxxxxxxxxxx:65534:65534:NFS generic user:/tmp:/bin/noshell
start:PG/qLJaYo/6mo:100:100:Initial login:/users/start:/bin/sh
startksh:PG/qLJaYo/6mo:100:100:Initial login:/users/start:/bin/ksh
startcsh:PG/qLJaYo/6mo:100:100:Initial login:/users/start:/bin/csh
jon:wjv0WWZ0v83xc:201:200:Working account:/users/jlh:/bin/sh
sysop:XR3knb2jVT9sk3:202:200:Admin account:/users/sysop:/bin/sh
```

Figure 12.2 An A/UX `/etc/passwd` file.

6. User's home directory.
7 Default shell: The user's default shell (`/bin/sh` for the Bourne shell, /bin/ksh for the Korn shell, `/bin/csh` for the C shell).

Account names are limited to 14 characters. They may contain any character that does not have special meaning to the shell (e.g., `/`, `\`, `@`, `$`, and spaces). In most cases, account names are short words that are easy to remember such as a user's initials or first name and last initial. As with file and directory names, the case of letters is significant.

The password that appears in `/etc/passwd` is encrypted by the `passwd` command. It can be decrypted only by the shell. The positive side to the encrypted password is that any user can read the contents of `etc/passwd` without worry that he or she can discover the password of any other account. However, if a user forgets his or her password, there is no way for even the superuser to decrypt what is in `/etc/passwd`. The only solution in that situation is to issue the user a new password.

When entering a new line in `/etc/passwd`, leave the password field empty. An initial password for the account should be entered from the superuser prompt (see the next section for details).

A user ID is a unique number assigned to the account name. Although user ID's are arbitrary, they must be unique within the system. The group ID is chosen from one of the groups defined in `/etc/group`.

The fifth field can be used for any text you wish to add to identify the account. In most cases, this is used to store the user's full name. The sixth field contains the path name of the account's home directory. Most systems create a directory named `/users` that will contain subdirectories with the names of each account. These subdirectories become each account's home directories.

The final field is the user's login shell. If no shell is entered, the account will default to the Bourne shell. Although most users will log in to either the Bourne, Korn, or C shell, additional shells are available. In particular, users whose access to the system needs to be severely restricted are assigned to the restricted shell (`/bin/rsh`). The restricted shell is discussed in detail in Chapter 13, System Security.

To add a new account, become the superuser. Use the command `vipw` to invoke `vi` on `/etc/passwd`. The `vipw` command locks the `/etc/passwd` file so that no other user can modify it at the same time. Type the line for the new account and write the file with `:w!` (`ZZ` will not work with `/etc/passwd`).

> The `/etc/passwd` file is documented in *A/UX Programmer's Reference*; see the section *File Formats (4)*, where the file names are in alphabetical order. Adding new accounts is described in *A/UX Local System Administration*; see pages 3-18 to 3-25. The `vipw` command is documented in *A/UX System Administrator's Reference*; see the section *Maintenance Commands (1M)*, where the commands are in alphabetical order.

Finish the process by creating the new account's home directory. For example, if the account `student65` will have a home directory of `/users/student65`, the superuser types:

```
mkdir /users/student65
```

Most system administrators keep a set of default `.profile` files. The appropriate `.profile` can then be copied into the new directory:

```
cp stud.profile /users/student65/.profile
```

Because the superuser has created the new user's default directory and `.profile`, the `root` account will be the owner of both; the file and directory will also be assigned to the `root`'s group. Therefore, change both the owners and groups to match the account name and the account's default group. Doing so for the `student65` account requires the following commands:

```
chown student65 /users/student65
chown student65 /users/student65/.profile
chgrp stdnts /users/student65
chgrp stdnts /users/student65/.profile
```

Setting Initial Passwords

If you look again at Figure 12.2, you will see that there are three root accounts, one for each of the three major shells. When A/UX is started for the first time, these accounts do not have passwords. Therefore, one of the first things that a system administrator should do is password the root accounts.

In addition, user accounts without passwords represent a significant security threat. Because `/etc/passwd` can be read by any user, accounts without passwords can be easily identified. All a user needs to do is log in to an account that has no password and then enter his or her password. The user then will control the account; only the superuser will be able to remove that access by changing the password again. For that reason, new user accounts should immediately be given passwords.

To set a password for an account other than the one to which you have logged in, become the superuser and type:

```
passwd <account name>
```

A/UX will prompt for the password twice. If the two entries agree, A/UX will encrypt the password and write the encrypted version to `/etc/passwd`. Note that the superuser is not prompted for a current password, nor are any rules about password composition enforced.

Managing File Systems

As shipped, A/UX comes with one file system: `/`. However, additional file systems can be created and added as needed. File systems may be stored on a floppy disk or on hard disks.

Understanding File Types

Most users interact with only regular files (text or binary) and directory files. However, A/UX also uses device files (also called special files), sockets, symbolic links, and named pipes. Like regular and directory files, the other types of files can be recognized by the first character in their permission string. The file type characters are:

1. `-` (Regular file.)
2. `d` (Directory file.)
3. `c` (Device file for a character device [a *raw* device]; character devices transfer data one character at a time.)
4. b (Device file for a block device; block devices transfer data one block [512 bytes] at a time.)
5. `p` (Named pipe.)
6. `s` (Socket.)
7. `l` (Symbolic link.)

Most peripheral devices are represented as both character and block device files. For example, a hard disk at `c1d0s2` will have the files:

```
/dev/dsk/c1d0s2
/dev/rsdk/c1d0s2
```

The `/dev/dsk` directory contains device files for block devices. The `/dev/rdsk` directory contains files for the character devices. In most cases, block I/0 is faster than character I/0. However, some programs (e.g., the backup utility `dump.bsd`) works faster on a character device.

Mounting and Unmounting File Systems

The process of getting A/UX to recognize a file system is called *mounting* the file system. File systems are detached, or *unmounted*, when they are no longer needed.[2]

A file system is mounted with the `mount` command. It has the general format:

```
mount  <file system name> <target directory>
```

The file system name is usually the file name assigned to the physical device on which the file system resides. For example, the Macintosh's first floppy drive has the file name `/dev/floppy0`. The target directory is the name of a directory to which the file system that is being mounted should be attached. The root of the mounted file system will appear as a subdirectory of the target directory. By convention, any file system added to A/UX is mounted as a subdirectory of `/mnt`. To mount a file system on the floppy disk, the command is typed:

```
mount /dev/floppy0 /dev/mnt
```

A/UX keeps a record of all mounted file systems in the file `/etc/fstab`. The entry for A/UX's root file system appears as:

```
/dev/dsk/c1d0s0 / 5,2 rw,noquota  1 2
```

The fields in the file are (from the left):

1. File system name.
2. Directory to which the root of the file system is attached when it is mounted.
3. File system type.
4. Mounting options.

---

2. The root file system, `/`, is always mounted.

5. Frequency (in days) with which the contents of the file system should be dumped.
6. Pass on which the file system should be checked during a file system checking operation (see the next section in this chapter for details).

A/UX recognizes five types of file systems:

1. `4.2` (A Berkeley UNIX (BSD) 4.2 file system.)
2. `5.2` (A UNIX System V file system.)
3. `NFS` (A "network file system"; i.e., a file system stored on another computer, but accessible over a local area network.)
4. `swap` (A file system used for virtual memory swap space.)
5. `ignore` (Instructs A/UX to ignore the rest of the entry; can be used to keep a record of file systems that are currently unused.)

To specify a file system type, use `mount`'s `-t` flag option. The command:

```
mount -t5.2 /dev/dsk/c1d0s2 /mnt
```

will mount a file system on an external hard drive (SCSI 1) as a UNIX System V file system.

`Mount` options determine the operations that can be performed on the file system. They include

1. `rw` (Permit reading and writing to the file system.)
2. `ro` (Permit reading but not writing to the file system.)
3. `quota` (Permit a limit to be placed on the size to which the file system can grow.)
4. `noquota` (Allow no limits on file system size; i.e., allow the file system to grow as large as the physical medium and the number of i-nodes will allow.)

Options are listed following the flag option `-o`, separated by commas. For example, if a file system on a floppy disk is to be mounted for reading only, the command can be issued as:

```
mount -o ro -t 5.2 /dev/floppy0 /mnt
```

The expression `-o ro` can also be replaced by the shorthand option `-r`.

If there are a number of file systems that should be mounted at one time, `mount` can be directed to take its parameters from the file `/etc/fstab`. This file has the same format as `/etc/mtab`. To instruct `mount` to read from `/etc/fstab`, use the `-f` flag option, as in:

```
mount -f
```

If file systems should be mounted at boot time, the commands to mount them are placed in a shell script named `/etc/rc` (Figure 12.3). This shell script is executed by `/etc/inittab` when A/UX is booted. Note that the root file system is mounted by this script. Any `mount`s that should be performed for your specific configuration can be added to this script with a text editor. (Because this file is processed before the system reaches init level `s`, it makes sense to edit it from the `sash` with `ed`.)

The `umount` command unmounts, or detaches, a files system. It can be issued as:

```
umount <file system name>
```

or

```
umount <directory to which file system is attached>
```

In other words, if `/dev/floppy0` has been attached to `/mnt`, it can be unmounted with either:

```
umount /dev/floppy0
```
or
```
umount /mnt
```

To unmount every attached file system (i.e., all those listed in `/etc/mtab`), use `umount`'s `-a` flag option:

```
umount -a
```

```
# top line left blank for csh ; don't delete it!
#         @(#)Copyright Apple Computer 1987      Version 1.7 of rc.sh
on 88/04/07 14:54:25 (ATT 1.12)#        Push line discipline/set the
device so it will print
/etc/line_sane 1set '/bin/who -r'
if [ "$7" = 2 ]
then
          # put mounts here (/usr, etc.)
          /etc/mount -at 5.2
          /usr/lib/ex3.9preserve -
          /bin/rm -f /tmp/*
          /bin/rm -f /usr/spool/uucp/LCK*
          /bin/rm -f /usr/spool/lp/SCHEDLOCK
          /bin/rm -f /usr/adm/acct/nite/lock*
          /bin/mv /usr/adm/sulog /usr/adm/OLDsulog
          /bin/mv /usr/lib/cron/log /usr/lib/cron/OLDlog
          if [ ! -f /etc/wtmp ]
          then
                    >/etc/wtmp
                    /bin/chmod 666 /etc/wtmp
                    /bin/chgrp adm /etc/wtmp
                    /bin/chown adm /etc/wtmp
          fi
          /bin/chmod 666 /etc/utmp
          /bin/su adm -c /usr/lib/acct/startup
          echo process accounting started
fi
# Enable these lines for dial-out UUCP lines - change the tty port
# to match the one you select as the dial-out port.
          /bin/chmod 666 /dev/tty0
          /bin/chown daemon /dev/tty0
          /bin/chgrp daemon /dev/tty0
```

Figure 12.3 The shell script `/etc/rc`.

The `mount` and `umount` commands are documented in *A/UX System Administrator's Reference*; see the `mount` pages in the section *Maintenance Commands (1M)*. The commands are in alphabetical order.

If the file system with which you are working is on a floppy disk, be sure to unmount it before ejecting the disk. Once the file system has been unmounted, eject it from the disk drive by typing `eject`.

The eject command is documented in *A/UX Command Reference (A–L)*. See the section *User Commands (1)*; the commands are in alphabetical order.

Checking File Systems

File systems can become corrupted for a variety of reasons. The number of free i-nodes, the size of individual files, and the number of free disk blocks may become inaccurate. A/UX provides the fsck utility to check the integrity of file systems and to repair them, if possible.

A/UX must be in single user mode before fsck can be run from the shell's prompt. For that reason, it is usually run when the system is first booted (e.g., respond y to A/UX's query about checking the root file system) or after something unusual has happened to the system (e.g., a power outage or a disk head crash). In addition, any file system that is mounted by /etc/rc can be checked when the system is brought to run level 2. If, at any other time, you have reason to believe that the file system might be inconsistent, first bring the system into single user mode with the shutdown command.

The fsck command has the general format:

```
fsck <file system name>
```

For example, to check the root file system (stored on an internal hard drive at SCSI address 0), the command is issued as:

```
fsck /dev/rdsk/c0d0s0
```

Because fsck works faster with a character device, the name of the file system is taken from the /dev/rdsk directory rather than /dev/dsk. A/UX responds with something like what appears in Figure 12.4.

If fsck finds file system inconsistencies, it will attempt to correct them (the transcript in Figure 12.4 was taken from a file system without inconsistencies). The first time you issue fsck, you may wish to simply view the status of the file system without attempting any repairs. In that case, use the -n flag option, as in:

```
/dev/rdsk/c1d0s0:
File System:  Volume:

** Phase 1 - Check Blocks and Sizes
** Phase 2 - Check Pathnames
** Phase 3 - Check Connectivity
** Phase 4 - Check Reference Counts
** Phase 5 - Check Free List
3577 files 69304 blocks 40140 free
```

Figure 12.4 The output of an uneventful `fsck` command.

```
fsck -n /dev/rdsk/c0d0s0
```

If you wish `fsck` to automatically attempt all repairs possible, use the `-y` option instead. If neither `-n` or `-y` are present, `fsck` will prompt for yes or no responses to questions about whether it should attempt repairs.

As you can see from the above transcript of an `fsck` execution, the utility has at least five phases:

1. Check blocks and sizes: `Fsck` examines the i-node list. The errors that may be detected include:
   a. Bad i-node type: Each i-node contains information about the type of file attached to that i-node (regular, directory, special block, special character, or FIFO). If `fsck` detects an unrecognizable type, it can repair the damage by clearing the i-node. If a file is actually attached to the i-node, clearing it will effectively delete the file.
   b. Bad or duplicate blocks: `Fsck` verifies the disk blocks used by each i-node. If it finds a block claimed by two i-nodes, it notes the occurrence. Ultimately, one of the i-nodes should be cleared (usually the one with the earliest time of last modification).
   c. I-node size errors: `Fsck` examines the portion of each i-node that contains the size of the file attached to it. If it detects an inconsistency, it will display:

```
POSSIBLE FILE SIZE ERROR I=i
```

where `i` is the i-node number with the bad file size. `Fsck` cannot correct error. The procedure for doing so is discussed later in this section. To complete the process, you will need the number of the offending i-node.

d. I-node format errors: Correctly formatted i-nodes will be either allocated or unallocated. I-nodes not in either state are in error. `Fsck` will clear them; any files that happen to be attached will be lost.

2. Check pathnames: `Fsck` removes directory entries for any i-nodes that were cleared during phase 1. In addition, it identifies other errors that relate to directories:
   a. Root i-node mode and status errors: Any error identified involving the root i-node indicates serious file system problems. `Fsck` may not be able to recover from such an error, especially if it discovers that the root i-node is unallocated.
   b. I-node number out of range: If `fsck` discovers an i-node number that is larger than the maximum i-node allocated for the file system, it can remove the error by deleting the directory entry that refers to the out-of-range i-node. A file may be lost when this occurs.
   c. I-nodes that point to bad directory entries: When `fsck` detects an invalid directory entry, it will clear the i-node by removing the directory entry. Again, file loss may occur.

3. Check connectivity: `Fsck` checks directory path names to ensure that there are no unattached directories. It will attach all unattached directories.

4. Check reference counts: `Fsck` looks again at the connectivity of the file system. The errors that are detected during this phase include:

a. Unreferenced files and/or directories: Files that are not connected to directories will be reconnected. If you decide not to reconnect the file, it can be cleared (i.e., deleted).
b. Free i-node count is wrong: If A/UX finds that the number of i-nodes that the file system thinks it has is different than the number of i-nodes it actually counted, it will correct the stored number.
c. Bad and duplicate blocks: If duplicate blocks remain in files and directories, `fsck` can fix the problem by clearing the i-node. Keep in mind that clearing an i-node effectively deletes the file or directory associated with it.

5. Check free list: `Fsck` checks the list of free (unused) i-nodes. No correction is made during this phase.

If errors are found in the list of free i-nodes, `fsck` will enter a sixth phase (Salvage free list) to rebuild the list.

The `fsck` command is documented in *A/UX System Administrator's Reference*. See the section *Maintenance Commands (1M)*; the commands are in alphabetical order. For example of `fsck` messages, see Chapter 8 of *A/UX Local System Administration*.

Fixing File Size Errors

Because `fsck` cannot automatically correct file size errors, you must do so manually after `fsck` has finished. If necessary, first mount the file system that contains the i-node with the problem. (The root system will be already mounted, but all others were unmounted when the system was brought to single user mode.)

To effect a repair, you will need the name of the file associated with the i-node. Use the `ncheck` command to do so:

```
ncheck -i <i-node number> <file system name>
```

The file system name must include the device file name for the file system, not its mount point. Therefore, to retrieve the file name for i-node 1024 of the file system on `/dev/dsk/c2d0s0`, the command is issued as:

```
ncheck -i 1024 /dev/dsk/c2d0s0
```

The `ncheck` command is documented in *A/UX System Administrator's Reference*. See the section *Maintenance Commands (1M)*; the commands are in alphabetical order.

Once you know the name of the file, copy to a new file under a different name (be sure to use `cp`, not `mv`). Then run `sync` (the program that forces a save of all I/O buffers to disk). At this point, take a look at the contents of the file. If it is something you want to keep, delete the original and rename of copy.

Creating New File Systems

Although the `mkfs` command will create new file systems, there is more to the process than running the command. First, the physical device on which the file system will reside must be formatted and, in the case of a hard disk, probably partioned.

Partitions and Slices

It is true that A/UX will recognize disk partitions created by non–Apple software. However, if you wish to be certain that the partitions will be A/UX compatible, use the program `HD SC Setup` that is shipped with Macintosh OS system software. `HS SC Setup` will initialize the hard disk and then partition the drive.

To create a file system, you must know the disk's SCSI ID, slice number of the partition, and size of the partition The SCSI ID is usually set on the back of the disk drive; note the number of kilobytes in the partition before quitting `HD SC Setup`. However, figuring out the slice number isn't quite as straightforward.

`HD SC Setup` will install a number of different types of partitions. Those that are compatible with A/UX are:

1. Eschatology
2. Eschatology2
3. Root
4. Root&User
5. Swap

6. Usr
7. Misc A/UX

A/UX automatically associates slice number 0 with Root and Root&User partitions. Swap partitions are slice 1; Usr partitions are slice 2. However, the remaining partition types are not associated with slice numbers.

If a disk contains partitions have the same slice number (e.g., Root and Root&User partitions on the same drive), then you must run the dp utility to assign unique partition names. Then, the pname command must be used to assign slice numbers to those partitions that are not given them automatically.

Before assigning unique partition names, you must know the index number that A/UX has assigned to each partition. Enter the command:

```
echo P | dp -q /dev/dsk/cnd0s31
```

where *n* is the SCSI ID of the drive. The echo passes a P command to dp, instructing it to print information about all named partitions. The -q flag option prevents dp from prompting for input. An entry for a typical partition looks like:

```
DPM Index: 7
Name: "Eschatology 2", Type: "Apple_UNIX_SVR2"
Physical: 6144 @ 150224, Logical: 6144 @ 0
Status:
         valid     alloc     in_use    not boot
         read      write
Eschatology File System (2) (critical)
Cluster:   0        Type: EFS Inode: 1
Made: [603161472] Fri Feb 10 19:51:12 1989
Mount: [603161638] Fri Feb 10 19:53:58 1989
Umount: [603161642] Fri Feb 10 19:54:02 1989
No AltBlk map
```

Note the name of the partition and its index number. Although the names may not be unique on a single disk, the index numbers will be.

You must then enter the dp program to change the partition names. Type:

```
dp /dev/dsk/cnd0s31
```

where *n* is the SCSI ID of the drive. When dp responds with:

```
Command?
```

enter c*n*, where *n* is the index number of a partition that has the same name as another partition. Dp responds with:

```
DPME Field?
```

Type n (for the Name field). Dp will then prompt for a new name for the partition. Enter a unique name of your choice; the name should contain no spaces. Then enter a q to return to the Command? prompt. Repeat the process for each partition that has a nonunique name. When finished, enter w at the Command? prompt to save the change you've made, followed by q to return to the shell.

The dp command is documented in *A/UX System Administrator's Reference*. See the section *Maintenance Commands (1M)*; the commands are in alphabetical order.

To assign slice numbers, use the pname command:

```
pname -a -cn <partition name>
```

where *n* is the SCSI ID of the disk drive. A/UX will give you the path name of the partition that should be used when referencing it. For example, the path name of a partition name Extra_Stuff on a disk at SCSI ID 5 would be retrieved with:

```
pname -a -c5 Extra_Stuff
```

A typical A/UX response is:

```
/dev/dsk/c5d0s4
```

If two partitions have automatically been assigned the same slice (e.g., Root and Root&User), then you must first find out which partition is actually recognized. Enter:

```
pname -p
```

to see all known partitions. Once you know which partition isn't recognized, use the procedure just described to give it a new slice number.

The `pname` command is documented in *A/UX System Administrator's Reference*. See the section *Maintenance Commands (1M)*; the commands are in alphabetical order.

Preparing Floppy Disks For File Systems

The discussion in the previous section focused on preparing hard disks for file systems. However, file systems can also be created on floppy disks. The only thing that needs to be done to prepare a floppy disk is to format it.

The A/UX floppy disk format is the same as the Macintosh OS system disk format. However, A/UX will not accept 1.44 Mb disks (only 400K and 800K), even though your Macintosh may be equipped with the high-density drive.

The easiest way to format a disk is to insert it into a disk drive from the Macintosh OS. If the disk is blank, the Macintosh OS will give you the chance to initialize it. If the disk has already been formatted, choose the Erase Disk option from the Special menu to reformat it.

If you must format a floppy disk while A/UX is running, use the `diskformat` command, as in:

```
diskformat /dev/rloppy0
```

To format a disk in a second floppy drive, use `/dev/rfloppy1` as the destination of the format.

The `diskformat` command is documented in *A/UX System Administrator's Reference*. See the section *Maintenance Commands (1M)*. the commands are in alphabetical order.

Creating the New File System

Assuming that you have partitioned the disk and assigned unique names and slice numbers, a file system is created with:

```
mkfs /dev/dsk/cnd0sy <size in blocks>
```

where *n* is the SCSI ID of the disk and *y* is the slice. The size of the new file system is equal to the total kilobytes allocated to the partition multiplied by 2. For example, a file system for a 20 Mb partition on `/dev/dsk/c5d0s4` is created with:

```
mkfs /dev/dsk/c5d0s4 40000
```

The `mkfs` command is documented in *A/UX System Administrator's Reference*. See the section *Maintenance Commands (1M)*; the commands are in alphabetical order. In addition, the entire process described in this section is covered in Chapter 5 of *A/UX Local System Administration.*

After creating a new file system, you may wish to test it. First, mount the file system. Then run `fsck` to verify its integrity. You may also wish to place an entry for the file system in `/etc/fstab` and a `mount` command in `/etc/rc`. The `/etc/fstab` entry will instruct A/UX to perform `fsck` on the file system if you answer `y` to the `Check file systems?` message when going to run level 2. A `mount` command in `/etc/rc` will automatically mount the file system when A/UX is booted.

Handling Printers

Printers may be attached to an A/UX system in two ways. They may use the Macintosh's serial ports (a direct serial connection) or they may use the AppleTalk Network. Unfortunately, A/UX does not support the Macintosh's built-in AppleTalk capability. Instead, AppleTalk access must be

provided on a plug-in board (e.g., the CommCard™] from SuperMac Technology).[3]

As discussed in Chapter 3, files are queued for printing with the `lp` command; the jobs that are queued can be viewed with `lpstat`. The queue itself is managed by the printer daemon, `lpsched`, which is started when the system is brought to multiuser mode. In addition, there are a number of commands that are used to administer the printing system. They may be performed by the superuser or by anyone logged in under the user name of `lp`. This account is shipped with A/UX and should be passworded as soon as possible to prevent unauthorized users from gaining access to the `lp` administrative commands.

For a tutorial on printer management, see pages 5-18 through 5-52 of *A/UX Local System Administration.*

Printer Destinations

When a user enters the `lp` command, the user's document is sent to the system's default printer. As shipped, A/UX expects an Apple ImageWriter connected to `tty1` (the serial port with a printer icon above it) with a serial cable. The printer has the name `iw2`.

Adding an Apple Laser Printer

Before an Apple laser printer can be accepted as a legal definition for a print job, the printer must be assigned an A/UX name. If it is not networked, the laser printer will generally occupy the same port as an ImageWriter (`tty1`). For that reason, the ImageWriter must be "removed" and the laser printer "added."[4]

The commands that add and remove printers are in the directory `/usr/spool/lp`. To remove the ImageWriter, type:

---

3. The advantage to spending the extra money on an AppleTalk board is the ability to print from Macintosh OS applications that are running under A/UX.

4. When connecting a LaserWriter using a serial cable, be sure to set the switch on the side of the printer to 9,600 baud, rather than AppleTalk.

```
RM_PR iw2
```

A/UX responds with the following:

```
destination "iw2" will no longer accept requests
printer "iw2" now disabled
scheduler stopped
scheduler is running
no system default destination
```

Notice that because the ImageWriter was the default printer, removing it means that there is no longer a default printer.

To add the LaserWriter, type:

```
ADD_LW laser tty1
```

The `laser` is the name that you are assigning to the printer; `tty1` is the port to which the printer is attached. After the command is issued, A/UX responds with:

```
scheduler stopped
destination "laser" now accepting requests
destination "PostScript" now accepting requests
printer "laser" now enabled
crw-rw----   2 lp       lp          0,  1 Dec  3  1987 /dev/laser
crw-rw----   2 lp       lp          0,  1 Dec  3  1987 /dev/tty1
```

The LaserWriter has two device addresses, `/dev/laser` and `/dev/tty1`. In addition, a user can address its destination as `laser` or `PostScript`. Notice also that while `RM_IW` restarted the `lp` scheduler, `ADD_LW` did not. Therefore, you should restart it with:

```
/usr/lib/lpsched &
```

If the LaserWriter you are using is a LaserWriter IINT or LaserWriter IINTX rather than a LaserWriter or LaserWriter Plus, you must make one additional change. Use a text editor to access the file `/usrspool/lp/model/psinterface`. Find the line `REVERSE=1` and change it to `REVERSE=0`. This change is necessary because the two classes of LaserWriters print on the opposite side of the paper.

To switch from a LaserWriter back to an ImageWriter, the process is similar. First, remove the LaserWriter with:

```
RM_PR laser
```

Then add the ImageWriter:

```
ADD_IW iw2 printer
```

A/UX can support multiple printers, either over a network or if an expansion board is plugged into one of the Macintosh's expansion slots. In the latter case, the ports on the board are named based on the slot in which the board is placed. For example, a board with four serial ports is plugged into slot 10, and the ports are named `ttya0`, `ttya1`, `ttya2`, and `ttya3` (`a` is the hexadecimal for 10). If attaching an Apple printer to one of these ports, use the correct device name (e.g., `/dev/ttya2`) in the `ADD` command.

The `RM` and `ADD` programs are shell scripts that perform a number of commands. If you are planning to add a different type of printer, you can perform the steps manually.

Adding a Printer Manually

If you are adding printers other than an ImageWriter or LaserWriter, then the `RM` and `ADD` scripts are not applicable. However, you can perform the process manually. The first step is to shut down `lpsched` with:

```
/usr/lib/lpshut
```

The `lpshut` command is documented along with the `lpsched` in *A/UX System Administrator's Reference*. See the section *Maintenance Commands (1M)*; the commands are in alphabetical order.

Then use the `lpsched` command with the general format:

```
lpadmin -p <name of the printer> -v <printer device file> -m <model>
```

A model is a shell script that acts as an interface between A/UX and the printer. For ImageWriters, the model is either `iw` or `imagewriter2`; for a PostScript printer like the LaserWriter, it is `psinterface`. In addition there are models named `dumb` (generic line printers), `1640` (Diablo 1640 terminal), `hp` (Hewlett-Packard 2631A line printer), and `prx` (Printronix printer)

Assume, for example, that you have attached a Diablo 1640 terminal to `tty1`.The command that instructs A/UX to recognize it as a valid `lp` destination is:

```
/usr/lib/lpadmin -pDiablo -v /dev/tty1 -m1640
```

The `lpadmin` command is documented in *A/UX System Administrator's Reference*. See the section *Maintenance Commands (1M)*; the commands are in alphabetical order.

At this point, `lpsched` will recognize the printer, but will not automatically allow print jobs to be scheduled. To permit printing, use the `accept` command:

```
/usr/lib/accept <printer name>
```

as in:

```
/usr/lib/accept Diablo
```

The `accept` command is documented in *A/UX System Administrator's Reference*. See the section *Maintenance Commands (1M)*; the commands are in alphabetical order.

Changing the Default Printer Destination

If you have more than one printer available, you have discretion over which one is the default printer. To change the default, type:

```
/usr/lib/lpadmin -d <printer name>
```

as in:

```
/user/lib/lpadmin -d1640
```

Denying Printer Requests

If, for some reason, print requests should not be queued, use the `reject` command:

```
/usr/lib/reject -r <reason for rejection> <printer name>
```

For example, to temporarily suspend print requests to the Diablo printer while the repair person is working on it, the command is issued as:

```
/usr/lib/reject -r"Repair man is working hard" Diablo
```

The `reject` command is documented in *A/UX System Administrator's Reference*. See the section *Maintenance Commands (1M)*; the commands are in alphabetical order.

Removing a Printer

To remove a printer, use the `-x` flag option of the `lpadmin` command:

```
/usr/lib/lpadmin -x <name of printer>
```

as in:

```
/usr/lib/lpadmin -x Diablo
```

Enabling and Disabling Printers

The `accept` and `reject` commands control whether or not print requests will be queued for printing. However, they do not affect whether or not the printer will print. If print requests are queued when the `reject` command is issued, no more requests will be queued but jobs already in the queue will be printed. To actually prevent a printer from printing, use the `disable` command:

```
enable -c -r <reason> <printer>
```

The `-c` option will cancel any print requests queued for the printer. Otherwise, they will remain in the queue.

If the Diablo has run out of paper, it will be disabled with:

```
enable -r"The Diable is out of paper" Diablo
```

To allow a printer to print again, use the `enable` command:

```
enable <printer name>
```

as in:

```
enable Diablo
```

The `enable` and `disable` commands are documented together under `enable` in *A/UX Command Reference (A–L)*. See the section *User Commands (1)*; the commands are in alphabetical order.

Installing and Using AppleTalk

As mentioned in Chapter 7, printing from a Macintosh OS application running under A/UX requires AppleTalk. However, A/UX cannot use the Macintosh's built-in AppleTalk hardware. Instead, an AppleTalk board, such as the SuperMac Technology CommCard, must be installed in one of the Macintosh's expansion slots. The discussion that follows, therefore,

assumes that the necessary board is installed according to the manufacturer's directions[5] and that it has been connected to an AppleTalk network that includes either a LaserWriter or an AppleTalk ImageWriter.

Configuring A/UX for AppleTalk

After the AppleTalk board has been installed, you will need to ensure that the AppleTalk daemon will be running. To do so, change the action field in the /etc/inittab entry below to respawn:

```
at0:2:off:/etc/at_nbpd >/dev/syscon 2>&1
```

The daemon (/etc/at_nbpd) will then be started when the system is brought to run level 2 and respawned whenever it is killed.

To make an AppleTalk printer the default system printer, become the superuser and run the /usr/spool/lp/ADD_AT shell script. In most cases, the default AppleTalk printer will be named atalk_printer. The command is, therefore, issued as:

```
ADD_AT atalk_printer
```

The ADD_AT script produces the following dialog:

```
scheduler stopped
/usr/lib/lpadmin: destination "atalk_printer" non-existant
destination "atalk_printer" now accepting requests
destination "AppleTalk" now accepting requests
printer "atalk_printer" now enabled
LP service atalk_printer now installed
```

Notice that the ADD_AT script does not specify any particular AppleTalk printer. If more than one is installed on the AppleTalk network, the lp

5. The instructions that come with the AppleTalk board should include building a new UNIX kernel that includes an AppleTalk driver. For example, the SuperMac CommCard is shipped with an INSTALL program that automatically builds and installs the new kernel.

command will send the file to the first available AppleTalk printer in the A/UX Macintosh's AppleTalk zone.

Choosing a Default AppleTalk Printer

As just mentioned, `lp` will choose the first available AppleTalk printer. (If that printer is a LaserWriter but the file being printed is a text file, `lp` will automatically convert the file to Postscript.) However, each user can select a specific AppleTalk printer with the `at_cho_prn` shell script.

The `at_cho_prn` script first checks to see if more than one AppleTalk zone is accessible. If there are multiple zones, it presents a list, as in:

```
Zone list:
1: Sales
2: Accounting
3: Shipping

ZONE number (0 for current zone) ?
```

Enter the zone number at the prompt.

After the zone has been selected (or if there is only one zone), `at_cho_prn` displays a list of available printers:

```
ITEM OBJECT   TYPE           ZONE  NET     NODE  SOCKET
1:    IW1     ImageWriter     *    0x1111  0x11  0xca
2:    IW2     ImageWriter     *    0x1111  0x12  0xcb
3:    LWII    LaserWriter     *    0x1111  0x13  0xcc

ITEM number (0 to make no selection) ?
```

Enter the number of the AppleTalk printer that should be used as the default destination for `lp` requests. `Lp` will then route print requests to the selected printer.

Macintosh Printing Notes

Once an AppleTalk card has been installed, users can print from Macintosh OS applications, just as they would if they were actually running under the Macintosh OS (i.e., using the Chooser desk accessory to select an AppleTalk printer). In addition, text selected in a `term` window can be printed in the same way.

Chapter 13

System Security

The phrase "system security" refers to anything that needs to be done to avoid the unauthorized disclosure, modification, or destruction of data. This chapter, therefore, covers a range of security issues, including system backup, assigning appropriate file and directory permissions, managing passwords, and using the restricted shell.

Password Security

For better or for worse, much of the security of any UNIX system relies on the security of its passwords. As mentioned earlier in this book, one of the first things a system administrator should do after installing A/UX is to create passwords for all of the accounts with which the system is shipped. User accounts should also be given passwords as soon as the accounts are created in `/etc/passwd`. However, simply creating the passwords is not enough to ensure that they will continue to be secure. They must be managed in such a way that they are difficult for unauthorized users to guess.

Password Management

Anyone who has even a little knowledge of UNIX will know that the ideal way to crack such a system is to figure out the superuser password. Once a cracker becomes the superuser, he or she has access to the entire system. However, there are some generally accepted principles for managing passwords that can help keep the superuser password, and other passwords, secure.

The ideal password should be easy to remember and, at the same time, difficult to guess. Experience has shown that passwords that are made up of two short, unrelated words linked by a special character best fits the requirements. Passwords of that type might be:

```
shout.green
book~grass
```

Because A/UX only insists that a password have one special character, it rests on the system administrator to ensure that users adhere to such a password standard.

Users should also be encouraged to change their passwords regularly. (See the next section for a way to force users to change their passwords.) In addition, they must be urged not to write their passwords down. If they feel they must put passwords on paper, they should keep them in a secure location, without any reference to the account name to which to the password applies. In no case should users be allowed to tape passwords to terminals. (Don't laugh; it happens.)

Password Aging

Users can be forced to change their passwords after a given period of time has passed by placing special characters in the password field of the `/etc/passwd` file. In addition, a minimum interval between password changes can also be enforced. This type of security scheme is known as *password aging.*

To enforce password aging, first create the `/etc/password` entry for the user and then give the user an initial password. The password aging characters can then be added to the end of the encrypted password field.

The aging characters are separated from the encrypted password by a comma. The next character represents, in weeks, how often the password must be changed. The following character is the minimum interval, in weeks, that must elapse between password changes. The remaining characters are the number of weeks that have passed since the last change. Although the system will maintain the number of weeks that have passed since the last change, you must enter the first two characters.

Unfortunately, you can't simply enter numbers of weeks as ordinary numbers. They must be coded according to the following scheme:

1. . (A period means 0. If the number of weeks between changes is a period, then the user will be forced to change his or her period the next time he or she logs in. If the password can be changed at any time (i.e., no minimum interval between changes) use a period for the second aging character.)
2. / (The slash represents a 1.)

3. `0` through `9` (The numbers represent 2 through 11.)
4. `A` through `Z` (The uppercase letters represent 12 through 37.)
5. `a` through `z` (The lowercase letters represent 38 through 63.)

If a user should change his or her password at least every four weeks, but no sooner than every two weeks, an `/etc/passwd` entry might appear as:

```
jon:1ci5kJLeo4LKW,20./:200:200:Jon Doe:/users/jon:/bin/sh
```

The `2` following the comma in the password field indicates that the password must be changed every four weeks; the `0` means that at least two weeks must elapse between changes. The `./` was entered by A/UX to indicate that the password was last changed a week ago.

For additional details on password aging, see the `passwd` entry in *A/UX Programmers Reference*. See the section *File Formats (4)*; the files are listed in alphabetical order.

Administrative File Security

In addition to passwords, a UNIX system's security relies heavily on the permissions given to files and directories. As you have discovered while reading Part III of this book, maintaining an A/UX system means that the system administrator is continually working with a large number of files that must be secured against unauthorized access. These files configure various parts of the system, keep logs of system activity, and run the daemons that automate regular activities.

Later in this section, you will find recommendations for permissions on a number of administrative files. Deciding which permissions to assign can be a challenging task. Consider, for example, a shell script that was written by a system administrator to summarize login/logout data. The final step in the script was to clean out the file `/etc/wtmp` (the place where login/logout data are stored). Because the system administrator wanted other users to see how the script was constructed, the script was given permissions of 744 (i.e., only the system administrator could modify or execute the script, but everyone could read it).

On the surface, there would appear to be no security risk in allowing other users to view the contents of the script. However, a regular user *copied* the script into his home directory. When he did so, he became the owner of the file and was then able to give himself execute permission. Executing the script to test it, he cleaned out `/etc/wtmp`, causing the loss of valuable system data. For the best protection of the system, the correct permissions for the script should have been 700 rather than 744!

A/UX is shipped with default permissions for its administrative files. As you will discover in the following sections, some of those permissions should be changed if you wish to restrict regular users from performing some administrative activities.

/etc Files

The `/etc` directory contains files like `passwd` and `group` that play important roles in system configuration. By default, these files are readable by everyone on the system and writable only by the superuser. However, it is often safer to make them writable by no one (i.e., read-only). The superuser can then override that restriction with `vi`'s `:w!` command. The effect is to guard against accidental writes that could inadvertently damage the files.

Suggested permissions for selected administrative files in `/etc` can be found in Table 13.1. At first glance, some of these permissions may not seem to make sense. Consider, for example, the `fsck` command. A file system check should only be performed by the system administrator while the system is in single user mode. That being the case, why do the file's group and the rest of the world have read and execute permission? The answer lies in the file's group and owner. Notice that they are `bin`, not `root`. Although `fsck` will not run unless the system is in single user mode, `root` will be unable to execute the command unless the rest of the world (into which `root` falls in this case) has execute permission. That is why many commands with an owner and group of `bin` have `755` permissions—to give `root` the right to execute them. Because these commands only run in single user mode, there is no chance that a regular user (logged in from a terminal or over a network) can have access to these commands.

Table 13.1
Suggested File Permissions for Selected Administrative Files in the Directory `/etc`

File	Owner	Group	Perm.
HOSTNAME	root	root	644
RELEASE_ID	bin	bin	644
TIMEZONE	root	root	644
dump.bsd	root	root	700
dumpdates	root	root	600
fsck	bin	bin	755
fstab	bin	bin	644
group	bin	bin	444
hosts	root	root	644
hosts.equiv	root	root	644
inittab	bin	bin	644
mkfs	bin	bin	755
mkfslib	bin	bin	755
mknod	bin	bin	755
mkslipuser	root	root	700
motd	bin	bin	644
mount	bin	bin	755
mtab	root	sys	644
newunix	bin	bin	755
passwd	root	root	444
powerdown	bin	bin	755
rc	bin	bin	755
reboot	bin	bin	755
shutdown	bin	bin	755
toolboxdaemon	bin	bin	755

/usr Files

The `/usr` directory is home to the major of the administrative files, including the system accounting files, the `cron` tables, the printing queue, and `uucp`. (Securing `uucp` is discussed later in this chapter).

Securing the Accounting Files

The majority of the accounting files are stored in `/usr/lib/acct`. With the exception of the `accton` program, all files are owned by `adm` and part of the group `adm`. The default permissions for these files can be seen in

Table 13.2
Default File Permissions for the System Accounting Files

acctcms	755
acctcon1	755
acctcon2	755
acctdisk	755
acctdusg	755
acctmerg	755
accton	755
acctprc1	755
acctprc2	755
acctwtmp	755
chargefee	755
ckpacct	755
diskusg	755
dodisk	755
fwtmp	755
holidays	755
lastlogin	755
monacct	755
nulladm	755
prctmp	755
prdaily	755
prtacct	755
ptecms.awk	755
ptelus.awk	755
remove	755
runacct	755
shutacct	755
startup	755
turnacct	755
wtmpfix	755

Table 13.2. Note that every file is executable by not only the owner and group, but by the rest of the world.

In a number of cases, you may wish to change these default permissions to prevent users other than the superuser from viewing accounting in data. In particular, `prdaily` should probably be changed to `770`, `chargefee` to `770`, and `shutacct` to `770`. Restricting `chargefee` will prevent regular users from malicously charging fees to other users; restricting `shutacct` will prevent regular users from stopping system accounting. (See Chapter 15 for details about how these files are used to collect and process accounting data.)

Table 13.3
Default Permissions for Cron Files

/usr/lib/OLDlog	644
/usr/lib/at.allow	644
/usr/lib/cron.allow	644
/usr/lib/log	644
/usr/lib/queuedefs	644
/usr/spool/cron/crontabs/adm	644
/usr/spool/cron/crontabs/crontab	644
/usr/spool/cron/crontabs/lp	444
/usr/spool/cron/crontabs/root	444
/usr/spool/cron/crontabs/uucp	644

Securing Cron Files

The cron files are stored in /usr/lib/cron and /usr/spool/cron. Their default permissions can be found in Table 13.3. If you wish to have a system that is more closed, change the permissions to restrict even read access by the rest of the world. In other words, files that have 644 permissions should be 640; files that have 444 permissions should be 440.

Securing Lp Files

The files that support printing are stored in /usr/lib and /usr/spool/lp. The default permissions appear in Table 13.4. Most of the lp commands (stored in /usr/lib) permit everyone to execute the commands. You may, however, wish to restrict execution right for commands such as accept and reject (commands that allow and disallow the queueng of lp requests).

Securing Uucp

Uucp presents two security challenges. First, you will need to secure your system from access by unauthorized external systems. Second, because some of the uucp files contain access information about systems that you call, those files must be isolated from both remote and local users.

As discussed in Chapter 13, the best way to control the access that remote systems have to yours is to use the /usr/spool/uucp/USERFILE.

Table 13.4
Default Permissions for `Lp` Files

/usr/spool/lp/ADD_AT	755
/usr/spool/lp/ADD_IW	755
/usr/spool/lp/ADD_LW	755
/usr/spool/lp/RM_PR	755
/usr/spool/lp/SCHEDLOCK	444
/usr/spool/lp/daily.ctl	644
/usr/spool/lp/default	644
/usr/spool/lp/hourly.ctl	644
/usr/spool/lp/hourly.log	644
/usr/spool/lp/log	644
/usr/spool/lp/oldlog	644
/usr/spool/lp/outputq	644
/usr/spool/lp/pstatus	644
/usr/spool/lp/seqfile	644
/usr/spool/lp/model/at_interface	755
/usr/spool/lp/model/*	644
/usr/spool/lp/class/*	644
/usr/spool/lp/member/*	644
/usr/spool/lp/request/Postscript/*	644
/usr/spool/lp/request/laser/*	644
/usr/spool/lp/transcript/laser-log	664
/usr/spool/lp/transctip/laser.opt	664
/usr/lib/accept	6755
/usr/lib/lpadmin	6755
/usr/lib/lpfx	755
/usr/lib/lpmove	6755
/usr/lib/lpshut	6755
/usr/lib/lpsched	6755
/usr/lib/pprx	6755
/usr/lib/prx	6755
/usr/lib/reject	6755

This file contains the names of systems that are allowed to call and the directories to which they will have access.

If your system is part of a network like Internet or USENET, you will probably be involved in forwarding mail and other files to other systems (i.e., you are in the middle of someones `uucp` path). By default, there is no restriction on the systems from which you will forward files and to which you will forward files. Any system that is listed in `USERFILE` and any system for which you have an L.sys entry can use you as an intermediary in a mail path. However, if you wish to restrict forwarding, use the FWDFILE and ORGFILE.

As long as neither file exists, forwarding is unrestricted. If the files exist but are empty, then no forwarding is permitted. To specify the systems to which you will forward files, enter the names of those systems in FWDFILE, one system to a line. To specify the systems and users from which you will accept files for forwarding, make an entry in ORGFILE for each. Enter the system name, followed by the names of users for whom you will forward files; separate the system name and user names by commas. For example, the line:

```
stech, sysop, tomw
```

means that files from stech sent by either sysop or tomw will be forwarded.

To secure the directories and files used by uucp, Apple recommends the permissions in Table 13.5. Notice that the binary file permissions include four numbers rather than the three you are used to seeing. The additional digit on the left governs the control a file has over its user ID and group ID when it runs. If set to 4, the file has the right to set its own user ID when it is executed. In most cases, files with this permission will set their user id to root and run as the superuser.[1]

The Restricted Shell

On occasion you may wish to set up accounts with very restricted access to the system. A convenient way to do this is to use the *restricted shell* (/bin/rsh). Users who have /bin/rsh as their login shell cannot:

1. change directory with the cd command;
2. change the value of $PATH;

1. The other available value for the sticky bit is 2. If the sticky bit is 2, then the file has the right to set its group ID. If the sticky bit is 6, then the file can set both its user and group IDs.

Table 13.5
Suggested Permissions for `uucp` Files and Directories

Directory permissions:

/usr/lib/uucp	755
/usr/spool/uucp	755
/usr/spool/uucp/.XQTDIR	777
/usr/spool/uucp/public	777
/usr/spool/uucppublic/receive	777

Binary file permissions:

/bin/uucp	4111
/bin/uulog	4111
/bin/uuname	4111
/bin/uustat	4111
/bin/uusub	4111
/bin/uux	4111
/bin/lib/uucp/uucico	4111
/bin/lib/uucp/uuclean	4111
/bin/lib/uucp/uuxqt	4111

Script files pemissions:

/usr/bin/uupick	755
/usr/bin/uuto	755
/usr/lib/uucp/uudemon.day	400
/usr/lib/uucp/uudemon.hr	400
/usr/lib/uucp/uudemon.wk	400
/usr/lib/uucp/uushell	755

`Uucp` system file permissions:

/lusr/lib/uucp/ADMIN	444
/usr/lib/uucp/FWDFILE	444
/usr/lib/uucp/L-devices	444
/usr/lib/uucp/L.cmds	444
/usr/lib/uucp/L.sys	400
/usr/lib/uucp/ORGFILE	444
/usr/lib/uucp/SQFILE	444
/usr/lib/uuc/USERFILE	444

3. issue path names containing `/`; and
4. redirect output with `>` or `>>`.

The `/bin/rsh` restrictions are enforced *after* the `.profile` has been executed. This means that the user's environment can be configured within the `.profile`. The most common scheme is to create a directory, `/usr/rbin`, and link into that directory all of the commands that the user should be able to use. The `/usr/rbin` directory is then assigned to `$PATH` within the `.profile`.

If the restricted shell is to provide effective security, then you must pay special attention to the commands that a restricted shell user is allowed to execute. The `ls` command, for example, is a "dangerous command," because it allows the user to see what files are in his or her current directory. The `rm` command is also extremely dangerous because it allows the user to delete files. In addition, the user should not own the directory in which he or she is working, nor should the user own the account's `.profile`.

To be most effective, the `/usr/rbin` directory should contain only compiled programs, shell scripts that perform a variety of functions for the user, and the commands used by the scripts. The user should have execute, but not read or write, access to the scripts. If it can be avoided, do not include the `ls` or `rm` commands in the restricted shell directory.

A system can contain more than one restricted shell directory. The use of /usr/rbin to contain restricted shell commands is merely convention. If you need to set up multiple restricted operating environments, use other directories to contain permitted commands. Then be sure to place the appropriate path name in `$PATH` in the user's `.profile`.

The restricted shell can be extremely useful when a system needs to permit full system access to some users but control others very closely. For example, when the system `stech` came on line in 1985, it had two purposes. The first was to permit the system administrator and a few associates to engage in software development activities. The second was to support a semiprivate bulletin board service (BBS). It was vitally important that the bulletin board users be isolated from the bulk of the system, protecting the development work in progress. Each bulletin board user, therefore, received a restricted shell account. The `/usr/rbin` directory contained shell scripts supporting BBS activity, the commands the shell

scripts used, the `passwd` command, and the `mail` command. The directory did not contain the `ls` command. Instead, the BBS administrator wrote a "help" script that explained what commands (i.e., scripts) were available. BBS users had write permission on only one directory, the directory set aside for uploaded software. They did not own their own login directories or `.profiles`.

The restricted shell is documented on page 16 of the `sh` documentation in *A/UX Command Reference (M–Z and Games)*. See the section *User Commands (1)*; the commands are in alphabetical order.

System Backup

Good system back up is even more important to a multiuser computer system than it is to a single user system. At least, if your stand-alone system loses a disk, you are the only one affected. On the other hand, when an A/UX system loses a disk, potentially many people are affected. For that reason, backup should be performed regularly.

Although there are many backup schemes, one generally accepted method is known as *grandparent-parent–child*. It means that you will keep three sets of backup disks or tapes. Each time you backup the system, you reuse the oldest of the three.

How often backups are made and how much of the system is backed up depends largely on system activity. Full system back ups require a great deal of time. It may be adequate for a moderately active system to be backed up completely only once a week, with incremental backups (backups of those files that have changed since the last backup was done) made once a day. Under that sort of scheme, you would keep three generations of complete backups as well as three sets of weekly incremental backups.

The easiest way to back up an A/UX system is to purchase an Apple Tape Backup 40SC. (Unfortunately, none of the other tape drives available today will recognize A/UX disk partitions.) This tape drive will back up both A/UX and Macintosh OS disk partitions. If you have the tape drive, follow the directions in its instruction manual to perform backups. There is one drawback to using the Apple Tape Backup 40 SC from the Macintosh OS: Its software will only back up and restore entire disk partitions;

therefore it isn't terribly practical for incremental backups. The alternative is to back up to floppy disks.

There are three A/UX utilities that can be used for backup: `cpio`, `tar`, and `dump.bsd`. (These utilities will also address the Apple Tape Backup 40SC, although it is much simpler to use the disk drive's software when backing up entire partitions.) `Cpio` is best suited to backups of individual files and directories; `dump.bsd` is best suited for full system backups, although it can also be used for incremental backups.[2]

Using Cpio

The `cpio` command is most useful for backing up small quantities of files or directories. Because it cannot spread its output over more than one disk or tape, the command can transfer only 800K to a disk or 38.5 Mb to an Apple SC40 Tape Drive tape. If the end of the media is encountered before the command is completed, you will be forced to abort and begin again.

Creating Cpio Archives

`Cpio` must be fed the names of the files and the directories that it is to copy. The easiest way to do this is to pipe it the results of an `ls` (to copy everything in a directory) or a `find` (to be more selective about what is copied). To copy the contents of the current directory to the disk in `floppy0`, the command is issued as:

```
ls | cpio -oB > /dev/rfloppy0
```

The `-o` flag option instructs `cpio` to produce output; the `B` option provides the correct record block size for a floppy disk. Notice also that the floppy

---

2. The `tar` command is slower than either `cpio` or `dump.bsd`. Its primary advantage is its ability to transfer files between a variety of UNIX machines. Because it is of less use as a backup tool than either `cpio` or `dump.bsd`, it is not discussed here. However, you can find documentation for using `tar` in Chapter 4 of *A/UX Local System Administration* and *A/UX Command Reference (M–Z and Commands)*; see the section *User Commands (1)*, where the commands are in alphabetical order.

drive device file has been specified as a raw (character) rather than a block device.

If the archive is to be created on tape, the process is slightly more complicated. The `cpio` output must be filtered through a program named `tcb` to obtain correct blocking of the tape records. Therefore, archiving the current directory to tape is typed as:

```
ls | cpio -o | tcb > /dev/rmt/tc1
```

This assumes that the tape drive has an, SCSI address of 1. If it does not, then replace the 1 in `tc1` with the correct SCSI ID.

When you need to archive selected files, use `find`. For example, incremental backups can be performed by using `find`'s `-mtime` option:

```
find -mtime 1 -exec ls "{}" ";" | cpio -o | tcb > /dev/rmt/tc1
```

The `-mtime` option will retrieve all files whose modification dates are more than one day old. The `-exec` portion of the command will pass the path name of any files identified through the pipe to `cpio`.

Restoring from a Cpio Archive

To restore the files and directories in a `cpio` archive, use the `-i` flag option. For example:

```
cpio -idum < /dev/rfloppy0
```

will copy everything from the disk in the Macintosh's right floppy drive into the current directory. The `d` option instructs `cpio` to create directories as needed; `u` means that all files from the archive will be copied, even if files with the same name and later modification dates exist in the current directory. The `m` option ensures that copied files and directories will retain the modification dates and times that they had when they were archived.

If you need to restore specific files or directories, place their names after the flag options, separated by a space:

```
cpio -idum NewLog OldLog < /dev/rfloppy0
```

If you can't remember which files are in an archive, ask `cpio` for a table of contents with:

```
cpio -it
```

The `cpio` command is documented in *A/UX Command Reference (A–L)*. See the section *User Commands (1)*; the commands are in alphabetical order.

Using Dump.bsd

Although `dump.bsd` is a bit harder to use than `cpio`, it is handy for full system backups. It can also be used for daily incremental backups. It has a companion program, `restore`, that is used to restore from disks or tapes created by `dump.bsd`.

Making Backups

Unlike `cpio`, `dump.bsd` will not format media as it is copying. You should, therefore, format a few more tapes or floppy disks than you think you will need before beginning..

`Dump.bsd` has the general format:

```
dump.bsd <keys> <arguments> <file system to back up>
```

Instead of flag options, the command uses *keys*. The major difference is that keys are not preceded by a dash. The most commonly used keys are:

1. dump level: The dump level is a number from 0 to 9. A dump level of 0 specifiies a full backup of the file system on the command line. Higher dump levels will back up those files that have been changed since the dump with the next lowest dump level was taken. For example, if a level 1 dump is taken on Monday, all files modified since the last level 0 backup was taken will be included. On Tuesday, a level 2 dump will back up all files that have been modified since Monday's level 1 dump. A common scheme is to perform a full system dump (level 0) at the end of the work week, level 1 on Monday, level 2 on Tuesday, level 3 on Wednesday, and so on.

2. c: The c key sets the blocking factor for the Apple SC40 Tape Drive. The tape drive (/dev/tape) is the default output device for dump.bsd.
3. f <device>: The f key indicates that some device other than an Apple SC40 Tape Drive should be used. It is followed by the name of the alternate device. In most cases, this will be the floppy disk, /dev/floppy0. (If the Macintosh has a second floppy drive and you wish to use that drive for the backup, the device file is /dev/floppy1).
4. F: The F key configures dump.bsd for use with the Macintosh's internal floppy. It assumes that you will be using 800K disks.
5. u: The u flag instructs dump.bsd to write the date, level of the dump, and file system that was backed up to the file /etc/dumpdates. The program will consult this file on subsequent dumps to determine exactly what files should be backed up. Dump.bsd expects /etc/dumpdates to exist and will abort if it does not. Therefore, before you run dump.bsd for the first time, type:

   ```
   touch /etc/dumpdates
   ```

   The touch command sets the modification date and time of a file to the current date and time; it creates the file if it does not exist.

To run dump.bsd to make a full system backup to tape, issue the command as:

```
dump.bsd 0uc /dev/rdsk/c1d0s0
```

In this particular command, the file system that is being backed up is on a disk with SCSI address 1. Notice that the device file name is given in the raw, or character, device format. If the block device file name (e.g., /dev/dsk/c1d0s0) is used, dump.bsd will nonetheless use the character device file.

To perform an incremental backup to floppy disk, the command might be typed:

```
dump.bsd 2uFf /dev/floppy0 /dev/rdsk/c1d0s0
```

Be sure to place the device file name for the target of the backup before the device file name of the file system that is to be backed up.

`Dump.bsd` keeps you informed of the progress of the dump and will ask you to change media as needed:

```
DUMP: Date of this level 2 dump: Tue Jun 13 13:02:56 1989
DUMP: Date of last level 0 dump: Fri Jun 9 17:02:55 1989
DUMP: Dumping /dev/rdsk/c1d0s0 to /dev/floppy0
DUMP: mapping (Pass I) [regular files]
DUMP: mapping (Pass II) [directories]
DUMP: estimated 25102 tape blocks on 15.65 tape(s).
DUMP: dumping (Pass III) [directories]
DUMP: dumping (Pass IV) [regular files]
DUMP: Floppy ejecting
DUMP: Change floppy: Mount floppy #2
DUMP: NEEDS ATTENTION: Is the new floppy mounted and ready to go?: ("yes" or
"no") yes
DUMP: floppy 2 begins with blocks from ino 21
DUMP: Floppy ejecting
DUMP: Change floppy: Mount floppy #3
DUMP: NEEDS ATTENTION: Is the new floppy mounted and ready to go?: ("yes" or
"no") yes
DUMP: floppy 3 begins with blocks from ino 59
DUMP: Floppy ejecting
DUMP: Change floppy: Mount floppy #4
DUMP: NEEDS ATTENTION: Is the new floppy mounted and ready to go?: ("yes" or
"no") yes
DUMP: floppy 4 begins with blocks from ino 104
DUMP: 36.99% done, finished in 0:42
DUMP: Floppy ejecting
DUMP: Change floppy: Mount floppy #5
DUMP: NEEDS ATTENTION: Is the new floppy mounted and ready to go?: ("yes" or
"no") yes
```

`Dump.bsd` first traverses the file system to determine which files and directories need to be backed up (the "mapping" steps). It then estimates the number of tapes or disks needed to complete the backup. (Even though the dialog says "tape," don't panic; if `/dev/floppy0` appeared on the command line as an argument to the `f` key, the backup will nonetheless be to floppy disk.) Unfortunately, `dump.bsd`'s estimates are often low. If you

have only the number of disks or tapes indicated by the command dialog, abort the dump with `CTRL-C` and format some more before restarting.

Periodically, `dump.bsd` will indicate the proportion of the backup that is completed and an estimate, in minutes, of how long it will take to complete the process. Just like the estimate of the number of disks or tapes needed, these estimates are also often low.

As you change media, number the disks or tapes carefully. The restore program will expect you to supply disks in the correct order.

Theoretically, `dump.bsd` should eject floppy disks whenever one is filled. However, even though the dialog indicates that the disk is being ejected, it stays firmly planted in the disk drive. If you are going to back up to floppy disks, be sure to have a manual Macintosh disk ejector handy. (A manual Macintosh disk ejector is nothing more than an unbent heavy-duty paper clip that you can stick into the little hole to the right of the disk drive.)

The `dump.bsd` command is documented in *A/UX System Administrator's Guide*. See the section *Maintenance Commands (1M)*; the commands are in alphabetical order.

Restoring From a Dump.bsd Backup

The `restore` program will restore all or some of the programs in a `dump.bsd` archive. If you need to restore all of the files from a set of backup disks, do the following:

1. Change the directory to the one into which the files are to be placed.
2. Place the first disk in the backup set into the drive. (By default, `restore` reads `/dev/floppy0`).
3. Type:

   ```
   restore r
   ```

   Change disks whenever `restore` prompts you to do so. Be sure to insert the disks in the correct order.

Be very careful when issuing the command in this manner. Because it restores to the current directory, there is a risk that you could accidentally overwrite portions of a file system that you did not intend to.

To restore from the tape drive, you must use the analog of `dump.bsd`'s `f` key, as in:

```
restore rf /dev/tape
```

This command restores from the Apple SC40 Tape Drive into the current directory.

To restore specific files, use the `x` key, as in:

```
restore x /usr/lib/uucp
```

The `restore` program searches the disk in `floppy0` for the directory `/usr/spool/uucp`. It will restore the directory, its file, all its subdirectories, and all their files and subdirectories, placing the top of the hierarchy in the current directory. If you wish to restore a directory but not its contents, issue the command with the `h` option:

```
restore xh /usr/lib/uucp
```

Keep in mind that it is up to you to place the correct `dump.bsd` archive disk in the disk drive. `Restore` has no way of knowing the disk on which a given file or directory is stored.

An entire restoration does not need to be performed in a single sitting. The `R` key permits you to specify a disk or tape number with which the process should begin. If, for example, you need to begin with disk 12, the command might be typed as:

```
restore rR 12
```

The `restore` command is documented in *A/UX System Administrator's Reference*. See the section *Maintenance Commands (1M)*; the commands are in alphabetical order.

Chapter 14

Communications Maintenance

A UNIX machine without some sort of communications is a sad computer. One of the things that makes UNIX so powerful is its ability to interact with other UNIX systems. A good portion of a system administrator's time is, therefore, usually occupied by handling communications. This chapter looks at setting up and maintaining `uucp` as well as working with B-NET and the "yellow pages."

Managing Uucp

As discussed in Chapter 7, `uucp` is a file transfer facility that can be invoked from the command line. It also handles the transfer of electronic mail. Setting up and maintaining `uucp` can be a bit of a challenge. Because `uucp` dials other computer automatically, A/UX must know the following each time it is instructed to call another system:

1. The name of the system being called.
2. The serial port through which the call is to be placed.
3. The telephone number that is to be dialed.
4. The sequence of commands required to log in to the remote system.

In addition, `uucp` maintains log files and spool directories that must be cleaned out every so often.

All of the information that `uucp` needs to operate is stored in a set of files that are modified, as needed, by the system administrator. These include:

1. `/etc/inittab`: Any port that will accept incoming calls must have a process called a `getty` started for that port. Ports that are to be used for outgoing calls must have their `getty` disabled.
2. `/usr/spool/cron/crontabs/uucp`: The `uucp cron` table contains entries for commands that perform regular maintenance on the `uucp` system.
3. `/usr/lib/uucp/L-devices`: The `L-devices` file identifies the ports that will be used for `uucp` communications.

4. /usr/lib/uucp/L.sys: The L.sys file describes system names, the ports that should be used to call remote systems, the numbers that should be called, and the login sequences. Developing L.sys entries that work is one of the greatest challenges of uucp management.

The uucp system uses a great many more files than the primary files just mentioned. For an exhaustive list, see Appendix A in *A/UX Local System Administration*.

Setting Up the Ports

The first part of any uucp system is the serial ports through which communications take place. Ports that should be polled to check for incoming calls must have a getty running; ports that will be used for outgoing calls should have the getty disabled.

As shipped, /etc/inittab contains the line:

```
00:2:off:/etc/getty tty0 at_9600  #Port tty0 (modem); set to "respawn
```

The port tty0 is intended for use by a modem (tty1 is intended to be used for a direct connection to a printer). Because the action field contains off, this port can be used for outgoing calls. However, if the port should be polled for incoming calls, the off must be replaced with respawn. As you will remember from Chapter 11, respawn will restart the getty whenever the system detects that the process has died.

The at_9600 indicates the maximum speed that is supported for the port. If the modem attached to the port cannot transmit at that speed, change at_9600 to reflect the modem's maximum speed. For a 2,400–baud modem, use at_2400.

If your system includes additional serial ports that will be used for communication, add lines for them to /etc/inittab. Assume that you have added a plug-in board with four serial ports (ttya0, ttya1, ttya2, and ttya3). Two of the ports will be used for outgoing calls, the other two for incoming calls. The /etc/inittab entries would be:

```
a0:2:off:/etc/getty ttya0 at_2400
a1:2:off:/etc/getty ttya1 at_4800
```

```
a2:2:respawn:/etc/getty ttya2 at_2400
a3:2:respawn:/etc/getty ttya3 at_4800
```

Notice that two of the lines (`ttya0` and `ttya2`) support transmission at up to 2,400 baud; the remaining two lines will handle 4,800 baud.

In addition to changes in `/etc/inittab`, make certain that the following lines in `/etc/rc` are not commented out (i.e., that they don't have pound signs as their first character):

```
/bin/chmod 666 /dev/tty0
/bin/chown daemon /dev/tty0
/bin/chown daemon /dev/tty0
```

If some port other than `tty0` is a dialout port, or if you have added more serial ports, insert analogous lines in `/etc/rc`. For example, if the port `ttya1` will be used for dialing out, then `/etc/rc` should contain:

```
/bin/chmod 666 /dev/ttya1
/bin/chown daemon /dev/ttya1
/bin/chown daemon /dev/ttya1
```

If these changes are not made, `uucp` will not have the right to access the device files that it needs to dial out.

Identifying Communications Devices

The entries in `/etc/inittab` identify what programs should be running for a communications port. However, they say nothing about what kind of device is attached to a port. That information is found in `/usr/lib/uucp/L-devices`.

In most cases, a serial port will have either a modem or a direct serial connection to another computer. Assuming that a 2,400–baud modem is connected to `tty0`, `L-devices` contains the following three lines:

```
DIR tty0 0 300
DIR tty0 0 1200
DIR tty0 0 2400
```

The column at the left identifies the type of device. In most cases this will be DIR, for a direct connection or a modem.[1] The second column contains the name of the port, followed by a placeholder (the zero)[2] and the speed with which a connection can be made. Notice that there is one entry for each speed at which the modem can transmit.

Creating L.sys Entries

The entries in /usr/lib/uucp/L.sys connect the names of systems you will be calling with the procedure for actually making the call. A typical line in the file looks like:

```
stech ANY tty0 2400 "" "" ATDT5551234^M  2400 ^MBREAK ogin: nuucp
```

The first field contains the name of the system that will be called. This does not necessarily need to be the actual name of the system. It is really just a name with which uucp can identify which line in L.sys to use. For example, if you call the same system, but use more than one login ID, you may set up a different L.sys entry for each. Give then unique names (e.g., stech1 and stech2) and then use whichever is appropriate when invoking uucp or mail.

The second field indicates what time calls may be placed. If the field contains ANY, then calls can be placed any time on any day. However, the calling time can also be restricted. The days of the week on which calling is permitted are listed as Mo, Tu, We, Th, Fr, Sa, and Su. The times during which calling is permitted are identified using a 24-hour clock. If calling is permitted only during nonworking hours, then the field would contain:

```
MoTuWeThFr1730-0800SaSu
```

---

1. In other UNIX systems, a modem is considered an ACU (automatic calling unit). However, A/UX insists that modems be treated as direct connections, making it a bit more difficult to arrive at a satisfactory L.sys dialing protocol.
2. If you have an ACU, use ACU in the leftmost field and replace the placeholder with the name of the ACU.

Notice that there are no spaces anywhere in this string. Because SaSu is not followed by any time interval, calling will be permitted at any time.

The third field contains the port through which the call should be made, followed by the calling speed. The pair of double quotes that follows is a placeholder for a telephone number (it is used only by an ACU). The remainder of the line is a sequence of items that uucp should send to the port and then expect to receive back from the communications line.

The sequence of actions begins with what uucp should receive from the line. In most cases, uucp expects nothing. Therefore, the send-receive sequence begins with a pair of double quotes with no spaces between them. Uucp must then send the modem dialing string:

```
ATDT5551234^M
```

The ^M is a carriage return. To type it using vi, don't simply press CTRL-M. Instead, type CTRL-V and then the CTRL-M. The above dialing string assumes that a Hayes-compatible modem is attached to tty0. If you have another type of modem, you will need to consult the modem's documentation to determine exactly how to send the command to dial the phone.

After sending the command to dial the phone, uucp waits for a message containing 2400. This is the last part of the CONNECT 2400 message that the modem on the other end of the line will send when a connection is made. In most cases, the message that uucp should expect to receive is written as the last few characters of the entire message; occasionally the first few characters will be lost.

Once the connection is made, uucp sends a carriage return followed by a break. The break is sent because stech's 2,400–baud modem answers at 1,200 baud and requires the break as a signal to cycle to the higher speed. At that point, the prompt login: should be received. That appears in L.sys as ogin:, leaving off the first character just in case it is lost in transmission. Finally, uucp sends the login name, nuucp. Stech has no password on its nuucp account; therefore, the L.sys entry does not expect to receive the password prompt nor does it transmit a password.

If the system that is being called has a password on the login name, the L.sys entry will end with:

```
ssword: fred
```

where `ssword:` is the last portion of the `Password:` prompt and `fred` is the password on the account in question.

Two very important things should be mentioned at this point. Because `L.sys` contains the phone numbers, account names, and passwords of other systems, it presents a serious security risk. Its permissions should be set so that only the superuser can read and write to the file; no other user should even have read access. Second, developing `L.sys` entries is a highly system-dependent process. The best strategy is to ask the system administrator of a system you will be calling to supply you with an entry that he or she believes will work. Then modify the entry to conform to A/UX's specific requirements.

Watching Uucp at Work

There is a significant element of trial and error involved with creating working `L.sys` entries. The process can be made a bit easier by using the `uucico` program with debugging turned on. When `uucico` is running in debugging mode, you will see the send-receive sequence from the `L.sys` entry.

In most cases, you will want to have a transcript of what occurred while you were trying to place a call. The easiest way to obtain one is to use the `term` utility, recording lines off the top of the screen. In a `term` window, become the superuser and type:

```
/usr/lib/uucp/uucico -r1 -s <system name> -x4 &
```

The -r flag option instructs `uucico` to place a remote call instead of working locally. The -s option is followed by the name of the `L.sys` entry you wish to test. Finally, the debugging level is set with the -x option. Level 4 is a moderate amount of information; to obtain the maximum verbosity, use level 9 (`-x9`). Notice also that this command is run in the background. If something goes wrong, you will then be able to use `kill` to terminate `uucico`.

Keeping Uucp Clean

Unless something is done about them, the uucp log files will continue to grow in size. In addition, there should be some limit to the length of time files will be allowed to stay in a queue for transfer. Although the cleanup can be handled manually, A/UX has three shell scripts (uudemon.hr, uudemon.day, and uudemon.wk) that can be used to automate the process. The functions that these scripts perform include:

1. uudemon.hr
   a. Runs uucico to transmit any files that are queued
2. uudemon.day
   a. Runs uuclean to remove any files that have been queued more that 168 hours. Mail will be sent to the user who queued the file, notifying him or her that the file has been deleted from the queue.
   b. Moves the daily log file, LOGFILE, to the end of the weekly log file, Log-WEEK. This process deletes LOGFILE.
   c. Runs uusub to gather statistics about uucp traffic during the past 24 hours.
3. uudemon.wk
   a. Adds the previous week's log file (stored in o.Log-WEEK) to o.SYSLOG.
   b. Moves the current week's log file (Log-WEEK) to o.Log-WEEK.
   c. Packs (compresses) the archival log files, o.Log-WEEK and o.SYSLOG.

The easiest way to manage the cleanup activities is to create a cron table named /usr/spool/cron/crontabs/uucp. It should contain the three lines:

```
56 * * * * /bin/su uucp -c "/usr/lib/uucp/uudemon.hr > /dev/null"
0 4 * * * /bin/su uucp -c "/usr/lib/uucp/uudemon.day > /dev/null"
30 5 * * 1 /bin/su uucp -c "/usr/lib/uucp/uudemon.wk > /dev/null"
```

The hourly daemon will run at 56 minutes after every hour, the daily

daemon at 4:00 a.m. every day, and the weekly daemon at 5:30 a.m. on the first of every month.

Letting Other Systems Call You

If other systems are to call you, they must have a login sequence for their own `L.sys` file. In most cases, they will logging in to the account named `nuucp`. This generic login is often left without a password to allow the greatest number of systems to exchange electronic mail. However, it is not as great a security risk as you might think.

The `/etc/passwd` entry for `nuucp` usually looks like:

```
nuucp::5:5:Open uucp login:/usr/spool/uucp:/usr/lib/uucp/uucico
```

Notice that the default shell is actually the program `uucico`. When a system logs in under `nuucp`, your system will automatically run `uucico`. When the program is terminated, whoever is logged in is logged out. The `nuucp` account has no access to the shell; the only thing that can be done with that login is run `nuucp`.

Even though `nuucp` may have no password, that is not enough to give calling system access to your system. Each remote system that should be allowed to exchange files with you must have an entry in `/usr/spool/uucp/USERFILE`. `USERFILE` indicates the directories to which a calling system has access. By default, it has only one line:

```
                    /usr/spool/uucppublic
```

The comma at the left is required. The line gives users on the local machine the right to send mail or to send files from the `/usr/spool/uucppublic` directory to another system. To give other systems access, `USERFILE` must be modified, as in:

```
stech, nuucp            /usr/spool/uucppublic
husc6, nuucp            /usr/spool/uucppublic
```

The left column contains the name of a system that is to be permitted to log in. It is followed by a comma and the login the system will use. The third field is a list of directories to which the remote system will have access. In most cases, access is restricted to `/usr/spool/uucppublic`. However, multiple directories can be supplied if they are separated by commas.

Enabling Incoming Mail

The file `/usr/lib/uucp/L.cmds` contains a list of the commands that a calling system can execute. If users on your machine are to be able to receive mail from other systems, then `L.cmds` should contain at least one line:

```
rmail
```

You may add other commands to this file if needed. However, leaving the file with only the `rmail` command will provide the maximum amount of security for the `uucp` system.

Local Area Networks and Internet

A/UX systems are often linked to one another in a local area network (LAN). LANs can be created with direct serial cabling (`slip` connections) or by equipping each A/UX machine with an Ethernet board and using coaxial cable.

If an LAN is never going to communicate with any other network, then there is no need to worry about uniquely identifying the machines on the network. However, most UNIX LANs have regular communications with the rest of the world via informal networks such as Internet or USENET. If your LAN falls into this category, then you will need an Internet address. You will need the Internet address when you configure A/UX for networking.

Internet addresses are assigned by SRI International without charge. To obtain one, call (800) 235-3155. While you are waiting for an official number, you can set up your network with a dummy number. The dummy number should adhere to one of the three following formats:

1. X, where X is between 1 and 126, as in:

   ```
   120
   ```

   This represents a class A (one–byte host number) network.
2. X.Y, where X is between 128 and 191 and Y is between 1 and 254, as in:

   ```
   150.2
   ```

   This represents a class B (two–byte host number) network.
3. X.Y.Z, where X is between 192 and 223 and Y and Z are between 1 and 254, as in:

   ```
   200.56.12
   ```

   Such a number represents a class C (three–byte host number) network.

The numbers discussed above identify an entire LAN, not the individual host machines that are part of the LAN. You must, therefore, add enough numbers to the Internet address to bring the length to four bytes. Assuming that a network has three host machines, then individual addresses can be assigned as:

Class A	120.1.1.1 120.1.1.2 120.1.1.3
Class B	150.2.1.1 150.2.2.1 150.2.3.1
Class C	220.56.12.1 220.56.12.2 220.56.12.3

These addresses represent the three host machines in a single LAN. In addition to the host computers, the LAN may also support terminals that access the host computers, modems, and printers.

A special form of the Internet address is the *Internet broadcast address*. This is an Internet address where the host portion, that portion that identifies the individual host machines on the LAN, is all 1s. For example, the following represent Internet broadcast addresses:

```
120.255.255.255
150.2.255.255
220.56.12,255
```

Each `255` represents a byte that is all 1s.

During the network configuration process, you may be asked for a *netmask*. A netmask is a string of 0s and 1s that can be used to isolate the network portion of an Internet address from the host system portion.[3] For a class A network the mask for a class A network is `0xFF000000`, for a class B network `0xFFFF00000`, and a class C network `0xFFFFFF00`. The `0x` indicates that the number that follows is in hexadecimal.

For additional information about Internet addresses, see pages 2-5 through 2-8 of *A/UX Network System Administration*.

Setting Up a Simple Network

A/UX supports two network protocols, B-NET (the TCP/IP protocol) and NFS (Network File System). The B-NET commands are supported by NFS. Unless you are short on main memory, you should install NFS. If you are creating your network with serial cables rather than Ethernet, you must also install the `slip` facility.

3. For those of you who understand binary operations, the mask is ANDed with the bits in the Internet address.

For more information about configuring networks, see Chapters 2 and 3 of *A/UX Network System Administration.*

To enable networking with NFS, do the following:

1. Modify `/etc/inittab` so that the network daemons will be started when the system is brought to run level 2.

Change:	To:
`nfs0:2:off:/etc/portmap`	`nfs:2:wait:/etc/portmap`
`net4:2:off:/usr/etc/in,routed`	`net4:2:wait:/usr/etc/in.routed`
`net5:2:off:/usr/etc/in.rwhod`	`net5:2:once:/usr/etc/in.rwhod`
`net9:2:off:/etc/inetd`	`net9:2:respawn:/etc/inetd`

2. Add the Internet addresses of other host systems on the network to `/etc/hosts`. As shipped, the file contains a single address (the loopback address that can be used to test networking without actually accessing another machine):

   ```
   0x7F.0x00.0x00.0x01      loop lo loo localhost
   ```

   For each host in addition to the machine with which you are working, add one line to the file. If the network has an Internet address of `150.2` and the current machine is `1.2`, then the other two machines are added as:

   ```
   150.2.1.1                dragon dg drag
   150.2.3.1                chimera ch chmra
   ```

   The first field contains a machine's Internet address. The remaining fields contain the machine's name and any aliases by which the system is known.
3. Create a new A/UX kernel with network support.
   a. Give the `root` account access to the shell scripts that will be used to create the new kernel:

```
chmod 755 /etc/newunix
chmod 755 /etc/install.d/*
```

b. If in multiuser mode, shut down to single user mode, then create the new kernel. If using Ethernet, type:

```
/etc/newunix nfs
```

If using serial cabling, type:

```
/etc/newunix nfs slip
```

c. Enter the commands:

```
sync
sync
reboot
```

Do not, however, allow A/UX to restart automatically. If your system is set up for automatic launch, cancel the launch so that you are left at the stand-alone shell. Then type:

```
launch newunix
```

Respond with `y` to the question about checking the root file system. Ignore any messages that you see. If the file system check forces a reboot, do not allow the system to reboot automatically. Instead, issue the `launch newunix` command again.

The `launch newunix` will force a reboot. In this case, allow A/UX to reboot in its normal manner. If your system does not boot automatically, boot by typing a command-b as usual.

d. Answer any questions that are asked during the system boot. If not already present, you will be asked for a host name (your system's name, e.g., `gryphon`) and a domain

name (a name for a group of systems that are identified as a unit, e.g., `mythicals` is the domain name for `gryphon`, `dragon`, and `chimera`).

If A/UX detects an Ethernet board, you will also be prompted for your machine's Internet address, the Internet broadcast address, and the netmask.

4. Enter multiuser mode and test the installation. Become the superuser and type:

   ```
   telnet loop
   ```

   Assuming that your system name is `gryphon`, you should see:

   ```
   A/UX Apple Computer, Inc. (gryphon)

   login:
   ```

   Press `CTRL-C` to exit the testing process.

For additional information on the `telnet` command, see *A/UX Command Reference (M–Z and Games)*. See the section *User Commands (1)*; the commands are in alphabetical order.

5. Repeat the installation process for each host on the network. Use the `ping` command to test the connections. For example, to test `gryphon`'s connection with `dragon`, type:

   ```
   /usr/etc/ping dragon
   ```

   The `ping` command attempts to send 64– byte packets of data to the remote system and then waits for an echo of the packet back to the local system. It reports its progress with output like:

   ```
   64 bytes from 150.2.1.1: icmp_seqno=0. time=18. ms
   64 bytes from 150.2.1.1: icmp_seqno=1: time=18. ms
   64 bytes from 150.2.1.1: icmp_seqno=2: time=18. ms
   64 bytes from 150.2.1.1: icmp_seqno=3: time=18. ms
   ```

Once four or more packets have been received back from the remote system, press `CTRL-C` to interrupt transmission. The `ping` command will then summarize its efforts:

```
----dragon PING Statistics----
4 packets transmitted, 4 packets received, 0% packet loss
round-trip (ms) min/avg/max = 18/18/18
```

Completing a Slip Installation

If your network will be using serial connections (either direct serial lines or modems), then there are four additional steps required before other machines can communicate with yours.

1. Add an Internet address to `/etc/slip.config` for each system that will be accessing yours over a serial line. Assume, for example, that `dragon` and `chimera` will be calling `gryphon`. The available serial ports are `ttya0` and `ttya2`. The `/etc/slip.config` file will contain:

   ```
   150.2.1.1
   150.2.1.1
   150.2.1.3
   150.2.1.3
   ```

   There is one entry for each serial line that can be used for a `slip` connection.
2. If you have not already done so, add the names of other slip hosts on your network to `/etc/hosts`. This file associates system names with Internet addresses.
3. Add an entry to `/etc/slip.hosts` for every user on every machine that will be calling yours using a `slip` connection. This file associates user names with Internet addresses. It has the general format:

```
<Internet address> <user name>
```

Users with accounts on `dragon` and `chimera` might be identified to `gryphon` with:

```
150.2.1.1   sysop
150.2.1.2   leslie
150.2.1.3   raoul
150.2.3.1   jackp
150.2.3.2   stoney
```

4. Complete the process by running `mkslipuser`. The `mkslipuser` command generates the file `/etc/slip.user`. (Don't try to look at the contents of this file; it's not a text file.)

Completing NFS Installation

Once you have completed the preceding steps for each host in your network, users will be able to use B-NET commands to log on to remote systems. NFS, however, allows a remote machine to mount and use a file system on a host machine (the *server*).

To become an NFS server, do the following:

1. Enable the NFS daemon by changing the action of the `nfs3` entry in `/etc/inittab` to `wait`. The line should appear as:

```
nfs3:2:wait:/etc/nfsd 4
```

2. Make sure that the line:

```
rpc   udp   /usr/etc/rpc.mountd 100005 1
```

appears in `/etc/servers`. The daemon `inetd` (also started by an entry in `etc/inittab`) runs all of the programs listed in that file.

3. Make entries in `/etc/exports` to indicate which of your file systems can be mounted by other machines on the network. The file

has the general format:

```
<file system name> <remote system name>
```

A/UX requires you to allow the entire root file system to be mounted. If everyone on the network should be able to mount your file system, the /etc/exports entry is simply:

```
/
```

If gryphon wants to allow dragon to mount its root file system (but not chimera), then the entry is written:

```
/       dragon
```

Setting Up an NFS Client

Machines that use NFS to mount file systems on servers are called *clients*. To complete configuration of a client, do the following:

1. Make sure that /etc/passwd has an entry for a user named nobody:

   ```
   nobody:xxxxxxxxxxxxx:65534:65543:NFS generic user:/tmp:/bin/noshell
   ```

2. Edit /etc/inittab, changing the action of nfs4 and nfs8 so that the lines appear as:

   ```
   nfs4:2:wait:/etc/biod 4
   nfs8:2:once:/etc/mount -at nfs >/dev/syscon 2>&1
   ```

3. Modify /etc/fstab to include the names of file systems on NFS servers that should be mounted by /etc/mount when the system is brought to multiuser mode. When adding a remote file system to /etc/fstab, preface the file system name with the name of the server; separate the server's name from the file sys-

tem name with a colon.

If dragon will be mounting gryphon's root file system, the entry would appear as:

```
gryphon:/ /mnt nfs rw 1 1
```

As you will remember from Chapter 12, the first field is the name of the file system being mounted. The second is its mount point on the local system. The third field contains the file system type (nfs for all systems mounted from NFS servers), followed by the mount options. In this particular example, the file system is mounted as a read/write file system (i.e., users on the remote machine can modify those files and directories for which they have write permission). The line ends with the dump level (see the discussion of dump.bsd in Chapter 15 for details) and the fsck pass number. The latter is ignored for remotely mounted file systems.

The NFS mount options are somewhat different from those used when mounting local file systems. Among the most commonly used are:

a. rw (read/write)
b. ro (read only)
c. hard (continue a mount attempt until it is successful)
d. soft (make only one attempt at mounting; if it fails, return an error message)

For additional details on NFS file system mounting options, see pages 3-13 through 31-15 in *A/UX Network System Administration*.

Configuring Network Mail

To enable the automatic transfer of mail within a network, you must modify /etc/inittab to start the mail daemon and optionally modify a configuration file. Begin by changing the action field of the sendmail entry in /etc/inittab so that entry reads as:

```
net8:2:once:/usr/lib/sendmail -bd -q30m
```

This version of the command will instruct `sendmail` to check the incoming mail port regularly and to check the mail queue for outgoing mail every 30 minutes.

If you wish to customize `sendmail`, use a text editor to modify the configuration file `/usr/lib/sendmail.m4`, a portion of which can be seen in Figure 14.1. As you can see from the documentation in the file, most of the lines that are not comments should begin with undefine for a simple network (e.g., one with a single domain).

The last four noncomment lines provide mail–forwarding information. The `L_USERREALY` field, for example, specifies the name of a machine on the network that should receive any mail addressed to a host not a part of the network; mail to unknown machines (not necessarily hosts) is sent to `L_RELAYHOST`.

If you have made changes to `sendmail.m4`, the changes must be installed with the command line:

```
m4 /usr/lib/sendmail.m4 > /usr/lib/sendmail.cf
```

The process is completed by freezing the new configuration with:

```
/usr/lib/sendmail -bz
```

For additional details on `sendmail`, see pages 7-32 through 7-34 and Appendix A of *A/UX Network System Administration*.

Monitoring a Network

Once a network is configured, the bulk of the system administrator's work involves making certain that the network is running as it should. A number of A/UX commands provide valuable monitoring information.

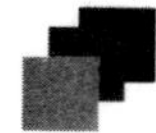

```
# local definitions

# define the simple local name.  If your domain server, etc.
#        are set up so that gethostname returns a simple name
#        don't define anything
undefine(L_SITE_M,salmon)
undefine(L_SITE_C,salmon)

# define the local domain.  L_DOMAIN_M is the main domain
#        name.  L_DOMAIN_C is a space separated list of
#        all the domains to be considered local.  If you aren't
#        using the name server this should only be defined if
#        gethostbyname(fully_qualified_name) will work.  Ie.
#        yp or /etc/hosts must have fully qualified names in
#        it.
undefine(L_DOMAIN_M,apple)
undefine(L_DOMAIN_C,apple)

# define the local universe.  As above UNIVERSE_M is the
#        main universe.  UNIVERSE_C is all universes to
#        be considered local.  Use undefine if site names
#        are only two deep.  (site.domain)
undefine(L_UNIVERSE_M,com)
undefine(L_UNIVERSE_C,com)

# define L_USERELAY to true to forward mail to unknown sites to
#        another site.  If no forwarding host exists or if your
#        name server contains MX records define it to be false.
define(L_USERELAY,false)

# define how to relay mailer.  If no relay site, change
#        define to undefine
undefine(L_RELAYMAILER,tcp)

# define who relays mail.  If no relay site, change
#        define to undefine
undefine(L_RELAYHOST,dragon)

# define how to hide this site.  Mail from this site will
#        appear to be from L_HIDEHOST.  If site hiding is
#        not defined change define to undefine
undefine(L_HIDEHOST,<@chimera>)
```

Figure 14.1 A portion of the file `/usr/lib/sendmail.m4`.

Network Status

The `netstat` command displays information about B-NET network activity. If issued with the `-i` flag option, it shows the active network interfaces, producing output like:

```
Name   Mtu   Network     Address        Ipkts Ierrs  Opkts  Oerrs  Coll
lo0    1536  loopback-ne loop             168     0    168      0     0
sl0*   1006  none        none             259     0    259      0     0
sl1*   1006  none        none               0     0      0      0     0
ae0    1500  150.2       dragon          1525     0   2346      0     0
ae1    1501  150.2       chimera          290     0    290      0     0
```

In this particular example, the computer has two slip interfaces (`sl0` and `sl1`), two NFS connections, and the loopback interface. The display includes the number of input packets (`Ipkts`), input errors (`Ierrs`), output packets (`Opkts`), output errors (`Oerrs`), and network collisions (`Coll`).

To see data about network sockets, as well as active network connections, use the `-a` flag option. The output appears something like:

```
Active Internet connections (including servers)
Proto Recv-Q Send-Q  Local Address        Foreign Address      (state)
tcp        0      0  loop.1060            loop.111           TIME_WAIT
tcp        0      0  loop.1059            loop.111           TIME_WAIT
tcp        0      0  loop.1058            loop.111           TIME_WAIT
tcp        0      0  dragon.1163          dragon.111         TIME_WAIT
tcp        0      0  dragon.1162          dragon.111         TIME_WAIT
tcp        0      0  dragon.1161          dragon.111         TIME_WAIT
tcp        0      0  chimera.1166         chimera.111        TIME_WAIT
tcp        0      0  chimera.1165         chimera.111        TIME_WAIT
tcp        0      0  chimera.1164         chimera.111        TIME_WAIT
tcp        0      0  *.smtp               *.*                   LISTEN
tcp        0      0  *.ftp                *.*                   LISTEN
tcp        0      0  *.telnet             *.*                   LISTEN
tcp        0      0  *.shell              *.*                   LISTEN
tcp        0      0  *.login              *.*                   LISTEN
tcp        0      0  *.exec               *.*                   LISTEN
```

```
tcp     0    0    *.finger         *.*                LISTEN
tcp     0    0    *.111            *.*                LISTEN
udp     0    0    *.tftp           *.*
udp     0    0    *.talk           *.*
udp     0    0    *.1044           *.*
udp     0    0    *.1042           *.*
udp     0    0    *.1040           *.*
udp     0    0    *.1037           *.*
udp     0    0    *.1035           *.*
udp     0    0    *.biff           *.*
udp     0    0    *.route          *.*
udp     0    0    *.111            *.*
```

In addition, `netstat` will display the status of the available communications protocols with the `-s` flag option, producing output such as:

```
ip:
        645 total packets received
        0 bad header checksums
        0 with size smaller than minimum
        0 with header length < data size
        0 with data length < header length
        0 fragments received
        0 fragments dropped (dup or out of space)
        0 fragments dropped after timeout
        0 packets forwarded
        0 packets not forwardable
        0 redirects sent
icmp:
        4 calls to icmp_error
        0 errors not generated 'cuz old message was icmp
        Output histogram:
             destination unreachable: 4
        0 messages with bad code fields
        0 messages < minimum length
        0 bad checksums
        0 messages with bad length
        Input histogram:
             destination unreachable: 4
```

```
          0 message responses generated
tcp:
          449 packets sent
               0 data packets (0 bytes)
               0 data packets (0 bytes) retransmitted
               236 ack-only packets (0 delayed)
               0 URG only packets
               0 window probe packets
               0 window update packets
               213 control packets
          485 packets received
               177 acks (for 177 bytes)
               118 duplicate acks
               0 acks for unsent data
               59 packets (0 bytes) received in-sequence
               0 completely duplicate packets (0 bytes)
               0 packets with some dup. data (0 bytes duped)
               59 out-of-order packets (0 bytes)
               0 packets (0 bytes) of data after window
               0 window probes
               0 window update packets
               0 packets received after close
               0 discarded for bad checksums
               0 discarded for bad header offset fields
               0 discarded because packet too short
          95 connection requests
          59 connection accepts
          118 connections established (including accepts)
          148 connections closed (including 0 drops)
          36 embryonic connections dropped
          177 segments updated rtt (of 272 attempts)
          0 retransmit timeouts
               0 connections dropped by rexmit timeout
          0 persist timeouts
          0 keepalive timeouts
               0 keepalive probes sent
               0 connections dropped by keepalive
udp:
          0 incomplete headers
          0 bad data length fields
```

```
0 bad checksums
156 Packets received
0 Big packets received
0 socket overflows
```

The `netstat` command is documented in *A/UX Command Reference (M–Z and Games)*. See the section *User Commands (1)*; the commands are in alphabetical order.

Host Status

The status of host machines on a network is displayed with the `ruptime` command. The output appears something like:

```
chimera  down     52+03.15
dragon   up         17.22
gryphon  up         12:25
```

It is important to realize that any machine that hasn't broadcast a network status report within the previous five minutes will be reported as `down`, even though the machine may actually be up. In addition, if the local host is not running `rwhod` (the remote `who` daemon), `ruptime` cannot function and will report:

```
no hosts!?!
```

The `ruptime` command is documented in *A/UX Command Reference (M–Z and Games)*. See the section *User Commands (1)*; the commands are in alphabetical order.

To see the names of the users logged in on all machines on the network, use the network version of the `who` command, `rwho`. Its output is the same as `who`, with the exception that user names are preceded by host names. Assuming that both `dragon` and `gryphon` are up, the output of `rwho` might be:

```
jon      gryphon:tty0     Jun 12  07:31
sysop    gryphon:console  Jun 12  08:00
raoul    dragon:tty0      Jun 12  12:20
admin    dragon:console   Jun 12  12:25
```

The rwho command is documented in *A/UX Command Reference (M–Z and Games)*. See the section *User Commands (1)*; the commands are in alphabetical order.

File System Status

To see all file systems mounted by a local system (host or client), use the df command. Remote file systems appear prefaced by their system name. If a user on chimera issues the command, the output might appear as:

```
/        /dev/dsk/c0d0s0   40143 blocks      13002 inodes
/usr2    grphon:/usr2      12444 blocks       1506 inodes
```

The df command is documented in *A/UX Command Reference (A–L)*. See the section *User Commands (1)*; the commands are in alphabetical order.

When you are logged in to a network server, all of the client machines that have mounted file systems from the server can be displayed with showmount. When used without arguments, the output of the command is simply a list of the client machines. The -a flag option displays the path name of the file systems that have been mounted, as in:

```
gryphon:/usr2
```

Note that this version of the command does not show which client or clients have mounted the local file system.

If you are logged in to a client, the showmount command can be used with a flag option of -e to display all the file systems exported by a given server. For example, a user logged in to dragon can see all the file systems that gryphon has exported by typing:

```
showmount -e gryphon
```

The showmount command is documented in *A/UX System Administrator's Reference*. See the section *Maintenance Commands (1M)*; the commands are in alphabetical order.

Chapter 15

System Accounting

A/UX has two separate packages to keep records of system usage, the *System Activity Package* and the *System Accounting Package*. The System Activity Package handles data about hardware use (e.g., CPU time, disk I/O) while the System Accounting Package gathers data about command use.

System Activity Data

System activity data are collected by `sadc` (System Activity Data Collector). It is invoked by two shell scripts, `sa` and `sa2`. The data are stored in a file named:

```
/usr/adm/sa/sadd
```

where *dd* is the current day of the month.

The easiest way to consistently collect system activity data is to use the `cron` facility. The `cron` table `/usr/lib/cron/crontab/adm` contains the following lines:

```
0 * * * 0,6 /usr/lib/sa/sa1
0 18-7 * * 1-5 /usr/lib/sa/sa1
0 8-17 * * 1-5 /usr/lib/sa/sa1 1200 3
5 18 * * 1-5 /usr/lib/sa/sa2 -s 8:00 -e 18:00 -i 3600 -uybd
```

The first line above runs `sa1` on the hour during weekends (0 = Sunday, 6 = Saturday). The next two lines apply to working days (1 through 5). During nonworking hours (18-7), `sa1` is run each hour on the hour; during working hours, the command is also run on the hour every hour. However, the arguments `1200 3` tell `sa1` to collect data three times at intervals of 1200 second (i.e., every 20 minutes). That means that data will be sampled every 20 minutes during working hours but only once an hour during nonworking hours.

The final line runs the `sa2` shell script at 6:06 p.m. each working day to produce a summary report. The report is stored in `/usr/adm/sa/sardd`, where *dd* is the day of the month on which the report was produced.

As shipped, these lines are "commented out" (i.e., they have pound signs (#) as their first character). To start system activity data collection, edit `/usr/lib/cron/crontab/adm` and remove the pound signs. Then run the `crontab` command on the file.

The `sa1` and `sa2` shell scripts are documented with `sadc` in *A/UX System Administrator's Reference*. See the section *Maintenance Commands (1M)*; the commands are in alphabetical order.

The System Activity Report

The report produced by `sa2` (a sample of which follows) provides a wealth of information. The report begins with a header that includes the system name, A/UX version, type of microprocessor, and date. The next paragraph summarizes CPU usage (percent time spend in user mode, system mode, waiting for I/O, and idle).

```
A/UX gryphon 1.1 SVR2 mc68020     06/09/89

11:00:05     %usr     %sys     %wio    %idle
12:00:02        2        5        2       91
13:00:02        0        4        1       95
14:00:02        0        3        1       96
15:00:02        0        3        1       96
16:00:03       21       13        1       64
17:00:01       15       11        1       72

Average         6        7        1       86
```

The report continues with data about peripheral devices. The columns list the I/O device (disk and tape drives) from which data were taken (device), percent of time that it was in use (%busy), average length of the queue of requests waiting for the device (avque), number of reads and writes performed by the device per second (r+w/s), number of 512-byte blocks transferred per second (blks/s), average time a processes must wait in the queue (avwait), and the average amount of time required to complete an I/O request (avserv).

```
11:00:05  device    %busy    avque    r+w/s  blks/s   avwait   avserv

12:00:02
13:00:02
14:00:02
15:00:02
16:00:03
17:00:01
Average
```

The section below contains data about queue length–the amount of time that processes must wait. From left to right, the columns represent the average time processes spent in the run queue, percent of time processes spent in a runable state but waiting to be swapped into the CPU, average time processes wait in the swap queue (swapped out of the CPU but runable), and percent of time processes spent in the swap queue.

```
11:00:05 runq-sz %runocc swpq-sz %swpocc
12:00:02     1.0      33
13:00:02     1.0      96
14:00:02     1.0     100
15:00:02     1.0      38
16:00:03     1.0      14
17:00:01     1.0      46

Average      1.0      54
```

The following section reports I/O buffer activity. From left to right, the first six columns represent the number of data transfers from a peripheral device to a buffer per second (bread/s), number of times the CPU read a buffer per second (lread/s), percent of read cache hits (%rcache), number of data transfers from a buffer to a peripheral device per second (bwrit/s), number of times the CPU wrote to a buffer per second (lwrit/s), and percent of write cache hits ($wcache). These data all relate to block data transfers (i.e., 512 bytes at a time). In addition, the last two columns contain the number of reads from a character device per second (pread/s) and number of writes to a character device per second (pwrit/s)

11:00:05	bread/s	lread/s	%rcache	bwrit/s	lwrit/s	%wcache	pread/s	pwrit/s
12:00:02	2	4	58	0	0	58	0	0
13:00:02	0	1	64	0	0	53	0	0
14:00:02	0	1	61	0	0	50	0	0
15:00:02	0	1	62	0	0	50	0	0
16:00:03	1	2	61	0	0	56	0	0
17:00:01	1	4	67	0	1	68	0	0
Average	1	2	62	0	0	58	0	0

Data about virtual memory activity (swapping and switching) appear in the next section. The columns represent the number of swaps into memory per second (swpin/s), number of 512-byte blocks swapped into memory per second (bswin/s), number of swaps out of memory per second (swopt/s), number of 512-byte blocks swapped out of memory per second (bswot/s), and number of process switches (pswch/s). The last column refers to the rate at which processes are swapped in and out to the CPU as the system implements multitasking.

11:00:05	swpin/s	bswin/s	swpot/s	bswot/s	pswch/s
12:00:02	0.00	0.0	0.00	0.0	20
13:00:02	0.00	0.0	0.00	0.0	57
14:00:02	0.00	0.0	0.00	0.0	59
15:00:02	0.00	0.0	0.00	0.0	23
16:00:03	0.00	0.0	0.00	0.0	15
17:00:01	0.00	0.0	0.00	0.0	34
Average	0.00	0.0	0.00	0.0	35

The system activity report also contains data about *system calls*. System calls are used within programs to interact with A/UX. They correspond to many of the commands that can be issued at the shell's prompt as well as special calls for I/O. From left to right, the columns represent the number of system calls per second (scalls/s), number of calls per second that read data (sread/s), number of calls per second that write data (swrit/s), number of forks per second (fork/s),[1] number of `exec` commands per second (exec/s), number of characters read by system calls per second (rchar/s), and number of characters written by system calls per second (wchars/s).

---

1. A fork creates a new process.

11:00:05	scall/s	sread/s	swrit/s	fork/s	exec/s	rchar/s	wchar/s
12:00:02	46	1	1	0.04	0.08	1359	46
13:00:02	115	0	0	0.01	0.02	226	5
14:00:02	119	0	0	0.01	0.02	149	3
15:00:02	46	0	0	0.01	0.02	149	3
16:00:03	73	5	36	0.02	0.04	814	459
17:00:01	90	5	10	0.03	0.06	1158	486
Average	81	2	8	0.02	0.04	642	167

Data about the use of file access system routines follow. The columns contain data about the number of times a request is made to an i-node per second (iget/s), number of requests for a specific file search path per second (namei/s), and number of requests for directory block reads per second (dirbk/s).

11:00:05	iget/s	namei/s	dirbk/s
12:00:02	0	0	0
13:00:02	0	0	0
14:00:02	0	0	0
15:00:02	0	0	0
16:00:03	0	0	0
17:00:01	0	0	0
Average	0	0	0

The next section of the report provides data about TTY activity. The columns contain the raw character input rate (rawch/s), the number of characters per second processed by canon (canch/s), the number of characters output per second (outch/s), the modem receive rate (rcvin/s), the modem transmit rate (xmtin/s), and the modem interrupt rate (mdmin/s).

11:00:05	rawch/s	canch/s	outch/s	rcvin/s	xmtin/s	mdmin/s
12:00:02	0	0	18	0	0	0
13:00:02	0	0	0	0	0	0
14:00:02	0	0	0	0	0	0
15:00:02	0	0	0	0	0	0
16:00:03	0	0	445	0	0	0
17:00:01	0	0	441	0	0	0
Average	0	0	151	0	0	0

Following TTY activity data, the System Activity Report presents status information about header tables for text, process, i-node, and file

header table. At the left you will find the number of entries per table for text (text-sz), processes (proc-sz), i-nodes (inod-sz), and files (file-sz). The four right columns record overflows of the tables.

```
11:00:05 text-sz proc-sz inod-sz file-sz text-ov proc-ov inod-ov file-ov
12:00:02    0/  0    6/ 50  14/100   48/100       0       0       0       0
13:00:02    0/  0    5/ 50  14/100   48/100       0       0       0       0
14:00:02    0/  0    4/ 50  14/100   48/100       0       0       0       0
15:00:02    0/  0    5/ 50  14/100   48/100       0       0       0       0
16:00:03    0/  0    5/ 50  14/100   48/100       0       0       0       0
17:00:01    0/  0    5/ 50  14/100   48/100       0       0       0       0
```

The final section of the report shows the rate of system messages (msg/s) and semaphores (sema/s) per second:

```
11:00:05    msg/s  sema/s
12:00:02     0.00    0.00
13:00:02     0.00    0.00
14:00:02     0.00    0.00
15:00:02     0.00    0.00
16:00:03     0.00    0.00
17:00:01     0.00    0.00

Average      0.00    0.00
```

For additional detail about the contents of the System Activity Report, see Chapter 10 of *A/UX Local System Administration*.

Interactive System Activity Data

There is no need to wait until 6:05 p.m. each day to view system activity data. The `sar` command will display all or some of the paragraphs of the system activity data collected up to the time at which the command is issued.

When used without flag options, `sar` displays the CPU utilization data from the first paragraph of the complete report. The remaining paragraphs are produced with the following flag options:

1. `-a` (file access system routines)
2. `-b` (buffer activity)

3. `-c` (system calls)
4. `-d` (I/O device activity)
5. `-m` (message and semaphore activity)
6. `-q` (queue length data)
7. `-v` (header table status)
8. `-y` (TTY device activity)
9. `-A` (all data, producing output like the System Activity Report)

The `sar` command is documented in *A/UX Command Reference (M–Z and Games)*. See the section *User Commands (1)*; the commands are in alphabetical order.

Process Use Data

The System Accounting Package provides data about process use. Reports are produced daily and monthly by entries in a `cron` table. In addition, process execution by user can be obtained with the `acctcom` command.

A tutorial on the System Accounting Package can be found in Chapter 9 of *A/UX Local System Administration.*

Starting Process Accounting

Process accounting is started by the program `/usr/lib/acct/startup`. To ensure that the `startup` is run every time A/UX is booted, make certain that the lines:

```
/bin/su adm -c /usr/lib/acct/startup
echo process accounting starting
```

in the file `/etc/rc` are not commented out (i.e., they should not have pound signs in front of them).

In addition, check `/usr/spool/cron/crontabs/adm` to make sure that the following lines are also not commented out:

```
0 4 * * 1-6 /usr/lib/acct/runacct 2> /user/adm/acct/nite/fdw2og
0 2 * * 4 /usr/lib/acct/dodisk
5 * * * * * /usr/lib/acct/ckpacct
15 5 1 * * /usr/lib/acct/monacct
```

A/UX will then run the programs that collect process accounting data and create accounting reports without human intervention.

Finally, give the adm login access to the accounting programs by placing the following line in /usr/adm/.profile:

```
PATH=/usr/lib/acct:/bin:/usr/bin
```

Process Accounting Data Collection

Once process accounting is started by /usr/lib/acct/startup, the A/UX kernel collects the accounting data and stores it in /usr/adm/pacct. The ckpacct program that runs at five minutes after every hour manages the size of the pacct file.

When pacct grows to larger than 1,000 512-byte blocks, ckpacct moves the data to a new file named:

/usr/adm/pacct/*n*

where *n* is an increment beginning with 1 and increasing by one for each file created. The original pacct file is then used again. Ckpacct uses the program turnacct to perform most of its functions.

Disk activity accounting is performed by the /usr/lib/acct/dodisk program. Unless you tell it otherwise, dodisk looks at /etc/fstab and /etc/inittab to identify all mounted file systems.

Working Versus Nonworking Hours

In many cases, accounting summary data are separated by working (prime) and nonworking (nonprime) hours. Weekends and holidays are considered nonworking hours. A/UX uses the file /usr/lib/acct/holidays to determine exactly what days and hours are nonprime.

```
*          @(#)holidays        UniPlus V.2.1.3     (ATT 1.3)
* Prime/Nonprime Table for UNIX Accounting System
*
* Curr     Prime      Non-Prime
* Year     Start      Start
*
  1989     0830       1730
*
* Day of              Calendar  Company
* Year                Date      Holiday
*
    1                 Jan 1     New Year's Day
   16                 Jan 16    Martin Luther King Jr.'s Birthday
   51                 Feb 20    President's Day
  149                 May 29    Memorial Day
  185                 Jul 4     Indepdence Day
  246                 Sep 4     Labor Day
  324                 Nov 23    Thanksgiving Day
  325                 Nov 24    day after Thanksgiving
  359                 Dec 25    Christmas Day
```

Figure 13.1 The file `/usr/lib/acct/holidays`.

In Figure 13.1 you will find a sample holidays file. The first noncomment line contains the current year, the start of working hours on a work day, and the start of nonworking hours on a work day. The remaining noncomment lines identify holidays by day of the year. The calendar date and name of the holiday are not used by A/UX, but exist to make the file more understandable. Add holidays as needed to configure the file to match the needs of your installation. Be sure to separate the fields with tabs rather than spaces.

Charging Fees

Some organizations charge their users fees, commonly either a flat fee per month or a computed fee based on connect time. The A/UX command `chargefee` will assess a user a fixed number of "units" and merge that data into the daily accounting report. How a unit is interpreted is up to you, although it is generally accepted to be one dollar.

`Chargefee`'s general syntax is:

```
/usr/lib/acct/chargefee <user name> <number of units>
```

For example, to charge jon five units, the command is issued as:

```
/usr/lib/acct/chargee jon 5
```

Unfortunately, A/UX does not allow you to set a rate for connect time and then compute the fee for all users who have logged on during the accounting period. Instead, chargefee must be run each time you wish to charge a user a fixed number of units.

The chargefee command is documented with acctsh in *A/UX System Administrator's Reference*. See the section *Maintenance Commands (1M)*; the commands are in alphabetical order.

The Daily Accounting Report

If the lines in /usr/spool/cron/crontab/adm are left as seen earlier, then a daily accounting report will be generated by runacct Monday through Saturday at 4:00 a.m. The output of runacct, however, is not a text file. Instead, to see the report, issue the command:

```
/usr/lib/acct/prdaily
```

from the shell's prompt. Since the report is lengthy, you may wish to view it with more or pg or redirect its output to a file that can be printed.

Each daily report begins with a header that gives the date and time when the report was created as well as the period it covers:

```
Jun  9 17:48 1989  DAILY REPORT FOR A/UX Page 1
from Tue Jun  6 13:20:06 1989
to   Fri Jun  9 17:41:54 1989
```

The next lines of the header report entries in the file /etc/wtmp that were produced by acctwtmp during the period the report covers. These include processes for system boots, changes in run level, and turning system accounting on and off.

```
7     system boot
16    run-level 2
5     run-level S
9     acctg on
```

Following the `/etc/wtmp` entries in the header are the commands that were used to produce the report:

```
1     runacct
1     acctcon1
```

The first major section of the daily report shows terminal usage and login/logout data. It begins with the total amount of time the system was in multiuser mode. The columns below present data for each port used for a login (LINE), the time the line was in use (MINUTES), the percent of multiuser time the line was in use (PERCENT), the number of logins on the line (# SESS, #ON), and the number of logouts (# OFF).

```
TOTAL DURATION IS 4582 MINUTES
LINE         MINUTES PERCENT     # SESS      # ON        # OFF
console      4123     90         10          10          18
ttyp0        1490     33         6           4           6
TOTALS       5613  -- 16         14          24
```

Section two of the report presents system utilization data by user. From the left the columns represent the user ID of the login (UID), the user name (LOGIN NAME), the amount of CPU time (PRIME for working hours, NPRIME for nonworking hours), the kilobytes of memory used per minutes (PRIME for working hours, NPRIME for nonworking hours), the connect time (PRIME for working hours, NPRIME for nonworking hours), a measure of disk usage (DISK BLOCKS, the number of processes contains the following information: created by the user (# OF PROCS), the number of logins (# OF SESS), number of times disk usage was sampled (# DISK SAMPLES), and the fee to be charged to the user, if any (FEE).

```
Jun   9 17:48 1989  DAILY USAGE REPORT FOR A/UX Page 1
      LOGIN     CPU (MINS)          KCORE-MINS     CONNECT (MINS)  DISK    # OF   # OF   # DISK  FEE
UID   NAME     PRIME  NPRIME        PRIME  NPRIME  PRIME  NPRIME   BLOCKS  PROCS  SESS   SAMPLES
0     TOTAL   42     2   17035      32     1853    2779   0        1299    14     0      0
0     root    5      1   156        5      0       0      0        755     0      0      0
1     daemon  0      0   2          0      0       0      0        21      0      0      0
2     bin     30     0   16831      23     0       0      0        3       0      0      0
4     adm     0      0   1          1      0       0      0        196     0      0      0
7     lp      0      0   2          1      0       0      0        102     0      0      0
201   jon     7      0   43         2      1853    2779   0        222     14     0      0
```

The fourth section provides data about individual command usage for the day on which the report was prepared. The first line contains totals across the columns. The remainder of the lines are sorted in descending order by the amount of memory used per second. The left column lists the name of the command (COMMAND NAME). It is followed by the number of times the command was used (NUMBER CMDS), the kilobytes per minute of memory used by the command (TOTAL KCOREMIN), the amount of CPU time used by the command in minutes (TOTAL CPU-MIN), the time taken to execute the command in minutes (TOTAL REAL-MIN), the average amount of memory used (MEAN SIZE-K = TOTAL KCOREMIN/NUMBER CMDS), average amount of CPU time (COMMAND MEAN CPU-MIN = NUMBER CMDS/TOTAL CPU-MIN), the percent of CPU time the command used while it was running (HOG FACTOR = TOTAL CPU-MIN/TOTAL REAL-MIN), number of characters transferred to and from peripheral devices (CHARS TRANS), and the number of 512-byte blocks read and written by a command (BLOCKS READ).

Jun 9 17:43 1989 DAILY COMMAND SUMMARY Page 1

					TOTAL COMMAND SUMMARY				
COMMAND NAME	NUMBER CMDS	TOTAL KCOREMIN	TOTAL CPU-MIN	TOTAL REAL-MIN	MEAN SIZE-K	MEAN CPU-MIN	HOG FACTOR	CHARS TRNSFD	BLOCKS READ
TOTALS	1299	17063.07	43.84	2273.63	389.20	0.03	0.02	0	63100
s9term	2	16828.87	29.60	391.43	568.59	14.80	0.08	0	1409
term	1	88.75	1.26	58.67	70.26	1.26	0.02	0	397
hfx	1	23.34	0.35	0.85	67.33	0.35	0.41	0	1204
vi	43	19.66	0.64	39.70	30.57	0.01	0.02	0	1479
sendmail	91	19.43	0.82	9.79	23.78	0.01	0.08	0	13909
rain	1	15.77	3.98	20.14	3.96	3.98	0.20	0	26
uucico	48	11.60	0.49	19.81	23.59	0.01	0.02	0	6761
sh	253	8.76	0.81	1248.49	10.84	0.00	0.00	0	4464
acctcom	34	8.34	0.64	6.88	13.04	0.02	0.09	0	3049
worms	1	6.90	1.56	9.92	4.42	1.56	0.16	0	29
ps	45	5.47	0.39	1.91	13.87	0.01	0.21	0	4480
more	16	3.45	0.56	10.26	6.15	0.04	0.05	0	737
ls	26	3.32	0.26	0.99	12.68	0.01	0.26	0	1656
mail	39	2.44	0.18	3.30	13.23	0.00	0.06	0	3376
uuxqt	28	2.11	0.11	1.04	19.25	0.00	0.11	0	2335
find	2	2.07	0.18	0.46	11.69	0.09	0.39	0	534
sar	77	1.77	0.23	1.21	7.58	0.00	0.19	0	1948
cu	2	0.85	0.21	17.32	4.03	0.11	0.01	0	51
lp	9	0.80	0.05	0.57	14.79	0.01	0.10	0	929
mailx	12	0.71	0.05	1.14	15.06	0.00	0.04	0	1004
lpsched	14	0.70	0.08	3.87	8.86	0.01	0.02	0	1387

cat	45	0.46	0.11	0.56	4.04	0.00	0.21	0	600
chown	19	0.39	0.04	0.28	9.68	0.00	0.15	0	777
rm	60	0.38	0.07	0.40	5.14	0.00	0.19	0	688
lpadmin	5	0.37	0.03	0.26	13.27	0.01	0.11	0	405
fish	15	0.37	0.11	38.25	3.32	0.01	0.00	0	113
uptime	4	0.32	0.05	0.12	6.30	0.01	0.41	0	319
bj	1	0.30	0.09	7.22	3.51	0.09	0.01	0	19
awk	10	0.29	0.03	0.61	10.11	0.00	0.05	0	760
who	5	0.29	0.03	0.08	9.22	0.01	0.38	0	158
uux	2	0.29	0.01	0.12	22.37	0.01	0.10	0	213
sadc	18	0.26	0.07	320.28	3.66	0.00	0.00	0	365
chgrp	17	0.26	0.03	0.21	8.20	0.00	0.15	0	647
news	9	0.20	0.02	0.34	10.79	0.00	0.06	0	442
cron	10	0.20	0.05	0.33	4.38	0.00	0.14	0	351
kill	31	0.20	0.03	0.14	5.76	0.00	0.24	0	417
crontab	5	0.18	0.01	0.12	12.20	0.00	0.12	0	289
date	25	0.18	0.03	0.15	5.97	0.00	0.20	0	255
chmod	34	0.18	0.04	0.13	4.12	0.00	0.32	0	317
portmap	19	0.18	0.04	1.01	4.07	0.00	0.04	0	510
df	22	0.16	0.03	0.36	4.86	0.00	0.09	0	337
errdemon	10	0.16	0.04	0.12	4.52	0.00	0.29	0	130
cp	21	0.15	0.03	0.17	5.39	0.00	0.16	0	336
tee	11	0.15	0.04	1.47	3.45	0.00	0.03	0	152
stty	12	0.15	0.02	0.23	8.05	0.00	0.08	0	352
uustat	4	0.14	0.01	0.06	12.34	0.00	0.19	0	138
timex	13	0.13	0.03	25.13	5.28	0.00	0.00	0	178
lpstat	2	0.11	0.01	0.11	14.22	0.00	0.07	0	165
cancel	2	0.11	0.01	0.11	11.13	0.00	0.09	0	145
hangman	2	0.10	0.03	17.22	4.02	0.01	0.00	0	132

The fifth section of the report has an identical structure to the fourth part. However, the data cover the beginning of the month to the current day.

Jun 9 17:43 1989 MONTHLY TOTAL COMMAND SUMMARY Page 1

TOTAL COMMAND SUMMARY

COMMAND NAME	NUMBER CMDS	TOTAL KCOREMIN	TOTAL CPU-MIN	TOTAL REAL-MIN	MEAN SIZE-K	MEAN CPU-MIN	HOG FACTOR	CHARS TRNSFD	BLOCKS READ
TOTALS	1299	17063.07	43.84	2273.63	389.20	0.03	0.02	0	63100
s9term	2	16828.87	29.60	391.43	568.59	14.80	0.08	0	1409
term	1	88.75	1.26	58.67	70.26	1.26	0.02	0	397
hfx	1	23.34	0.35	0.85	67.33	0.35	0.41	0	1204
vi	43	19.66	0.64	39.70	30.57	0.01	0.02	0	1479
sendmail	91	19.43	0.82	9.79	23.78	0.01	0.08	0	13909
rain	1	15.77	3.98	20.14	3.96	3.98	0.20	0	26
uucico	48	11.60	0.49	19.81	23.59	0.01	0.02	0	6761
sh	253	8.76	0.81	1248.49	10.84	0.00	0.00	0	4464
acctcom	34	8.34	0.64	6.88	13.04	0.02	0.09	0	3049

worms	1	6.90	1.56	9.92	4.42	1.56	0.16	0	29
ps	45	5.47	0.39	1.91	13.87	0.01	0.21	0	4480
more	16	3.45	0.56	10.26	6.15	0.04	0.05	0	737
ls	26	3.32	0.26	0.99	12.68	0.01	0.26	0	1656
mail	39	2.44	0.18	3.30	13.23	0.00	0.06	0	3376
uuxqt	28	2.11	0.11	1.04	19.25	0.00	0.11	0	2335
find	2	2.07	0.18	0.46	11.69	0.09	0.39	0	534
sar	77	1.77	0.23	1.21	7.58	0.00	0.19	0	1948
cu	2	0.85	0.21	17.32	4.03	0.11	0.01	0	51
lp	9	0.80	0.05	0.57	14.79	0.01	0.10	0	929
mailx	12	0.71	0.05	1.14	15.06	0.00	0.04	0	1004
lpsched	14	0.70	0.08	3.87	8.86	0.01	0.02	0	1387
cat	45	0.46	0.11	0.56	4.04	0.00	0.21	0	600
chown	19	0.39	0.04	0.28	9.68	0.00	0.15	0	777
rm	60	0.38	0.07	0.40	5.14	0.00	0.19	0	688
lpadmin	5	0.37	0.03	0.26	13.27	0.01	0.11	0	405
fish	15	0.37	0.11	38.25	3.32	0.01	0.00	0	113
uptime	4	0.32	0.05	0.12	6.30	0.01	0.41	0	319
bj	1	0.30	0.09	7.22	3.51	0.09	0.01	0	19
awk	10	0.29	0.03	0.61	10.11	0.00	0.05	0	760
who	5	0.29	0.03	0.08	9.22	0.01	0.38	0	158
uux	2	0.29	0.01	0.12	22.37	0.01	0.10	0	213
sadc	18	0.26	0.07	320.28	3.66	0.00	0.00	0	365
chgrp	17	0.26	0.03	0.21	8.20	0.00	0.15	0	647
news	9	0.20	0.02	0.34	10.79	0.00	0.06	0	442
cron	10	0.20	0.05	0.33	4.38	0.00	0.14	0	351
kill	31	0.20	0.03	0.14	5.76	0.00	0.24	0	417
crontab	5	0.18	0.01	0.12	12.20	0.00	0.12	0	289
date	25	0.18	0.03	0.15	5.97	0.00	0.20	0	255
chmod	34	0.18	0.04	0.13	4.12	0.00	0.32	0	317
portmap	19	0.18	0.04	1.01	4.07	0.00	0.04	0	510
df	22	0.16	0.03	0.36	4.86	0.00	0.09	0	337
errdemon	10	0.16	0.04	0.12	4.52	0.00	0.29	0	130
cp	21	0.15	0.03	0.17	5.39	0.00	0.16	0	336
tee	11	0.15	0.04	1.47	3.45	0.00	0.03	0	152
stty	12	0.15	0.02	0.23	8.05	0.00	0.08	0	352
uustat	4	0.14	0.01	0.06	12.34	0.00	0.19	0	138
timex	13	0.13	0.03	25.13	5.28	0.00	0.00	0	178
lpstat	2	0.11	0.01	0.11	14.22	0.00	0.07	0	165
cancel	2	0.11	0.01	0.11	11.13	0.00	0.09	0	145
hangman	2	0.10	0.03	17.22	4.02	0.01	0.00	0	132

The final section of the report shows date of last login for each user. Users that have not logged in since the last time the system was booted will show as 00-00-00.

```
Jun  9 17:43 1989  LAST LOGIN Page 1
```

```
Fri Jun  9 17:41:46 EDT 1989
-rw-r--r--   1 adm      adm        13312 Jun  9 11:20 /etc/wtmp
-rw-rw-r--   1 adm      adm        41312 Jun  9 17:41 pacct
files setups complete
wtmp processing complete
connect acctg complete
process acctg complete for /usr/adm/Spacct1.0609
all process actg complete for 0609
tacct merge to create daytacct complete
no fees
no disk records
WARNING: recreating /usr/adm/sum/tacct
updated sum/tacct
WARNING: recreating /usr/adm/sum/cms
command summaries complete
system accounting completed at Fri Jun  9 17:43:32 EDT 1989
```

Figure 13.2 A sample `active` **file.**

```
00-00-00  adm      00-00-00  root      00-00-00  startksh
00-00-00  bin      00-00-00  rootcsh   00-00-00  sys
00-00-00  daemon   00-00-00  rootksh   00-00-00  uucp
00-00-00  ftp      00-00-00  start     00-00-00  who
00-00-00  lp       00-00-00  startcsh  89-06-09  jon
00-00-00  nobody
```

The `runacct` and `prdaily` commands are documented in *A/UX System Administrator's Reference*. See the section *Maintenance Commands (1M)*, where the commands are in alphabetical order. Note that `prdaily` is documented in the `acctsh` section.

Runacct Status Messages

While it is producing the daily accounting report, `runacct` writes status messages to `/usr/adm/acct/nite/active`. A sample of this file can be seen in Figure 13.2. The lines in this file are not error messages. They report the progress of `runacct`, including warnings of the summary files that will be cleared.

The Monthly Report

If you have not changed the default entries in `/usr/spool/cron/crontabs/adm`, a monthly accounting summary will be generated at 5:15 a.m.

on the first day of every month by the program `monacct`. The report is placed in a file named `/usr/adm/acct/fiscal/fiscrp`*mm*, where *mm* is the month for which the report was generated. In addition, `monacct` restarts the summary files in `/usr/adm/acct/sum` that are used by `runacct` to print the month-to-date summary section of the daily accounting report.

The monthly report has a structure very similar to the daily report. The columns have the same meaning.

Jun 10 09:47 1989 Page 1

UID	LOGIN NAME	CPU (MINS) PRIME	NPRIME	KCORE-MINS PRIME	NPRIME	CONNECT (MINS) PRIME	NPRIME	DISK BLOCKS	# OF PROCS	# OF SESS	# DISK SAMPLES	FEE
0	TOTAL	42	2	17035	32	1853	2779	0	1299	14	0	0
0	root	5	1	156	5	0	0	0	755	0	0	0
1	daemon	0	0	2	0	0	0	0	21	0	0	0
2	bin	30	0	16831	23	0	0	0	3	0	0	0
4	adm	0	0	1	1	0	0	0	196	0	0	0
7	lp	0	0	2	1	0	0	0	102	0	0	0
201	jlh	7	0	43	2	1853	2779	0	222	14	0	0

Jun 10 09:47 1989 TOTAL COMMAND SUMMARY FOR FISCAL 06 Page 1

TOTAL COMMAND SUMMARY

COMMAND NAME	NUMBER CMDS	TOTAL KCOREMIN	TOTAL CPU-MIN	TOTAL REAL-MIN	MEAN SIZE-K	MEAN CPU-MIN	HOG FACTOR	CHARS TRNSFD	BLOCKS READ
TOTALS	1299	17063.07	43.84	2273.63	389.20	0.03	0.02	0	63100
s9term	2	16828.87	29.60	391.43	568.59	14.80	0.08	0	1409
term	1	88.75	1.26	58.67	70.26	1.26	0.02	0	397
hfx	1	23.34	0.35	0.85	67.33	0.35	0.41	0	1204
vi	43	19.66	0.64	39.70	30.57	0.01	0.02	0	1479
sendmail	91	19.43	0.82	9.79	23.78	0.01	0.08	0	13909
rain	1	15.77	3.98	20.14	3.96	3.98	0.20	0	26
uucico	48	11.60	0.49	19.81	23.59	0.01	0.02	0	6761
sh	253	8.76	0.81	1248.49	10.84	0.00	0.00	0	4464
acctcom	34	8.34	0.64	6.88	13.04	0.02	0.09	0	3049
worms	1	6.90	1.56	9.92	4.42	1.56	0.16	0	29
ps	45	5.47	0.39	1.91	13.87	0.01	0.21	0	4480
more	16	3.45	0.56	10.26	6.15	0.04	0.05	0	737
ls	26	3.32	0.26	0.99	12.68	0.01	0.26	0	1656
mail	39	2.44	0.18	3.30	13.23	0.00	0.06	0	3376
uuxqt	28	2.11	0.11	1.04	19.25	0.00	0.11	0	2335
find	2	2.07	0.18	0.46	11.69	0.09	0.39	0	534
sar	77	1.77	0.23	1.21	7.58	0.00	0.19	0	1948
cu	2	0.85	0.21	17.32	4.03	0.11	0.01	0	51
lp	9	0.80	0.05	0.57	14.79	0.01	0.10	0	929
mailx	12	0.71	0.05	1.14	15.06	0.00	0.04	0	1004
lpsched	14	0.70	0.08	3.87	8.86	0.01	0.02	0	1387
cat	45	0.46	0.11	0.56	4.04	0.00	0.21	0	600
chown	19	0.39	0.04	0.28	9.68	0.00	0.15	0	777
rm	60	0.38	0.07	0.40	5.14	0.00	0.19	0	688
lpadmin	5	0.37	0.03	0.26	13.27	0.01	0.11	0	405
fish	15	0.37	0.11	38.25	3.32	0.01	0.00	0	113
uptime	4	0.32	0.05	0.12	6.30	0.01	0.41	0	319
bj	1	0.30	0.09	7.22	3.51	0.09	0.01	0	19
awk	10	0.29	0.03	0.61	10.11	0.00	0.05	0	760

who	5	0.29	0.03	0.08	9.22	0.01	0.38	0	158
uux	2	0.29	0.01	0.12	22.37	0.01	0.10	0	213
sadc	18	0.26	0.07	320.28	3.66	0.00	0.00	0	365
chgrp	17	0.26	0.03	0.21	8.20	0.00	0.15	0	647
news	9	0.20	0.02	0.34	10.79	0.00	0.06	0	442
cron	10	0.20	0.05	0.33	4.38	0.00	0.14	0	351
kill	31	0.20	0.03	0.14	5.76	0.00	0.24	0	417
crontab	5	0.18	0.01	0.12	12.20	0.00	0.12	0	289
date	25	0.18	0.03	0.15	5.97	0.00	0.20	0	255
chmod	34	0.18	0.04	0.13	4.12	0.00	0.32	0	317
portmap	19	0.18	0.04	1.01	4.07	0.00	0.04	0	510
df	22	0.16	0.03	0.36	4.86	0.00	0.09	0	337
errdemon	10	0.16	0.04	0.12	4.52	0.00	0.29	0	130
cp	21	0.15	0.03	0.17	5.39	0.00	0.16	0	336
tee	11	0.15	0.04	1.47	3.45	0.00	0.03	0	152
stty	12	0.15	0.02	0.23	8.05	0.00	0.08	0	352
uustat	4	0.14	0.01	0.06	12.34	0.00	0.19	0	138
timex	13	0.13	0.03	25.13	5.28	0.00	0.00	0	178
lpstat	2	0.11	0.01	0.11	14.22	0.00	0.07	0	165
cancel	2	0.11	0.01	0.11	11.13	0.00	0.09	0	145
hangman	2	0.10	0.03	17.22	4.02	0.01	0.00	0	132

Jun 10 09:47 1989 TOTAL COMMAND SUMMARY FOR FISCAL 06 Page 2

ln	18	0.09	0.02	0.10	4.79	0.00	0.19	0	189
expr	18	0.09	0.02	0.02	5.71	0.00	0.76	0	47
sed	9	0.08	0.01	0.22	5.45	0.00	0.07	0	243
uulog	4	0.08	0.01	0.05	8.59	0.00	0.18	0	96
quiz	2	0.08	0.02	2.60	4.29	0.01	0.01	0	25
wc	10	0.07	0.02	0.21	4.07	0.00	0.08	0	153
col	1	0.06	0.01	0.05	4.34	0.01	0.29	0	17
accton	10	0.06	0.01	0.04	5.56	0.00	0.25	0	146
disable	1	0.06	0.01	0.05	11.53	0.01	0.12	0	75
ttt	1	0.06	0.02	4.10	3.76	0.02	0.00	0	21
du	9	0.05	0.01	0.15	5.29	0.00	0.07	0	155
lpshut	2	0.05	0.00	0.03	11.50	0.00	0.13	0	100
uuclean	1	0.05	0.00	0.02	15.05	0.00	0.13	0	58
ul	1	0.04	0.01	0.06	5.59	0.01	0.12	0	38
id	2	0.04	0.00	0.03	10.03	0.00	0.14	0	88
tail	4	0.04	0.01	0.13	4.95	0.00	0.07	0	83
reject	1	0.04	0.00	0.03	11.68	0.00	0.12	0	60
mastermi	2	0.03	0.01	1.87	4.63	0.00	0.00	0	18
sync	5	0.03	0.00	0.04	5.88	0.00	0.11	0	111
accept	1	0.03	0.00	0.08	6.61	0.00	0.05	0	67
pcat	1	0.02	0.01	0.04	2.79	0.01	0.22	0	20
psbanner	1	0.02	0.00	0.03	9.75	0.00	0.08	0	59
toolboxd	1	0.02	0.00	0.11	4.60	0.00	0.04	0	72
mkdir	3	0.02	0.00	0.02	7.61	0.00	0.12	0	49
enable	1	0.02	0.00	0.02	5.85	0.00	0.18	0	35
sag	1	0.02	0.00	0.05	8.21	0.00	0.04	0	35
whoami	1	0.01	0.00	0.01	8.33	0.00	0.15	0	35
time	2	0.01	0.00	0.02	3.75	0.00	0.22	0	21
getopt	2	0.01	0.00	0.01	6.43	0.00	0.26	0	25
mv	1	0.01	0.00	0.01	5.67	0.00	0.24	0	20
rmmail	1	0.01	0.00	0.00	4.67	0.00	0.35	0	12
echo	1	0.01	0.00	0.01	6.87	0.00	0.17	0	11
cut	1	0.01	0.00	0.01	4.58	0.00	0.14	0	25
line	1	0.01	0.00	0.01	5.62	0.00	0.11	0	6
sleep	1	0.00	0.00	0.06	8.00	0.00	0.01	0	11

Jun 9 17:43 1989 LAST LOGIN Page 1

00-00-00	adm	00-00-00	root	00-00-00	startksh
00-00-00	bin	00-00-00	rootcsh	00-00-00	sys
00-00-00	daemon	00-00-00	rootksh	00-00-00	uucp
00-00-00	ftp	00-00-00	start	00-00-00	who
00-00-00	lp	00-00-00	startcsh	89-06-09	jlh
00-00-00	nobody				

The `monact` command is documented as part of `acctsh` in *A/UX System Administrator's Reference*. See the section *Maintenance Commands (1M)*; the commands are in alphabetical order.

Processes by User

As much information as the daily accounting report can provide, it doesn't tell you exactly what each user has been doing. Theoretically, the `acctcom` command should solve that problem. The command:

```
acctcom -u <user name>
```

should display all of the processes run by a given user since the last daily accounting report was run. However, it doesn't appear to work as documented.

Consider the following output, a report of processes executed by the user `root`:

```
ACCOUNTING RECORDS FROM:  Tue Jun  6 13:20:28 1989
COMMAND                           START    END         REAL     CPU    MEAN
NAME        USER      TTYNAME     TIME     TIME       (SECS)  (SECS)  SIZE(K)
#accton     root         .       13:20:28 13:20:28     0.43    0.08     5.10
chmod       root         .       13:20:30 13:20:30     0.32    0.08     5.50
chown       root         .       13:20:30 13:20:30     0.83    0.12    13.43
#chgrp      root         .       13:20:31 13:20:31     0.73    0.12    10.00
sh          root         .       13:20:16 13:20:31    15.80    0.47    11.54
sh          root         .       13:20:32 13:20:32     0.83    0.17     8.25
errdemon    root         .       13:20:33 13:20:33     0.70    0.23     4.04
cron        root         .       13:20:34 13:20:35     1.82    0.28     3.88
portmap     root         .       13:20:41 13:20:47     6.88    0.22     3.88
portmap     root         .       13:20:48 13:20:48     0.92    0.05     6.67
sendmail    root         .       13:20:49 13:21:00    11.15    0.52    11.69
sendmail    root         .       13:21:00 13:21:03     3.10    0.47    23.14
sendmail    root         .       13:21:02 13:21:02     0.90    0.10    26.08
#accton     root         .       14:19:38 14:19:38     0.25    0.07     6.88
#chmod      root         .       14:19:39 14:19:39     0.23    0.08     5.10
```

```
#chown      root     .     14:19:40 14:19:41     1.02     0.12    10.71
#chgrp      root     .     14:19:41 14:19:41     0.75     0.12     8.21
sh          root     .     14:19:28 14:19:41    13.25     0.63     9.08
```

During the time these data were collected, the `root` issued the `ps` command several times, as well as `hfx`. As a matter of fact, none of the commands that the `root` issued from the pound sign prompt are included.

When `acctcom` is run with a user other than the `root`, the only processes that appear are those spawned by commands, not the commands themselves. In other words, generally all you see are instances of `sh`.

The `acctcom` command is documented in *A/UX System Administrator's Reference*. See the section *Maintenance Commands (1M)*; the commands are in alphabetical order.

Appendix
Working with C

Although you may not be a programmer, you may acquire the C source code for programs that have been placed in the public domain by their authors. Many useful programs are available for downloading from UNIX networks like USENET. Before these programs can be used on an A/UX system they must be *compiled*, *linked*, and *loaded*.

Despite the fact that C is the most portable programming language available, a given C program will not necessarily run under A/UX without modification. If a program will not run, the problem can usually be traced to input and output (I/O) statements. Fortunately, most of the C programs that are available in the public domain have been written with "vanilla" I/O (input and output that does not rely on any special terminal or machine characteristics).

If you are not a C programmer, there is no easy way to determine just by looking at the source code whether or not a program will run under A/UX. The best thing to do is to attempt to compile the program and then see if it runs.

Preparing a Program

Unlike shell scripts, C programs are compiled by a *compiler*. A compiler is a program that takes the text version of a program (the source code) and translates it into binary so that it can be executed. However, just compiling a program is not enough to make it executable.

The input and output commands included in most compiled languages are actually the names of programs that have been written by others to interact with the hardware. These programs (*external functions*) are gathered together in *libraries* and supplied with the compiler. Therefore, to run properly, a compiled program must be *linked* with the libraries that contain the functions it has used. The final step in the program preparation process involves loading the compiled program and the links to the libraries into an executable program module.

On many computer systems, compiling, linking, and loading are three separate steps. However, in most cases, A/UX will perform all three with a single command: `cc`.

The `cc` command expects files to be named in the following manner:

1. C source code: file name with a `.c` extension, as in `dimmer.c`
2. Compiler output (object file): file name with a `.o` externsion, as in `dimmer.o`
3. Default executable file: file named `a.out` unless another name is supplied on the `cc` command line

The program in `dimmer.c` (the source code appears in Appendix 9.A) will dim the screen of an A/UX system's console monitor after a specified interval has passed. To compile the program, type:

```
cc -o dimmer dimmer.c
```

The `-o` flag option specifies an output file (`dimmer`) different from the default of `a.out`. When `cc` has finished, `dimmer` will be an exectuable file. (Documentation for `dimmer` is part of the program itself.)

Make and Make Files

Preparing the `dimmer` program for execution is simpler than doing so for most C programs because the entire program is contained in a single file. More commonly, C programs are split between several files. Each source file must be compiled separately and then linked together with any needed libraries. Program constants used by one or more of the files may also be gathered together into a *header* file, identified by its `.h` extension.

To simplify the compiling, linking, and loading of programs that are spread between many files, many programmers use the `make` command. `Make` uses the contents of a file named `makefile` to determine the order in which files should be compiled.

As an example, look at the `make` file in Listing 1 at the end of this section. This file controls the compilation, linking, and loading of a program named `month`. Month is an event scheduler. It records appointments by day and time over multiple years. In addition, users on the system can check each other's calendars to find out when individuals are free. This feature is particularly useful when you are trying to schedule a meeting for more than two people. (The documentation for `month` can be found in Chapter 5, where it is used as an example of formatting a text file under A/UX.)

The make file first assigns options and arguments to shell variables. It then specifies the output files (*targets*) that should be produced and what files they are dependent upon. The final output file is month. It is created by linking the files:

```
display.o help.o lunar.o meet.o month.o appt.c psched.o
    schedule.o time.o user.o
```

The .o extension indicates that these are *object* files. (An object file is the compiled (binary) version of a C source file.) In this particular make file, these file names have been previously stored in a shell variable, MONTH_OBJS.

The name of each target is followed by a colon and then a list of the files that are required to produce the target. The line below contains the command that will create the target. As you can see from Listing 1, month requires ten source files (those with the .c extensions). Seven of those files must be compiled with the header file, month.h.

The final two lines of the make file do not relate to files that are part of month. Instead, they contain the shell command rm to delete all of the object files.

To use a make file, first place the make file and all of the source and header files it uses in a separate subdirectory. Then type:

```
make
```

The make program searches for a file named makefile, Makefile, s.makefile, or s.Makefile. If the make file has a name other than one of the four just mentioned, its name can appear on the command line with the -f option, as in:

```
make -f MakeIt
```

Make will compile the source files in order. If an error is found, it will cease execution and print an error message on the standard output. If you wish to continue processing rather than stopping when an error is de-

tected, use a `-k` flag option. `Make` will not complete its work with the file that caused the error, but will process all others.

Listing 1: Sample Makefile for the Month Program

```
#*
#* Original Author: Tom Stoehn
#* Modifications by: Marc Ries
#*

MONTH_OBJS = display.o help.o lunar.o meet.o \
	month.o appt.o psched.o schedule.o time.o user.o
#Define OSFLAG = -DBSD if target system is Berkeley 4.2
#Undefine LIB2 if target system is Pyramid System V Universe
#Note: some systems may require termlib instead of termcap
#  GETFIELD is you don't have getfield()
CC    = cc
#OSFLAG = -DBSD
CFLAGS = -O -c $(OSFLAG) -DGETFIELD
LDFLAGS = -s -n
LIBS  = -lm -lcurses $(LIB2)
LIB@  = -ltermcap

month: $(MONTH_OBJS)
	$(CC) $(MONTH_OBJS) $(LIBS) $(LDFLAGS) -o month

appt.o: appt.c month.h
	$(CC) $(CFLAGS) appt.c

display.o: display.c month.h
	$(CC) $(CFLAGS) display.c

help.o: help.c month.h
	$(CC) $(CFLAGS) help.c

lunar.o: lunar.c
```

```
        $(CC) $(CFLAGS) lunar.c

psched.o: psched.c month.h
        $(CC) $(CFLAGS) psched.c

month.o: month.c month.h
        $(CC) $(CFLAGS) month.c

meet.o: meet.c
        $(CC) $(CFLAGS) meet.c

schedule.o: schedule.c month.h
        $(CC) $(CFLAGS) schedule.c

time.o: time.c month.h
        $(CC) $(CFLAGS) time.c

user.o: user.c month.h
        $(CC) $(CFLAGS) user.c

clean:
        rm *.0
```

Reading C Programs

If you are comfortable with another high-level language, you can read C programs to understrand how they work just by knowing a few things about C syntax. This section will introduce you to the syntax C uses to express common programming constructs. Familiarity with these syntax rules with enable you to read and understand how the sample programs `dimmer` and `month` work.

Many C language concepts will seem familiar; they have been presented earlier in this book in the context of A/UX commands and shell programming. Keep in mind that the operating system has borrowed from C, and not the other way around.

C Variables

C variable must be declared as one of the following types:

1. `int` (iinteger)
2. `char` (one character)
3. `float` (floating point, real)
4. `double` (double–precision floating point

Arrays use brackets around the subscripts (rather than the parentheses used by most other languages). Character strings are defined as an array of type `char`.

Structures

C *structures* are the equivalent of Pascal and COBOL records. They have the general format:

```
struct {
     variable1 declaration
     :
     :
     variablen declaration
     }
StructureName;
```

The individual variables within a structure are referenced by preceding them with the structure name and a period:

```
StructureName.variable
```

Pointers

Pointer variables contain the addresses of other variables. Pointer variable names begin with asterisks, as in:

```
*ptr
```

Each pointer is defined as a specific variable type and will only point to variables of that type.

The address of a variable is assigned to a pointer across an equals sign by preceding the variable with an ampersand. For example:

```
*ptr=&WindowRec
```

will place the address of the variable or structure `WindowRec` into the pointer variable `*ptr`.

Operators

C supports all of the operators present in high-level programming languages, as well as some that are unique to C.

Assignment

Values are assigned to variables across an equals sign, as in:

```
counter=1;
```

The assignment operator can also be used on the right–hand side of an expression. For example,

```
starter=(counter-1);
```

performs two assignment operations. A 1 is assigned to counter; the same value is then assigned to starter.

C provides a shorthand for assignment statements that have a target variable that is the same as the variable to the right of the assignment operator. For example, the statement:

```
counter=counter+1;
```

can be written:

```
counter+=1
```

Arithmetic

The C arithmetic operators are:

1. + (addition)
2. - (minus)
3. * (multiplcation)
4. / (division)
5. % (modulo–the remainder of an integer division)

Relational

The C relational operators are:

1. == (equal to)
2. != (not equal to)
3. < (less than)
4. <= (less than or equal to)
5. > (greater than)
6. >= (greater than or equal to)

Logical

C provides the following logical operators:

1. && (AND)
2. || (OR)
3. ! (NOT)

Bit

One of the characteristics that programmers like most is c's ability to interact at the bit level (i.e., setting the values of individual bits). These types of operations are not available with most high-level languages and rely on concepts that are more commonly used in assembly language programming.

The bit operators are:

1. & (AND the bits of two integers)
2. | (OR the bits of two integers)

3. ^ (exclusive–OR the bits of two integers)
4. << (left shift)
5. >> (right shift)
6. ~ (one's complement)

Increment and Decrement

As well as the bit operators, C provides increment and decrement operators. The *prefix* operators increment or decrement a variable by 1 before the expression in which the operator is used is evaluated. The *postfix* operators increment and decrement by 1 after the expression in which the operator is used has been evaluated.

The increment and decrement operators are:

1. `i++` (increment `i` postfix)
2. `++i` (increment `i` prefix)
3. `i--` (decrement `i` postfix)
4. `--i` (decrement `i` prefix)

Conditional

The conditional operator is a shorthand for an `if/then/else` statement. It has the general format:

```
expression1 ? expression2 : expression3
```

If `expression1` is true, the value of the statement is `expression2`. If `expression1` is false, the statement returns `expression3`.

Comma

C statements may contain more than one expression, each separated by commas. C evaluates each expression, but returns only the value of the last one. For example, the statement:

```
counter += 1, starter -=1
```

will add 1 to `counter` and subtract 1 from `starter`, but return the value of `starter`.

Statement Structure

C statements end with semicolons. Statements that should be grouped together to form a block (e.g., within an `if/then/else` construct or a `while` loop) are surrounded by braces (`{` and `}`). A block has the general format:

```
{
contents of the block
}
```

Blocks can be nested as needed. Opening and closing braces, however, must be paired.

Selection

The syntax for C's `if/then/else` construct is:

```
if (expression)
    {
        statements to execute if expression is true
    }
else
    {
        statements to execute if expression is false
    }
```

These constructs can be nested as needed.

C also provides a version of the `case` statement known as `switch`. `Switch` will only accept integer control variables. Its format is:

```
switch (integer expression)
    {
        case value1:
            statements to execute
        :
        :
        case valuen:
```

```
            statements to execute
        default:
            statements to execute
    }
```

The label `default` will catch any values of the integer expression in the `switch` statement that don't match any of the `case` statement values.

Iteration

C supports three contructs for iteration: `while`, `do while` (similar to `until`), and `for`.

A `while` loop has the structure:

```
while (expression)
    {
        body of loop
    }
```

The loop will continue as long as `expression` is true (i.e., not equal to zero). If `expression` is false when the program first encounters the `while` statement, the loop will never execute.

The `do while` loop functions much like `until` in other languages. The test of the control expression is at the bottom of the loop. Although the loop will continue as long as the control expression is true, a `do while` will always execute at least once. It has the structure:

```
do
    {
        body of loop
    }
while (expression)
```

C also supports a `for` loop. It has the format:

```
for (initial value, ending value, incrememt)
    {
```

```
        body of loop
    }
```

For example, the loop:

```
for (counter=0,counter<10,counter++)
    {
        body of loop
    }
```

will execute ten times. The variable `counter` will be assigned an initial value of zero. It will be incremented by 1 each time the loop executes. As long as its value is less than ten, the loop will continue.

C looping can also be controlled with `continue` and `break`. `Continue` cause the loop to iterate immediately; `break` exists from the loop.

Functions

Programmers give structure to C programs by writing functions. In fact, a C program is nothing more than a group of function, one of which has the name `main`. Functions are used where BASIC programs use functions or subroutines and where Pascal programs use functions and procedures.

A function has the general structure:

```
type FunctionName (parameters)
parameter declarations
     {
     body of function
     return expression
     }
```

The `type` is the data type of the value returned by the function (e.g., `int` for an integer value, `char` for a character value). The function has a name followed by a list of the parameters that are passed into the function.

The lines preceding the opening brace are used to declare the data types of the parameters. Any parameter that isn't declared defaults to `int`. The body of the function begins with a declaration of local variables (those used only within the function) and ends with a `return` statement. The expression following `return` defines the value that is returned by the function. If no `return` is present, the function will terminate without sending any value back to the calling function.

Functions are called by using their names followed by the parameters to be passed:

```
FunctionName (parameters);
```

By default, all parameters are passed by value. To pass by reference, the parameter is defined within the function as a pointer variable, as in:

```
char *response
```

When called, the parameter must be sent as an address, as in:

```
GetSum (&response);
```

C programs all include a function with the name `main()`. This function comprises the main program and may exist only once in a given program.

I/O

Most of the C source code that is in the public domain contains "vanilla" I/O statements. In other words, the I/O is suitable for line-oriented terminals and makes no assumptions about terminal characteristics. For that reason, programs written in this way won't be very Mac-like (i.e., they don't provide the menus and windows characteristic of the Macintosh Operating System). Nonetheless, they are very portable and, in most cases, will run under A/UX without modification in their I/O statements. Keep in mind that the C I/O statements are functions; they are stored in a C library that is linked to the compiled source code.

Two functions manage I/O one character at a time:

`getchar()` (Read one character from the standard input, the keyboard.)

`putchar(x)` (Write the character x on the standard output, the screen.)

An entire line of formatted output is displayed with the `printf()` function:

```
printf(control_string, value1, value2, ... valuen);
```

The control string contains formatting information. It may be included in the `printf()` function call as a literal surrounded by double quotes or it may be a pointer to a variable that contains the control string.

The input analog to `printf()` is `scanf()`:

```
scanf(control_string, &var1, &var2, ... &varn);
```

The control string is similar to that used with `printf()`. It is followed by the addresses of the variables into which data are to be stored.

File Functions

The following functions are used to manipulate files:

1. `fopen()` (open a buffered file)
2. `fclose()` (close a buffered file)
3. `getc()` (get one character from a buffered file)
4. `putc()` (write one character to a buffered file)
5. `fprintf()` (write formatted to a buffered file)
6. `fscanf()` (read formatted from a buffered file)
7. `create()` (create a file for unbuffered I/O)
8. `open()` (open an existing unbuffered file)
9. `close()` (close an unbuffered file)
10. `read()` (read from an unbuffered file)
11. `write()` (write to an unbuffered file)
12. `unlink()` (delete a file)

Preprocessor Statements

Before compiling, the `cc` command runs a C program through a *preprocessor*. The preprocessor recognizes statements preceded by a pound sign (#)

and replaces them with actúal C code. The preprocessor statements that you are most likely to encounter are:

1. `#define` (Define a C macro. C macros are true programming macros. The body of the macro is inserted in the source code wherever the macro name is used.)
2. `#include` (Include an external file. This is commonly used to include header files.)
3. `#if, #else, #endif` (Conditional compilation. The statements between `#if` and `#else` will be compiled if the expression following `#if` is true. Otherwise, the statements between `#else` and `#endif` will be compiled.)
4. `#ifdef` (Conditional compilation. Compile the following statements if the name after `#ifdef` has been defined in a `#define` statement.)
5. `#undef` (Undefine. Removes the statements assigned to a macro name with `#define`)

To Learn More About C

If you want to learn more about C programming, you may wish to consult one of the following books:

Kermighan, Brian W. and Dennis M. Ritchie, *The C Programming Language*. Prentice-Hall, Inc. Englewood Cliffs; NJ: 1978.

Pugh, Kenneth. *C Language for Programmers*. Scott, Foresman and Company. Glenview, IL: 1985.

Ward, Terry A. *Applied Programming Techniques in C*. Scott, Foreman and Company. Glenview, IL: 1985.

Ytree: A Sample C Program

`Ytree` is one of many utility programs written for UNIX and placed in the public domain by its author. Although it is short for a C program, it is typical of the kind of software available from networks such as USENET.

```
/usr/spool
__________
|
|
L____cron
L____lp_______________model
|     L_______________class
|     L_______________interface
|     L_______________member
|     L_______________request__________laser
|                     L________________PostScript
|     L_______________transcript
L____uucp_____________.XQTDIR
L____uucppublic
L____netmail
L____rwho
L____ftp______________bin
|     L_______________etc
|     L_______________pub
L____mqueue
```

Figure A.1 A directory tree displayed by `ytree`.

`Ytree` displays a directory hierarchy on the screen. The tree in Figure A.1 was produced by typing the name of the program followed by the path name of the top level directory with which output should begin:

```
ytree /usr/spool
```

Notice that the program displays only directories; it does not display any files those directories contain.

Because `ytree` is a short program, the source code fits in one file, `ytree.c`.; no `makefile` is required. To compile, link, and load the program, issue the command:

```
cc -o ytree ytree.c
```

This will compile the program, link it to the needed libraries, and store the executable module in `ytree`.

Source Code for Ytree

```
     "vtree path" draws the directory tree structure starting at the path
     given as the parameter.
     Gene Lee  UUCP: ...ihnp4!{meccts,dayton,rosevax}!ems!minnow!lee
     UNISYS Corporation     ATT:  (612) 635-6334
*/
#include <stdio.h>
#include <ftw.h>
#include <sys/types.h> /* included because <sys/stat.h> needs it */
#include <sys/stat.h>  /* included to use STAT(2) structure in fn() */
#include <errno.h>     /* included to pick up error number */
#include <string.h>   /* included to use string functions */
int fn();
char *tail();
#define MAXDEPTH 100     /* maximum directory depth allowed */
#define DIRNAME_LENGTH 15 /* maximum number of chars in a directory name */
#define LEADGAP 5   /* number of spaces in to start drawing first col */
#define CONNECT_CHAR "_" /* char used to connect node names in drawing */
#define BLANK_CHAR " "   /* char used to draw blanks when drawing */
#define BRANCH_CHAR "L"  /* char used to draw branch from parent node */
#define NEWLINE_CHAR "\n" /* char used to perform a line feed-carriage ret */
#define VERT_CONNECT "|"  /* char used to draw vertical lines */
main(argc,argv)
int argc;
char *argv[];
{
      int ftw_stat;
      int i;
      if (argc != 2) {
            fprintf(stderr, "Call: vtree path\n");
            exit(-1);
      }
      fprintf(stdout, "VTREE\n\n\n%s\n", argv[1]);
      for (i=0; i < strlen(argv[1]); i++)
            fprintf(stdout, "_");
      fprintf(stdout, "\n%s\n%s", VERT_CONNECT, VERT_CONNECT);
      ftw_stat = ftw(argv[1], fn, 10);
      fprintf(stdout, "%s%s", NEWLINE_CHAR, NEWLINE_CHAR);
      if (ftw_stat != 0)
            printf("FTW error = %d\n",errno);
/*
             VTREE
}
/*________________________________________________________________________*/
int fn(name,ptr,type)
char *name;          /* name of the directory entity */
struct stat *ptr;    /* pointer to a STAT(2) structure */
int type;            /* entity type according to <ftw.h> */
{
      static char table[MAXDEPTH][DIRNAME_LENGTH];
      static int tablecount=0;  /* count of how many entries in the table
                  are currently valid */
      static int column=0;  /* what column are we printing output in */
```

```
	static match_found;  /* has a match been found yet */
	static firsttime=1;  /* the first time this routine is called */
	switch (type) {
	case FTW_D:
		/* printf("%s\n",name); */
		break;
	case FTW_DNR:
		/* printf("%s",name);
		printf("    directory that can't be read\n"); */
		break;
	default:
		return(0);  /* other types of entity need no processing */
	}
	if (firsttime) {
		loadtable(table, &tablecount, name);
		firsttime =0;
		return(0);
	}
	match_found=0;
	do {
		/* if this path is a extension of the last path */
		if (tablecount == 0 || match(table,tablecount, name) ==0) {
			strcpy(table[tablecount++], tail(name)); /* add last node to
								table */
			column++;  /* were going to print new name in next column */
			drawlevel(column, tail(name));
			match_found =1;  /* we just found a new directory level */
		} else {
			tablecount--;  /* back up one node level and try again */
			column--;    /* printout column goes back with dir level */
		}
	if (tablecount < 0) {
		fprintf(stderr, "Internal Program Error\n");
		exit(-1);
	}
	} while (!match_found);
	return(0);
}
/* ______________________________________________________________________ */
/*
  This function returns a pointer into path of the last node in the path
*/
char *tail(path)
char *path;
{
	char *ptr;
	if ((ptr =strrchr(path,'/')) == NULL)
		return(path);       /* it didn't have a path seperator */
	else
		return(ptr +1);    /* return pointer to last node in path */
}
/* ______________________________________________________________________ */
/*
	match checks to see if the first nodes in the path name match to
```

```
      node names in the table
*/
int match(table,tablecount,name)
char table[MAXDEPTH][DIRNAME_LENGTH];
int tablecount;     /* how many entries in the table are valid and need to be
checked */
char *name;         /* the directory path of node names */
{
      int i;
      char *ptr;
      char path[200];    /* make a copy of their pathname to strtok on */
      strcpy(path, name);
      /* check first node name against first table entry */
      if (strcmp(table[0], (ptr =strtok(path,"/"))) != 0) {
            return(-1); /* return no match */
      }
      /* check the rest of the table up to the last valid entry against
            each node name in the path */
      for (i=1; i < tablecount; i++)
            if (strcmp(table[i], strtok(NULL, "/")) != 0)
                  return(-1);      /* return no match */
      return(0);
}
/* ________________________________________________________________________ */
loadtable(table, tablecount, name)
char table[MAXDEPTH][DIRNAME_LENGTH];
int *tablecount;
char *name;
{
      char path[160];    /* make a copy of the path so as not to chg it */
      char *ptr;
      strcpy(path, name);
      *tablecount =0;          /* nothing in the table yet */
      if ((ptr = strtok(path, "/")) == NULL)   /* if only a '/' for ex */
            return;
      else {
            strcpy(table[*tablecount], ptr); /* load table entry */
            (*tablecount)++;   /* add the node name found to the count */
      }
      while ((ptr = strtok(NULL, "/")) != NULL) { /* while a node name is
      found */
            strcpy(table[*tablecount], ptr);
            (*tablecount)++;
      }
}
/* ________________________________________________________________________ */
drawlevel(column,name)
int column;    /* column to print nodename in */
char *name;    /* nodename to print */
{
      static int lastcolumn=MAXDEPTH;  /* last column a name was printed in */
      static int lastlength;    /* length of last nodename printed */
      if (column <= lastcolumn)     /* this means we need to start a new row */
            startnewrow(column, name);
```

```
        else                            /* add name to end of last row */
              addtorow(lastlength, name);
        lastcolumn =column;       /* remember the last column printed in */
        lastlength =strlen(name); /* remember length of last name printed */
}
/*____________________________________________________________________________*/
addtorow(lastlength, name)
int lastlength;       /* length of the previously printed name */
char *name;              /* name to be printed */
{
        int i;
        /* move over and print it */
        for (i=0; i < DIRNAME_LENGTH +1 -lastlength; i++)
              fprintf(stdout, CONNECT_CHAR);
        fprintf(stdout, name);     /* print the node name */
}
/*____________________________________________________________________________*/
startnewrow(column, name)
int column;    /* column to print nodename in */
char *name;    /* nodename to print */
{
        int i,j;
        fprintf(stdout, NEWLINE_CHAR);    /* start the new line */
           /* move away from left edge */
        if (column ==1) {  /* if printing in first column */
              fprintf(stdout, BRANCH_CHAR);  /* char along left edge */
              for (i=0; i < LEADGAP -1; i++)
                    fprintf(stdout, CONNECT_CHAR);
        } else {
              fprintf(stdout, VERT_CONNECT);  /* char along left edge */
              for (i=0; i < LEADGAP -1; i++)
                    fprintf(stdout, BLANK_CHAR);
        }
        /* move over to its parents column in above row */
        for (i=0; i < (column -2); i++)
              for (j=0; j < DIRNAME_LENGTH +1; j++)
                    fprintf(stdout, BLANK_CHAR);
        if (column > 1) {  /* LEADGAP did this already for column ones */
              fprintf(stdout, BRANCH_CHAR); /* branch down from prev row */
              for (i=0; i < DIRNAME_LENGTH; i++)
                    fprintf(stdout, CONNECT_CHAR);
        }
        fprintf(stdout, name);     /* print the node name */
}
/*  ----------------- end of source ------------------------------------ */
--
Gene Lee  UUCP: ...ihnp4!{meccts,dayton,rosevax}!ems!minnow!lee
UNISYS Corporation      ATT:  (612) 635-6334
If not for the courage of the fearless crew, the minnow would be lost.
s!minnow!lee
UNISYS Corporation      ATT:  (612) 635-6334
If not for the courage of the fearless crew, the minnow would be lost.
```

Index

A

B

C

D

E

F

G

H

I

J

K

L

Q

R

S

T

U

V

W

Y

Z

About the Author

Jan L. Harrington is a faculty member of the Division of Computer Science and Mathematics at Marist College in Poughkeepsie, NY, where she teaches courses in database management to both graduate and undergraduate students. Dr. Harrington is the author of several database textbooks, including *Relational Database Management for Microcomputers: Design and Implementation.*

Dr. Harrington has been involved with UNIX since 1984, when she designed and wrote software for a UNIX bulletin board system. Until her move from Massachusetts in July, 1989, she served as the system administrator of a UNIX installation. A/UX has given her the chance to combine her passion for the Macintosh and her interest in UNIX.

Current writing projects include an update of her Brady publication, *Database Management with Double Helix,* and a Macintosh version of a textbook based on Microsoft Works. Her most recent research projects include a longitudinal study of the computer experience of incoming college freshmen and an evaluation of concurrency control mechanisms in multiuser microcomputer database management systems.

Inside the Apple Macintosh

Jim Heid
and
Peter Norton

At last, the book that Mac users have long been waiting for, *Inside the Apple Macintosh*. Master the basics and understand the inner workings of the Macintosh with the computer authorities, Jim Heid and Peter Norton. *Inside the Apple Macintosh* provides the beginning Mac user with an understanding of how the Mac operates and gives practical technical advice on troubleshooting disk and file problems.

Experienced IBM users new to the Mac will benefit from comparisons of DOS and Mac features for business and personal applications. Even those already familiar with the Mac will find plenty of interesting and useful information here. The discussion of the toolbox and the architecture primer gives aspiring Mac developers the background needed to begin programming.

Also included:

- Networking Mac to Mac, Mac to PC, and Mac to mainframe
- Using MultiFinder and mulitasking
- Navigating around the desktop
- Comparing the Mac SE, Mac II
- Customizing Macros
- And much more.

Jim Heid is a contributing editor to *MacWorld* and the author of *dBASE Mac in Business*. Peter Norton is microcomputer's best known author of *Inside the IBM, Peter Norton's Inside OS/2,* and *Peter Norton's DOS Guide*.

ISBN: 0-13-467622-X
$24.95